Learn Rust Programming Today

Learn Rust Programming Today

From Building Blocks to a Working Application

Jere Käpyaho

FSC
www.fsc.org
MIX
Paperi vastuul-
lisista lähteistä
Paper from
responsible sources
FSC® C105338

Editing and cover design: Conifer Productions Oy, Tampere, Finland

Publisher: BoD · Books on Demand, Mannerheimintie 12 B, 00100 Helsinki, bod@bod.fi

Printing press: Libri Plureos GmbH, Friedensallee 273, 22763 Hamburg, Germany

ISBN: 978-952-89-0298-0

Table of Contents

List of Examples

Introduction

Ten years after the release of version 1.0, Rust has become a force to be reckoned with. When advocating Rust, the usual statistics and anecdotes are rolled out:

- Rust has nine consecutive years as the most loved / admired programming language in the Stack Overflow annual survey.
- As this book is being completed Rust has reached an all-time high position in the TIOBE Index[1] (June 2026, 12th).
- Rust is now core part of the Linux kernel[2] (not without controversy, of course).
- Microsoft is reducing the attack surface of shipping products using Rust or lessons learned from it[3].
- Amazon Web Services has developed the Bottlerocket container operating system mostly in Rust[4].
- AdaCore is diversifying from Ada and SPARK to include Rust[5].

This kind of reporting really belongs in InfoWorld, Ars Technica or The Register instead of a Rust programming book, but it cannot be denied that there is momentum.

Before we head straight into practical Rust programming, let's have a quick look at how Rust can be compared with other languages that might be more familiar to the reader.

---

[1] https://www.tiobe.com/tiobe-index/
[2] https://rust-for-linux.com
[3] https://techcommunity.microsoft.com/blog/surfaceitpro/safer-drivers-stronger-devices/4431411
[4] https://bottlerocket.dev
[5] https://www.adacore.com/languages/rust

Rust in a nutshell

If you already have some (or a lot of) programming experience, you have come across many features that somehow define programming languages. It can be useful to frame Rust in terms of those features.

Here are some of the most obvious differences between Rust and other current programming languages. You can skip this section if you want to get straight to the action.

Notational differences

While Rust looks at least a little familiar to those coming from "curly brackets" languages, it's good to know about some notational differences that can make your work a little easier.

- *Curly brackets:* Like C, C++, Java, JavaScript, Swift, and many others, Rust uses curly brackets to delimit blocks. However, unlike Python, whitespace is not significant.
- *Less parentheses:* Rust does not need parentheses around expressions in conditional statements. They can be used to provide clarity or force an evaluation order, but the traditional outer parentheses are not needed.
- *Semicolons for statements only:* The semicolon is used to terminate a statement, but not after an expression. This has an interesting application in functions, where the last expression in the function body becomes the return value.
- *Commas allowed:* Commas are allowed after the last item in arrays and other list-like constructs. This is to avoid a compiler error when you add an item to the end of the list, but forget to add the comma.
- *Terseness:* Rust uses short keywords and symbols for common semantic elements, such as `fn`, `struct`, and `impl` instead of `function`, `record`, or `implementation`.
- *Pattern matching:* Rust has no traditional `switch` statement. Instead the `match` expression uses pattern matching to select between alternatives.

- *No function overloading:* Functions with the same name but different argument lists are not allowed in Rust.
- *No default arguments in functions,* and no named arguments either.
- *Explicit block structure:* curly brackets are always needed in if expressions and loops.

Conceptual differences

- *Errors, not exceptions:* Rust does not have exceptions like C++ or Java, so there is no `try...catch` construct either. Errors are handled using a dedicated `Result` generic enumeration type with `Ok` and `Err` variants.
- *No `null`:* Rust does not have the `null` value, so the same kind of null pointer exceptions that are common in Java can't occur. Instead Rust has the `Option` type which can be inspected.
- *Stack instead of heap:* Memory for values in the program is usually allocated on the stack, unless dynamic allocation on the heap is specifically asked for.
- *No garbage collection:* The Rust compiler checks the program for memory usage. Allocated memory is freed when the variables go out of scope. The compiler detects cases where memory would be used after it has been freed.
- *Powerful macro system:* Rust macros are different from traditional C-language macros that do text substitution. They generate code when they are expanded early in the compilation process.

Learning Rust by doing

There is no getting around the fact that Rust can be a difficult language to learn. It has what is known as a "steep learning curve". Even though it is an imperative language that at least superficially looks a bit like the "curly bracket languages"—C, C++, Java, C#, JavaScript—there are many concepts that are very different from those more established languages.

It is also somewhat challenging to find a linear ordering for all the features of Rust that matter in everyday software development. When learning Rust new things come up all the time, and you will either have to deal with them on the spot, or defer them to some future time. Both of these approaches have their problems.

In this book I've decided to approach Rust programming from the viewpoint of learning by doing, instead of isolated examples that you "just have to remember" or "keep in mind". Apart from the very first small examples of Rust programs, almost everything in this book is aimed towards a single end result: a working application that does a well-defined thing.

The Today application is large enough to provide an opportunity to meet most, if not all, the important concepts of Rust in action, and to show a way to take advantage of them in the context of real software development.

It is my hope that by the time you finish this book you have a much better idea about what Rust is good for, and how to use that goodness to your advantage. You will also have a useful, flexible application that can serve as the basis for further development or as a source of building blocks for other applications.

Who this book is for

This book is intended primarily for programmers who already have a good command of one or more programming languages, and who are approaching Rust as a possible "second language", maybe even with thoughts of making it the first. This book will probably not work for you if you are a complete beginner, but go ahead and pick it up anyway, out of curiosity. You can fill in the gaps with other books in the Rust lexicon, like *The Rust Programming Language* [Kla2026].

If you have ever felt frustrated with programming books that present seemingly disconnected facts about language syntax but never a coherent picture of what can be achieved with the concepts of the language, this could be the book for you. Instead of isolated examples this book has a long arc, where even the first small ideas are somehow connected to the end result (read on and you shall see).

This book is primarily about Rust the language, but it is also about Rust the enabler. Rust is one of the few current languages where everything comes together nicely, once you have given it a little bit of time and practice. The language is coherent, the tools are excellent, and the results are great.

Source code repositories

All the programs developed in this book are available on GitHub under the MIT License. The main repository[6] has all the source code for every chapter, in a format that should get you up and running with just `cargo run` (see Chapter 5, *Getting to know Cargo* for details).

The book repository has a chapter key that connects the chapter numbers to the directories in the repository. See the `README.md` in the repository for details.

The Today program is developed separately, starting from where this book ends, in its own repository[7]. It is anticipated that this repository will soon leave the book repository behind in terms of features.

Acknowledgments

Thanks to all the numerous open source developers who made the tools that enabled this book: the Rust compiler and tools, Visual Studio Code, Emacs, Vim, DocBook XML, DocBook XSL stylesheets, Apache FOP, SQLite, xmllint, Darwin, Linux, the utilities we use daily, and so much more. Thanks also to all the closed-source authors who write software that manages traffic, finance, municipalities, vehicles, and entertainment.

Thanks to the friends, colleagues, and students who listened politely to my enthusiastic rants about Rust and this book.

Thanks to the music makers who provided the soundtrack to writing this book, including but not limited to: Beach House, Carbon Based Lifeforms, Yellow Magic Orchestra, Hiroshi Yoshimura, Rudy Adrian, and many more.

And as always, a hug/e thank you to my love Virpi for the support and encouragement.

[6]https://github.com/coniferprod/learn-rust
[7]https://github.com/coniferprod/today-rs

Part I. Getting Started with Rust

In this part of the book we will look at installing the Rust tools, and then go for a test drive at the Rust Playground. We'll also get to know how to invoke the Rust compiler to turn source code into an executable file, and take a look at how to edit Rust source code with a programmer's editor. Finally, we'll introduce Cargo, the build system and package manager of Rust.

Table of Contents

Chapter 1. Using the Rust Playground

Learn about

- How to run your first Rust program in the Playground
- How to use the `println!` macro
- How to print the value of a variable
- The difference between immutable and mutable variables

In order to get your first taste of Rust programming you don't even need to install anything. Instead, point your web browser at the Rust Playground[1]. You will see a editor-like text area with some Rust source code, along with some buttons to perform operations.

[1]https://play.rust-lang.org

Figure 1.1. The Rust Playground

If the text area contains anything, select it all with the mouse or a keyboard shortcut and delete it; we want to start with a clean slate.

Enter the following program into the text area:

Example 1.1. The classic "Hello, world!" program in Rust

```
fn main() {
    println!("Hello, world!");
}
```

Then click the Run button above the editor text area and to the left. You should see another area below the editor, containing messages from the Rust compiler, followed by the output of the program. Under the heading Standard Error you will see something lke this:

```
Compiling playground v0.0.1 (/playground)
```

```
    Finished `dev` profile [unoptimized + debuginfo] target(s) in 0.66s
     Running `target/debug/playground`
```

Below that, under the heading Standard Output you should see the output:

```
Hello, world!
```

If this is not the case, then you will see some error messages from the Rust compiler listed under Standard Error. Fix them as you best can, and try again.

The program above is the classic "Hello, world!" program, originally devised by Brian Kernighan [Ker2019]. It has become the standard as the very first program you write when you're learning a new programming language. It lets you test that your setup works, so that you can move on to greater things. Let's analyze the Rust version of this (very short) program line by line.

Every Rust program must have an entry point called `main`, defined as a Rust function using the `fn` keyword. This function has no parameters, but the parameter list (in parentheses) must always be there, even if it is empty. The function header is followed by the function body, in the curly brackets `{` and `}`. The body can contain statements and expressions. In this program the only statement is an invocation of the `println!` macro—you can tell that it is a macro from the exclamation mark after its name. Later we will meet many more Rust macros.

When the program is compiled, the `println!` macro will be expanded into more Rust source code. Here it prints the text `Hello, world!`, expressed here as a static string enclosed in quotes, to the standard output, with an added newline. The semicolon marks the end of the statement. There is also another version of this macro without the trailing newline, called `print!`.

Let's try something else. Change the program in the playground to read:

Example 1.2. Printing a variable in Rust

```
fn main() {
    let message = "Hello, world!";
    println!("{}", message);
}
```

The let expression declares a named variable, which here is called `message`. The `println!` macro can also print the value of a variable instead of just a literal string, provided that there is a placeholder in the format string that can be replaced by the value of the variable. When you run this program, it displays the exact same text as the earlier one.

We will be seeing more than enough error messages by the compiler later on, but just to get an idea of how they look, add a line to the program to change the value of the `message` variable and print it again:

Example 1.3. Trying to assign to an immutable variable

```
fn main() {
    let message = "Hello, world!";
    println!("{}", message);
    message = "How are you today?";
    println!("{}", message);
}
```

If you now run the program, you will find that it does not even compile, let alone run. Instead, you will get a lengthy error message:

```
Compiling playground v0.0.1 (/playground)
error[E0384]: cannot assign twice to immutable variable `message`
 --> src/main.rs:4:5
  |
2 |     let message = "Hello, world!";
  |         ------- first assignment to `message`
3 |     println!("{}", message);
4 |     message = "How are you today?";
  |     ^^^^^^^^^^^^^^^^^^^^^^^^^^^^^^ cannot assign twice to immutable variable
  |
help: consider making this binding mutable
  |
2 |     let mut message = "Hello, world!";
  |         +++
```

The Rust compiler has found a problem, reported about it and even offered a way to fix it. The problem is that the `let` keyword defines an *immutable* variable. This is the default in Rust. Once an immutable variable is initialized, it cannot be changed, or "mutated". To be able to change the value later, the variable needs to be defined with an additional `mut` keyword, as suggested by the compiler:

Example 1.4. Changing the variable to be mutable

```
fn main() {
    let mut message = "Hello, world!";
    println!("{}", message);
    message = "How are you today?";
    println!("{}", message);
}
```

Now there are no compiler errors, and the output is as expected:

```
Hello, world!
How are you today?
```

Note that when the `message` variable was defined, there was no indication of its data type. However, Rust is a statically typed language, and the type of every variable must be known and fixed at the time the program is compiled, either by specifying it or letting the compiler infer it from the context.

We were able to leave out the data type because Rust has *type inference*, meaning that it can decide the data type of the variable based on the value used to initialize it. In most cases the inferred data type is exactly what we intended, but in some situations (which we will see later) Rust needs the data type to be explicitly specified. In this case the text in quotes can only be a string.

The Playground is essentially the Rust compiler and the Cargo tool packaged into a web application that can be driven with your web browser. We will have a look at both the compiler and Cargo soon, but first let's make a couple of small Rust programs just to get familiar with some of the basic building blocks.

You can create much more elaborate programs with the Playground than just the traditional "Hello, world!", because it also provides you with some of the most common Rust libraries. It also has many of the utilities that are part of the standard Rust tools, such as `rustfmt` for formatting your Rust source code according to the guidelines in the Rust style guide, and Clippy for checking your code for common mistakes.

The Rust Playground is excellent for getting familiar with Rust, but it does have its limitations. At some point you will want to start working on Rust programs with tools installed locally on your computer. In the next chapter we will have a look at how to download, install and test drive the official Rust development tools.

Chapter 2. Getting the Rust tools

Learn about

- How to download and install the Rust development tools
- How to update the tools after installation

When you are ready to download the Rust development tools on your computer and start to use them locally, go to the Rust home page[1] and click the Get Started button. You will be directed to the official method of installing Rust, which is done using a tool called `rustup`. This tool will need to be downloaded first and executed, in a manner that is dependent on the operating system on your computer.

Figure 2.1. Installing Rust

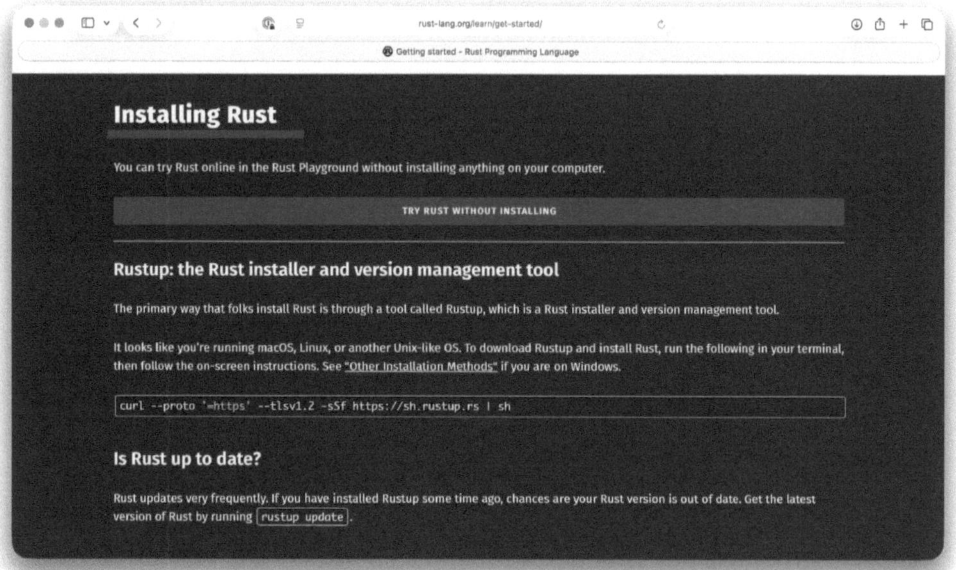

[1]https://rust-lang.org

The Rust home page will most likely detect your operating system, and offer you a suitable way of getting `rustup`. On Unix-like systems, like Linux and macOS, you will use `curl` to download a shell script and execute it. You can also download the shell script using the URL shown, and audit it before executing it. On Windows you will need to download the `rustup-init.exe` program, which requires the Visual C++ Build Tools. There are also standalone installers, so you will need to make a choice that best suits your environment. The Rust documentation has plenty of up-to-date material about installation on various platforms.

For the sake of discussion, let's assume that you are running Linux or macOS, and you execute the `rustup` initialization script. This will result in the `rustup` tool being installed, and then used to download and install the rest of the Rust tools, including the Rust compiler. The `rustup` tool will also be your method of keeping the Rust tools up to date, and it will be installed in a directory that ends up in your search path.

After the installation is complete, you can use the command `rustup show` to check that the Rust toolchain has been installed. On the author's machine (Apple MacBook Air M4), at the time of this writing, the result looks like this:

```
% rustup show
Default host: aarch64-apple-darwin
rustup home:  /Users/me/.rustup

installed toolchains
--------------------
stable-aarch64-apple-darwin (active, default)

active toolchain
----------------
name: stable-aarch64-apple-darwin
active because: it's the default toolchain
installed targets:
  aarch64-apple-darwin
  x86_64-unknown-linux-gnu
```

There are several versions of the Rust toolchain, with the "stable" version being the latest official release version. Since Rust is developing all the time, there are also "nightly" versions that you can use if you want to use features that may not be ready for prime time yet. In this book we will only use the stable toolchain.

Even the stable toolchain gets updates every six weeks. You can use `rustup` to check for them and install them. At the time of writing this, a new version of the stable toolchain had just been released, so the `rustup update stable` command resulted in downloading and installing the new version 1.92.0:

```
% rustup update stable
info: syncing channel updates for 'stable-aarch64-apple-darwin'
info: latest update on 2025-12-11, rust version 1.92.0 (ded5c06cf 2025-12-08)
info: downloading component 'rust-std' for 'x86_64-unknown-linux-gnu'
 28.0 MiB /  28.0 MiB (100 %)   4.5 MiB/s in  6s
info: downloading component 'rust-src'
  3.4 MiB /   3.4 MiB (100 %)   2.6 MiB/s in  1s
info: downloading component 'cargo'
  8.2 MiB /   8.2 MiB (100 %)   2.8 MiB/s in  3s
info: downloading component 'clippy'
  2.8 MiB /   2.8 MiB (100 %)   1.2 MiB/s in  2s
info: downloading component 'rust-docs'
 20.5 MiB /  20.5 MiB (100 %)   3.6 MiB/s in  7s
info: downloading component 'rust-std'
 26.0 MiB /  26.0 MiB (100 %)   2.7 MiB/s in  9s
info: downloading component 'rustc'
 60.9 MiB /  60.9 MiB (100 %)   3.4 MiB/s in 19s
info: downloading component 'rustfmt'
  1.5 MiB /   1.5 MiB (100 %)   1.3 MiB/s in  1s
info: removing previous version of component 'rust-std' for 'x86_64-unknown-linux-gnu'
info: removing previous version of component 'rust-src'
info: removing previous version of component 'cargo'
info: removing previous version of component 'clippy'
info: removing previous version of component 'rust-docs'
info: removing previous version of component 'rust-std'
info: removing previous version of component 'rustc'
info: removing previous version of component 'rustfmt'
info: installing component 'rust-std' for 'x86_64-unknown-linux-gnu'
 28.0 MiB /  28.0 MiB (100 %)  26.5 MiB/s in  1s
info: installing component 'rust-src'
info: installing component 'cargo'
info: installing component 'clippy'
info: installing component 'rust-docs'
 20.5 MiB /  20.5 MiB (100 %)   5.0 MiB/s in  2s
```

```
info: installing component 'rust-std'
info: installing component 'rustc'
 60.9 MiB /  60.9 MiB (100 %)  27.8 MiB/s in  2s
info: installing component 'rustfmt'

  stable-aarch64-apple-darwin updated - rustc 1.92.0 (ded5c06cf 2025-12-08) (from rustc
 1.91.1 (ed61e7d7e 2025-11-07))

info: checking for self-update
```

The output shows that all the Rust tools were updated. As a last step, `rustup` also tried to update itself, but there was no update available for it. You may want to issue the `rustup update stable` command from time to time to get the latest tools. Check the Rust language blog on the home page regularly for news about new releases, features and bug fixes.

Chapter 3. Using the Rust compiler

Learn about

- How to invoke the Rust compiler

One of the most important tools in the Rust toolchain is the compiler, `rustc`. It is responsible for transforming your Rust source code into executable programs, with the help of many other tools. However, you are less likely to use the compiler directly than through the Cargo tool, which we will look at in detail in the next chapter. Still, it's a good idea to find out a little bit how the executable version of your program is actually made.

Following the installation of the Rust tools in the previous chapter, you should now have the stable Rust toolchain on your computer. The relevant directories should also be in your search path, so that you can directly run any of the Rust development tools from inside your terminal window using the shell of your choice (most likely `bash` in Linux, `zsh` on macOS, and `PowerShell` or `Command Prompt` in Windows).

Change to a suitable working directory (your home directory, or maybe some other location dedicated to programming projects). Using your favorite text editor, prepare a file called `hello.rs`, with the same content as the first example in the chapter about the Rust Playground. We're going to make an executable file out of that using the Rust compiler.

The standard file extension for Rust source code is `.rs`. As a reminder, here is what the file should contain:

Example 3.1. The traditional "Hello, world!" program

```
fn main() {
    println!("Hello, world!");
}
```

Once you have the file created, enter the following command:

```
rustc hello.rs
```

The Rust compiler reads the contents of the source code file `hello.rs`, parses it, generates object code and links it with the standard library. The result is an executable file called `hello` (in Linux and macOS) or `hello.exe` (in Windows). To execute this file, enter one of the following commands:

```
./hello  # Linux, macOS
hello    # Windows (Command Prompt)
.\hello  # Windows (PowerShell)
```

You will need to mention the current directory in Unix and Windows PowerShell, unless you have it in your `PATH` (and if you do, you should probably remove it immediately). You should see the familiar greeting printed out in the terminal.

You will not be using the Rust compiler directly too often, but it is an essential part of the Rust toolchain. In a while we will be looking at Cargo, the Rust project management tool, but first we'll take a look at editing Rust source code.

Chapter 4. Editors for Rust source code

Learn about

- Various editors for Rust source code

Editing Rust source code

You may already have a favorite programming editor, and there is no need to give it up. There is excellent support for writing Rust source code in all the most popular editors.

Visual Studio Code

For Visual Studio Code[1] there is the `rust-analyzer` extension, which is the official extension for Rust. It provides syntax coloring, code completion, and source navigation. Visual Studio Code is one of the most popular editors for Rust programming, so you should have next to no difficulty in getting up to speed. You may want to tweak the settings a little bit, because there is a lot going on, and especially the inlay hints may turn out to be a little bit distracting.

[1]https://code.visualstudio.com

One of the things that makes Visual Studio Code so compelling is the Language Server Protocol or LSP[2], originally from Microsoft. It has proven so useful that other editors and various programming language communities have also started adopting it.

Vim, Neovim, and Emacs

For Vim[3] (and Neovim) there is ample choice for Rust support based on Language Server Protocol. If you want a similar level of functionality as Visual Studio Code, there are several plugins based on `rust-analyzer`. You may also be familiar with Conquer of Completion or coc, and there is a version of `rust-analyzer` that works with it.

[2]https://microsoft.github.io/language-server-protocol/
[3]https://www.vim.org

For Emacs[4], LSP rules again, so you'll probably want lsp-mode and rustic[5].

Zed

There is also an up-and-coming programmer's editor called Zed[6], which is actually made with Rust. Zed is available for all the major platforms, and already has a sizable collection of extensions.

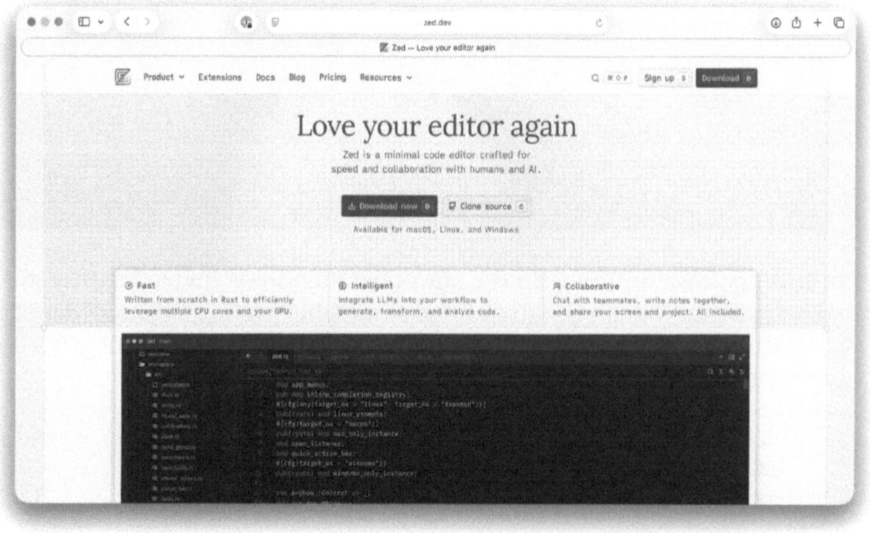

RustRover

There are not that many dedicated Rust IDEs out there, but RustRover by JetBrains (released in 2024) is the one to try out if you're looking for an experience similar to IntelliJ IDEA for Java. See the RustRover home page[7] for details.

[4] https://www.gnu.org/software/emacs/
[5] https://arjenwiersma.nl/notes/rust-emacs/
[6] https://zed.dev
[7] https://www.jetbrains.com/rust/

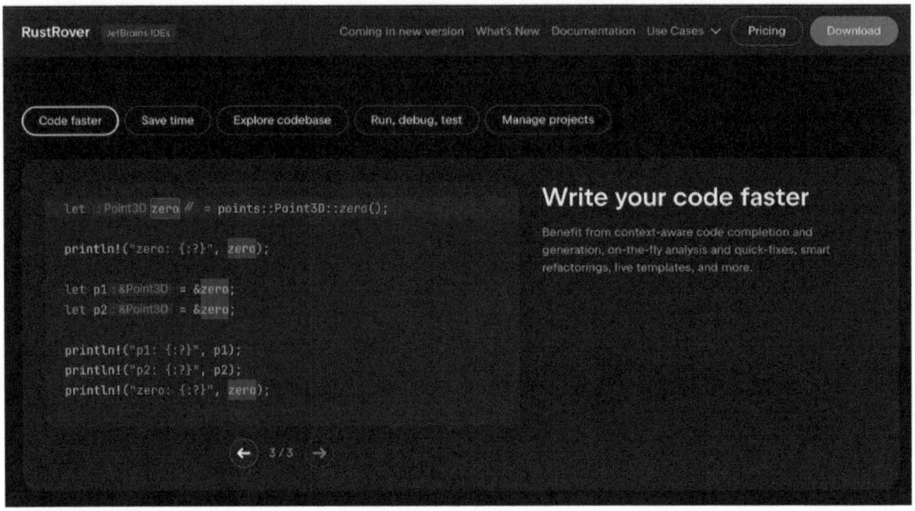

In this book we will rely on the standard Rust tools, paired with your favorite editor, so that we can be sure of knowing where to look for problems and how to fix things when something goes wrong, without having to learn a completely new tool along with a new programming language.

Chapter 5. Getting to know Cargo

Learn about

- Making a new package with Cargo
- Building and running a program with Cargo
- Editing the `Cargo.toml` configuration file

Hello, Cargo

You will not have travelled very far into the land of Rust when you come across Cargo, the official build system and package manager for Rust. It is the most convenient way to handle all the steps required to collect, compile, test, execute, and even install your Rust programs.

Cargo is designed to handle everything between editing and debugging, and can be extended to do more. You make a new Cargo project, configure it to suit your needs, and then prepare your Rust source code in your favorite editor. Cargo then gives you a set of convenient subcommands to compile, test, or run your program.

Cargo is installed along with the standard Rust toolchain, so it is available to you right after you have installed Rust on your computer. You can verify this with the command

```
cargo --version
```

which should result in something like this:

```
cargo 1.94.1 (29ea6fb6a 2026-03-24)
```

To get started with Cargo, let's remake the "Hello, world!" program as a Cargo project. If you took a test drive of the Rust compiler in Chapter 3, *Using the Rust compiler*, you will have the files `hello.rs` and `hello` (or `hello.exe`) in your working directory. Delete them now, so that we can create a project with the same name, with one of the following commands:

```
rm hello.rs hello  # in Linux or macOS
del hello.*  # in Windows
```

To create a new Cargo project named `hello`, enter the following command:

```
cargo new hello
```

Cargo responds with:

```
    Creating binary (application) `hello` package
note: see more `Cargo.toml` keys and their definitions
   at https://doc.rust-lang.org/cargo/reference/manifest.html
```

Cargo has created a new directory called `hello`, so change your working directory to that and list its contents. You should see the `Cargo.toml` file, which is the project's configuration file for Cargo, and the `src` directory, which contains the Rust source code of the project. If you list the contents of the `src` directory, you will find that Cargo has already generated a file called `main.rs` for you.

```
% cd hello
% ls -l
total 8
-rw-r--r--  1 me    staff  76 Jan  4 09:41 Cargo.toml
drwxr-xr-x  3 me    staff  96 Jan  4 09:41 src
% ls -l src
total 8
-rw-r--r--  1 me    staff  45 Jan  4 09:41 main.rs
% cat src/main.rs
fn main() {
    println!("Hello, world!");
}
```

The `main.rs` file contains exactly the same "Hello, world!" program that we made earlier in the Rust Playground and with the Rust compiler. This is not a coincidence, of course.

We'll take a look at the `Cargo.toml` configuration file soon, but first let's build and run the program with Cargo. To build an executable file with Cargo, you use the `cargo build` subcommand in the project directory, like this:

```
% cargo build
   Compiling hello v0.1.0 (/Users/me/learn-rust/ch-cargo/hello)
    Finished `dev` profile [unoptimized + debuginfo] target(s) in 0.51s
```

By default, Cargo makes a debug build of the executable, matching the name of the project, and puts the results in a subdirectory called `target/debug` in the project directory. (Release builds would go to `target/release`.) You can run the program now with one of the following commands:

```
target/debug/hello  # in Linux or macOS
target\debug\hello  # in Windows
```

In addition to building the program, you can also run it with Cargo, using the `cargo run` subcommand:

```
% cargo run
    Finished `dev` profile [unoptimized + debuginfo] target(s) in 0.00s
     Running `target/debug/hello`
Hello, world!
```

As you can see, Cargo reports about what it is doing, but if you want to see just the program output and nothing else, use the `--quiet` (or `-q`) option to suppress the reporting:

```
% cargo run --quiet
Hello, world!
```

If you want to check your program for errors without building an executable, use `cargo check`. To build a release version of the program, without embedded debug information, use `cargo build --release`, and to run the release version use `cargo run --release`. If you need more information about the various Cargo subcommands and their options, use the `cargo help` command, or consult *The Cargo Book*[1].

We will learn more about Cargo subcommands later, but now let's have a quick look at the Cargo configuration file.

The Cargo configuration file

When Cargo created the project, it also added a configuration file in the TOML format[2], called `Cargo.toml`. It has the following content:

[1] https://doc.rust-lang.org/cargo/
[2] https://toml.io/en/

Example 5.1. The `Cargo.toml` configuration file

```
[package]
name = "hello"
version = "0.1.0"
edition = "2024"

[dependencies]
```

As you can see, the configuration file is as minimal as the `hello.rs` source code file we saw earlier. At this point, it basically just has the name and version of the project, the edition of Rust to use. Here it is 2024 (the latest as of this writing), but also the 2021, 2018, 2015 editions can be used - see the Rust Edition Guide[3] for details.

You can edit this file by hand, or use the appropriate Cargo subcommands. The most important thing here in the coming chapters is the section that is still empty, namely `[dependencies]`. This is where you will specify which crates your program depends on. We will learn more about crates in Chapter 19, *Crates*.

[3] https://doc.rust-lang.org/edition-guide/

Part II. Building Blocks of Rust Programs

In this part we will make a few small Rust programs that get us familiar with the building blocks used to construct Rust programs. We can use these programs, or at least sections of them, later as parts of a larger application, once we have learned how to put together some smaller programs with all the necessary parts.

Table of Contents

Chapter 6. Strings and numbers

Learn about

- How to use strings for storing text
- How to use numeric data types for storing numbers

Storing text and numbers

In this chapter we're going to take a look at two of the most common data types in variables found in Rust programs: strings for storing text, and numeric types like integer and floating-point types for storing numbers. Of course these are not the only data types in Rust, and later we will have a look at Boolean values and user-defined data types.

Strings

Unless you are doing only heavy-duty numeric programming, you will likely have to deal mostly with text, and in programming terms that means *strings*. Strings can be surprisingly complicated, especially when you need to represent text in various human languages, or incorporate emoji in your material. Both of those tasks require that you use the Unicode[1] standard, which is a collection of definitions and algorithms that lay down the basics of modern text processing.

Rust fully embraces Unicode, and gets all the good things from it, but also inherits many of the necessary complexities of Unicode text processing. Even if your application can manage with just ASCII text, you still need to know about how Rust manages strings.

Internally, strings in Rust are represented in the UTF-8 encoding of Unicode, which is the most common encoding used on the web, both in the HTML

[1]https://home.unicode.org

markup for web pages and also JSON data for web APIs. In most cases you don't need to explicitly specify that you use UTF-8 encoding.

There are actually two kinds of Unicode-backed strings in Rust: immutable strings, and heap-allocated, dynamic strings. We will have a closer look at both of these types later.

We already saw a string literal, enclosed in quotation marks, in one of our very first Rust programs, where we declared a variable called `message` with a string value:

Example 6.1. Using a string variable

```
fn main() {
    let message = "Hello, world!";
    println!("{}", message);
}
```

To make better use of strings, let's make a new project with Cargo and call it `events`. If you are in the `hello` directory, use `cd ..` to go the parent directory, so that the new project is next to the previous one, and not inside it:

```
% cd ..
% cargo new events
% cd events
```

Cargo has again created the `src/main.rs` source code file. Edit the contents of the file to look like this:

Example 6.2. Using the `println!` macro

```
fn main() {
    let description = "Rust 1.0.0 released";
    println!("{}", description);
}
```

If you build and run the program now, it will be boring, because it just prints out the value of the `description`. We'll make it more interesting when we look at numbers soon.

String slices

Often you will want to get just a part of a string. In Rust this is called a *slice*. The extent of the slice is determined using a *range*. Ranges are actually values of the `Range` type in the Rust standard library, and they have a special notation. A range has a start index and an end index, but the end index is one past the last slice position. So, a range expressed as `0..4` would cover 0, 1, 2, and 3, but not 4. To get a range that includes the end point you use the equals sign, as in `0..=4`.

Let's say we have a string in a variable called `description`, like above. It has the text `Rust 1.0.0 released`, but we want just the word "Rust". The characters in a string are indexed from zero, so the range that gets the slice we want is `0..4` (or `0..=3` if you prefer).

The actual slice is obtained with a reference to the original string, followed by the range in square brackets. That is why the following code:

Example 6.3. Using a string slice

```
fn main() {
    let description = "Rust 1.0.0 released";
    let language = &description[0..4];
    println!("Now learning: {language}");
}
```

is going to print out

```
Now learning: Rust
```

Since the range starts at the first index, it does not need to be mentioned, so just `..4` would be fine here too.

Note

> The `println!` is a *macro* used to print formatted strings. In the example above, the part in curly brackets, `{language}` means that the printed text should contain the current value of the `language` variable.

The & sign or ampersand means a reference. Later we will expand on the importance of references.

Numbers

Like most other programming languages, Rust has both integer and floating-point data types for storing numerical data.

Integers

Integers, or just ints for short, are found in just about every programming language. They come in various sizes and shapes: 32-bit, 64-bit, 16-bit, 8-bit, and even 128-bit integers, signed or unsigned. Rust takes a pragmatic view of integers: if you don't mention anything else, an integer literal like `42` is taken to mean a signed 32-bit integer. Its data type is called `i32`.

Other integer types are named with a similar pattern: the data type for unsigned 32-bit integer is `u32`, and there are also `i128`, `u128`, `i64`, `u64`, `i16`, `u16`, `i8` and `u8`. As if these were not enough, there are also the architecture-specific `usize` and `isize` types, which are usually 32 or 64 bits wide depending on the processor.

To see an integer in action, edit `src/main.rs` to look like this:

Example 6.4. Using an integer variable

```
fn main() {
    let description = "Rust 1.0.0 released";
    let date = 2015_05_15;
    println!("{}: {}", date, description);
}
```

The variable `date` is initialized with an integer literal. Rust will *infer* the data type of the variable to be `i32`, because there is no type mentioned, and the literal value fits into 32 bits (with lots of bits to spare). The literal may look strange, but it is legal—it just has embedded underscores to make it more readable, because the digits are now in presented as groups (year, month, and day in that order). This integer literal is intended to represent a date, as you can guess from the name of the variable. The date is 15 May 2015, the day when version 1.0.0 of Rust was released.

Here we are taking advantage of the fact that a date can be represented in a way that resembles the format of ISO 8601, the international standard for date and time representation [ISO2019]. In the standard, the date is actually text, and dates are usually stored by a program as values of some suitable abstract data type, but in Rust that would require us to define some new data types or use an external crate, and we're not ready for either of those options yet. So let's use this way for now.

This date representation is quite handy, because the chronological order of the dates is the same as their numerical order. The date components (year, month, and day) are in order from the most significant to the least. However, there is a potential problem: if we accidentally used dashes instead of underscores, they would be taken as minus signs, so `2015-05-15` would actually mean 2015 *minus* five *minus* fifteen, or 1995—not at all what was intended! There is no way the compiler could know what we meant, and later we will definitely use a proper abstract data type for the date.

If you now run the program, it will be slightly more interesting. The underscores don't appear in the output, because they are only intended for someone who reads the source code. The `println!` macro has converted the integer to a text string, and displays it alongside the description:

```
% cargo -q run
20150515: Rust 1.0.0 released
```

Floating-point numbers

Rust has two floating-point types based on the IEEE 754 standard[2]: the 32-bit `f32` and the 64-bit `f64`. The latter is the default floating-point type inferred by the Rust compiler when it sees a floating-point literal (a numeric literal with a decimal point).

The programs we are developing in this book don't have much use for floating-point numbers, but of course they are the basis of any numerical work

[2]https://standards.ieee.org/ieee/754/6210/

in many application areas. Even just calculating percentages or averages requires floating-point types to retain accuracy.

Dividing a floating-point value with an integer value is not going to work due to Rust's rigid typing. In the next example it is necessary to explicitly treat the integer as a floating-point value to perform the division:

Example 6.5. Using floating-point variables

```
fn main() {
    let sum = 49.0;  // inferred type is f64
    let count = 8;   // inferred type is i32
    let average = sum / count as f64;  // convert to f64
    println!("average = {average}");
}
```

If you try to divide `sum` with `count` using just the expression `sum / count`, you will get an error from the Rust compiler:

```
error[E0277]: cannot divide `{float}` by `{integer}`
```

Instead of casting the integer to floating-point with the `as` keyword, you can use the `f64::from` method to avoid accidental truncation:

```
    let average = sum / f64::from(count);
```

If you were to later change the type of the divisor to a floating-point number, it would be truncated by the `as` operator.

The default floating-point type in Rust is `f64` and not `f32` because, generally speaking, in modern CPUs it allows more precision with nearly the same performance. However, there are many factors at play, so when in doubt, benchmark. If we don't need the extra precision, but could use the memory savings, we can explicitly declare a floating-point variable as `f32`.

If we wanted an `f32` instead of the default `f64`, we could add a *type suffix* to the floating-point literal, like `49.0f32`.

You can find out the limits of the numeric types by printing out their `MIN` and `MAX` values, like `u32::MAX` or `f64::MAX`.

Chapter summary

Strings are how text is stored and processed in Rust. Numbers are either integer or floating-point, with various bit sizes.

Chapter 7. Tuples and arrays

Learn about

- Using tuples to represent a few related values
- Using arrays to store many items of the same type

Storing data in tuples and arrays

In this chapter we'll take a look at ways of getting some more data into the program and organizing it. First we'll introduce the tuple data type for collecting various values together into an entity, and then we'll have a look at the array data type, so that we can collect a number of those entities together.

Tuples

A *tuple* is a collection of related values, which don't necessarily have the same data type. A tuple could be a pair, a triple, a quartet, and so on (there are actually also one-element and zero-element tuples).

In the previous chapter we had two variables, `date` and `description`. We can collect their values into a tuple and assign that to a single variable. Since there are two values, they make up a pair. Tuple members are placed between normal parentheses, and separated with commas. To retrieve the individual items of the tuple we need to refer to them with their numeric indices, starting from zero:

Example 7.1. Using a tuple variable

```
fn main() {
    let event = (2015_05_15, "Rust 1.0.0 released");
    println!("{}: {}", event.0, event.1);
}
```

Here, `event.0` is the first member of the tuple (the date, an `i32` value), while `event.1` is the second item (the description, a string or `&str`). Note that we still haven't specified any data types, but if we wanted to be explicit about it, we could declare the event variable like this:

```
let event: (i32, &str) = (2015_05_15, "Rust 1.0.0 released");
```

The & indicates a reference, and `str` is the Rust string type, which is usually found attached to a reference; more on that later.

A tuple is fixed in length, meaning that we can't add any new members after the tuple is initialized, and we can't remove any of them either. However, that does not mean that a tuple can't be *changed*. If we make the variable that is holding the tuple *mutable* by using the `let mut` statement, we will be able to change the members. The following example uses a mutable tuple variable called `location` to hold a geographic location, with the floating-point number components listed latitude first, longitude second—but then swaps the components:

Example 7.2. Swapping the components of two tuples

```
fn main() {
    let mut location = (61.4982, 23.7608);
    println!("Original = {},{}", location.0, location.1);
    location = (location.1, location.0);
    println!("Swapped  = {},{}", location.0, location.1);
}
```

The program prints out the two locations, original and swapped:

```
Original = 61.4982,23.7608
Swapped  = 23.7608,61.4982
```

This can be quickly verified in the Rust Playground.

Arrays

Just one event does not do us much good, even if it is as important as the release of Rust 1.0.0. We can make many more events, but we don't need to have a dedicated variable for each of them. Instead, we can put many of them in an *array*.

As in many other programming languages, an array in Rust is a contiguous area of memory with items of the same data type, laid end to end. The items, called array *elements*, can be accessed using their numerical *index*. In Rust, as in many other languages, the index of the first element is zero, and the index of the last element is the number of elements minus one.

Arrays can be declared beforehand with a fixed size and data type. The type of each element must be the same. The elements can also be given on the spot using an *array literal*, with all the values inside square brackets, and separated by commas. The Rust compiler will figure out how many elements there are. The array can also be initialized all at once, giving an identical value to each of them. Either way, the array must be initialized before it can be used.

Here is how we could use an array to hold some more tuples representing important events:

Example 7.3. Making an array with tuple values as elements

```
fn main() {
    let events = [
        (2008_12_03, "Python 3.0 released"), // the modern version of Python
        (1996_01_23, "JDK 1.0 released"),    // the first version of Java
        (2015_05_15, "Rust 1.0.0 released"),
    ];
    println!("{:#?}", events);
    println!("{} events", events.len());
    println!("Most important event: {:?}", events[2]);
}
```

Run this version of the program and observe the output:

```
% cargo -q run
[
    (
        19960123,
        "JDK 1.0 released",
    ),
```

```
    (
        20081203,
        "Python 3.0 released",
    ),
    (
        20150515,
        "Rust 1.0.0 released",
    ),
]
3 events
Most important event: (20150515, "Rust 1.0.0 released")
```

The events are shown almost like the tuples that were used to initialize them, but they are "pretty-printed", so that the result is easier to read. The number of events is printed out, and one of the elements (the last one) is printed out again.

There are a couple of things worth noting in the source code. First, the array elements are laid out on separate lines to make the program more readable, and the last array element is followed by a comma. This is intentional, because we may want to add another element to the array, but then forget to add the comma after the previous element. By allowing this additional comma here, the Rust compiler saves us from another failed compilation round. Second, the whole array is printed using a special placeholder `{:#?}`, which stands for "pretty-print". If you try to print the whole array with the usual `{}` placeholder, you will get a compiler error:

```
error[E0277]: `[({integer}, &str); 3]` doesn't implement `std::fmt::Display`
 --> src/main.rs:7:20
  |
7 |     println!("{}", events);
  |                --    ^^^^^^ `[({integer}, &str); 3]` cannot be formatted with the
 default formatter
  |                |
  |                required by this formatting parameter
  |
  = help: the trait `std::fmt::Display` is not implemented for `[({integer}, &str); 3]`
  = note: in format strings you may be able to use `{:?}` (or {:#?} for pretty-print)
 instead
  = note: this error originates in the macro `$crate::format_args_nl` which comes from
 the
```

```
  expansion of the macro `println` (in Nightly builds, run with -Z macro-backtrace for
 more info)

For more information about this error, try `rustc --explain E0277`.
error: could not compile `events` (bin "events") due to 1 previous error
```

That's one lengthy error message, but it is full of useful information. The reason for the error seems clear enough: the type of the array is `[({integer}, &str); 3]`, or "an array of three tuples with an integer (`i32` to be exact) and a `&str` as elements". This type does not have the capability to print itself, because it does not implement the trait called `std::fmt::Display`. Later on we will learn more about traits, and make our own data types implement the `Display` trait, but right now we will solve the problem just as the compiler suggests: using the `{:#?}` placeholder. We could also try the ordinary debug printout with the `{:?}` placeholder; it is more compact than the pretty-print, and in this case it might be clearer.

The last line printed by the program picks out the most important event of the lot: the release of Rust 1.0.0. It is the last element of the array, so it has the index value of 2. The index is put inside square brackets after the name of the array variable. The same thing we saw earlier about printing applies to the tuple as well; its data type does not implement the `Display` trait, so it is printed with the `{:?}` placeholder.

What if we tried to access an array element that does not exist? Let's see what happens if we add the following line to the program:

```
println!("Non-existent element: {:?}", events[3]);
```

Given that the valid array elements are 0, 1, and 2, because the array has three elements, it turns out that the program will not even compile, let alone run:

```
% cargo -q run
error: this operation will panic at runtime
  --> src/main.rs:10:44
   |
10 |     println!("Non-existent element: {:?}", events[3]);
   |                                            ^^^^^^^^^ index out of bounds: the
 length is 3 but the index is 3
   |
   = note: `#[deny(unconditional_panic)]` on by default
```

```
error: could not compile `hello` (bin "hello") due to 1 previous error
```

After analyzing this program, the Rust compiler is sure that this will not end well, and stops the madness before something bad could happen at runtime. The Rust term "panic" means an unrecoverable error. When a panic occurs, the Rust runtime tries to clean up and terminate the program in an orderly fashion. We will have a lot more to say about error handling later.

Sorting the array

Since tuples have a natural ordering based on their components, it is quite easy to sort the array of events in place, provided that it is mutable. Here we have added some events and organized them by language, so that we can observer the results of the sorting:

Example 7.4. Sorting an array of tuples

```
fn main() {
    let mut events = [
        (2025_09_16, "Java 25 released"),
        (1996_01_23, "JDK 1.0 released"),
        (2025_10_07, "Python 3.14 released"),
        (2008_12_03, "Python 3.0 released"),
        (2025_12_11, "Rust 1.92.0 released"),
        (2015_05_15, "Rust 1.0.0 released"),
    ];

    events.sort();
    //events.reverse();

    println!("{:?}", events);
}
```

When this array is printed out, we can see that the items are now in ascending order by date, which is just an integer after all:

```
[(19960123, "JDK 1.0 released"), (20081203, "Python 3.0 released"),
 (20150515, "Rust 1.0.0 released"), (20250916, "Java 25 released"),
```

```
(20251007, "Python 3.14 released"), (20251211, "Rust 1.92.0 released")]
```

To get the events printed in descending order by date (latest first), we could reverse the array in place after sorting by uncommenting the line with the `reverse` call:

```
events.sort();
events.reverse();
println!("{:?}", events);
```

This would result in the events being printed in reverse order:

```
[(20251211, "Rust 1.92.0 released"), (20251007, "Python 3.14 released"),
(20250916, "Java 25 released"), (20150515, "Rust 1.0.0 released"),
(20081203, "Python 3.0 released"), (19960123, "JDK 1.0 released")]
```

Chapter summary

Tuples let us put together a small number of values with different data types, and refer to them by their ordinal number. Arrays are random-access collections of a fixed number of elements of the same data type.

Data types that don't implement the `Display` trait can be printed using the special `{:?}` or `{:#?}` placeholders.

Arrays have some useful methods like `sort` and `reverse` that operate on mutable instances. The `len` always returns the number of array elements.

Chapter 8. Iteration and looping

Learn about

- Iterating the items of an array
- Using the `for` statement to loop through an array

Looping through the elements

As a result of the previous chapter about tuples and arrays, we have a number of events in an array, represented by pairs (tuples with two items in each). We can make more events in the same form and put them in the array. The Rust compiler will allocate memory for them on the stack when the program is run.

A Rust array knows its own length, and as we saw briefly in the previous chapter, it can be queried with the `len` method. Let's add a few more events, representing the latest that has happened in Rust, Python, and Java at the time of this writing, and then print them all using a `while` loop:

Example 8.1. Iterating the elements of an array with a `while` loop

```
fn main() {
    let events = [
        (1996_01_23, "JDK 1.0 released"),
        (2008_12_03, "Python 3.0 released"),
        (2015_05_15, "Rust 1.0.0 released"),
        (2025_09_16, "Java 25 released"),
        (2025_10_07, "Python 3.14 released"),
        (2025_12_11, "Rust 1.92.0 released"),
    ];
    let mut index = 0;
    while index < events.len() {
        println!("[{}] {}: {}", index + 1, events[index].0, events[index].1);
        index += 1;
    }
```

```
}
```

The output is predictable; all the events printed in exactly the order they occur in the array:

```
[1] 19960123: JDK 1.0 released
[2] 20081203: Python 3.0 released
[3] 20150515: Rust 1.0.0 released
[4] 20250916: Java 25 released
[5] 20251007: Python 3.14 released
[6] 20251211: Rust 1.92.0 released
```

The while loop uses the variable `index` to indicate an array element, starting from zero up to one less than the array length. This approach works, but it has some inconveniences. You need:

- to know that the indexing starts at zero
- to have a dedicated index variable
- to manually increment the index on every loop round, and
- make the while loop run only until the indexes run out, to avoid an out-of-bounds error.

This kind of loop is not typically used in Rust when processing *every* item in a collection such as an array.

The traditional `for` loop, as found in "curly-bracket" languages (like C, C++, C#, Java, or JavaScript) is not the typical Rust approach either. That would also mean maintaining an index. Instead, Rust uses *iterators* with the `for` keyword. They work much like the enhanced `for` loop in Java.

An *iterator* is a construct that is implemented by the collection data types in Rust. We can also get an iterator for our own types by implementing the `Iterator` trait. To actually use an iterator in a `for` loop, we need to pick a name for the variable that will hold each item in the collection in turn, and then call the `iter` method of the collection:

Example 8.2. Using an iterator and the `for` statement on the array

```
fn main() {
    let events = [
        (1996_01_23, "JDK 1.0 released"),
        (2008_12_03, "Python 3.0 released"),
        (2015_05_15, "Rust 1.0.0 released"),
        (2025_09_16, "Java 25 released"),
        (2025_10_07, "Python 3.14 released"),
        (2025_12_11, "Rust 1.92.0 released"),
    ];

    // With index number:
    /*
    for (index, event) in events.iter().enumerate() {
        println!("[{}] {}: {}", index + 1, event.0, event.1);
    }
    */

    for event in events {
        println!("{}: {}", event.0, event.1);
    }
}
```

The program prints out every event in the array:

```
19960123: JDK 1.0 released
20081203: Python 3.0 released
20150515: Rust 1.0.0 released
20250916: Java 25 released
20251007: Python 3.14 released
20251211: Rust 1.92.0 released
```

Actually, we cheated a little, since with the iterator we lost the counter that was in the `while` version. Not to worry—we can get the index of each element by using the `enumerate` method of the iterator. The indexed version of the `for` loop then looks like this:

```
for (index, event) in events.iter().enumerate() {
    println!("[{}] {}: {}", index + 1, event.0, event.1);
}
```

The `enumerate` method returns pairs (tuples of two items) with the index of the current item and the actual element. As we will see later on, method chaining in the style of `events.iter().enumerate()` is a common idiom in Rust.

If we only need the element, and not its index number, we don't actually have to explicitly get the iterator. The version without the index number could be written like this:

```
for event in events {
    println!("{}: {}", event.0, event.1);
}
```

Chapter summary

Items in an array can be processed with either a `while` loop, maintaining an index, or with a `for` loop, using an iterator we get with the `iter` method of the array. If we need array indices with a `for` loop, we use the `enumerate` method of the iterator.

Chapter 9. Making decisions

Learn about

- The `bool` data type in Rust for truth values
- The `if` expression for making decisions, with an optional `else` part

Truth values

Apart from repetition with loops, a key feature of programs is the ability make decisions based on some condition being true or false. Rust has a dedicated data type for truth values, called `bool` after the English mathematician George Boole, and it also has an `if` expression with an optional `else` part.

In the previous chapter we saw how a `while` loop had a condition for its termination:

```
let mut index = 0;
while index < events.len() {
   // ...
   index += 1;
}
```

This `while` loop will execute as long as `index` is smaller than the number of events, which we get from `events.len()`. This is an example of a condition that reduces to a truth value, either `true` or `false`. These are also the only values allowed for the `bool` data type.

Deciding which statements to execute

You can declare variables of type `bool`, but typically Boolean values are used implicitly as conditions like in the `while` loop above. For decisions that don't involve repetition, Rust has the `if` expression. Unlike in most other programming languages, it is not a statement, but an expression, with a value of either `true` or `false`, so the type of the expression is `bool`. The `if` expression also has an optional `else` part, and both parts must produce an expression of the same type.

Let's build up a situation where we check if any of the events in our array have a date that matches some given date. We don't care about the year, only about the month and the day of month. So, if today was May 15th, then we would want to find out if any of the events have a month component corresponding to the month of May, and a day component with the value 15.

We want to print out only those events that happened today, for some definition of "today". Today's date could be taken from the real-time clock of the computer that is running the program, hard-coded into the program (only for testing purposes, of course), or taken from a command-line argument (also for testing).

Regardless of where the date comes from, we want to filter out those events that have a matching date. First we'll find a way to store the month and day of the filter date. Then we'll extract the months and days from each event, and compare them to the filter date. If there is a match, we print out the event's date and description.

This is going to take some preparation, and we'll need to learn a few things ahead. Our dates are expressed as large integers, but there is really no easy way to extract the month and day using some arithmetic operation. If we could convert a date into a string, we could use string slices (see Chapter 6, *Strings and numbers*) to extract the relevant parts, and turn them back into integers for the purposes of comparing them.

It turns out to be quite easy to turn the `i32` that holds the date into a string; just call its `to_string` method. Testing in the Rust Playground, the results are promising:

```
let date = 2015_05_15;
println!("date as i32   :  {date} ");
let date_string = date.to_string();
println!("date as string: '{date_string}'");
```

The output shows both the integer version and the string equivalent:

```
date as i32   :  20150515
date as string: '20150515'
```

To extract the month and the day, we can take slices of the date string and convert them back into integers using the `parse` method of `i32`:

```
let month_string = &date_string[4..6];
let month: i32 = month_string.parse().unwrap();
let day_string = &date_string[6..8];
let day: i32 = day_string.parse().unwrap();
println!("month={month} day={day}");
```

The type annotations are needed, or the Rust compiler will complain, since it is not obvious what kind of integer should be produced by the `parse` method. However, now we do have variables of type `i32` that hold the month and the day. This method will work for any of the dates in our event array, provided that they are correct, in the sense that they have four digits for the year, two digits for the month, and two digits for the day—in exactly that order.

What if there was an error in the literal? An `i32` value of `2015515`, when converted to a string, would be only seven characters long, and the month would come out as `51`! Even worse, an attempt to take a slice with the range `6..8` would panic due to an out-of-bounds error. As we can see, this way of storing dates is full of dangers, so it will soon be time to find something better.

Let's get back to our original business of matching events to a date. If we put the month and the day into a tuple, it will be easier to compare them. However, we will also need to do the same for the date of each event in our array, so there will be a bit of repetition. We'll fix that in Chapter 10, *Functions*. Right now we just want to build up towards an if expression that can tell us if the date matches that of some event:

Example 9.1. Listing events that match a target date

```
fn main() {
    let events = [
        (1996_01_23, "JDK 1.0 released"),
        (2008_12_03, "Python 3.0 released"),
        (2015_05_15, "Rust 1.0.0 released"),
        (2025_09_16, "Java 25 released"),
        (2025_10_07, "Python 3.14 released"),
        (2025_12_11, "Rust 1.92.0 released"),
    ];
```

```
    // Get the month and day from our target date:
    let date = 20150515;
    let date_string = date.to_string();
    let month_string = &date_string[4..6];
    let month: i32 = month_string.parse().unwrap();
    let day_string = &date_string[6..8];
    let day: i32 = day_string.parse().unwrap();
    let month_day = (month, day);

    let mut any_luck = false;  // Boolean flag

    for event in events {
        // Get the month and day from the event's date:
        let event_date_string = event.0.to_string();
        let event_month_string = &event_date_string[4..6];
        let event_month: i32 = event_month_string.parse().unwrap();
        let event_day_string = &event_date_string[6..8];
        let event_day: i32 = event_day_string.parse().unwrap();
        let event_month_day = (event_month, event_day);

        // Get the event year separately for printing:
        let year_string = &event_date_string[..4];
        let year: i32 = year_string.parse().unwrap();

        // Compare the month-day pairs and print
        // event year and description if equal:
        if event_month_day == month_day {
            println!("{}: {}", year, event.1);
            any_luck = true;
        }
    }

    if !any_luck {
        println!("No events for {date}");
    }
}
```

There it is, the conditional expression—buried inside the for loop. This is the longest Rust program we have written so far, and it is getting rather long-winded. In Chapter 10, *Functions* we'll look at how to make a function to avoid the repetition.

There is another conditional expression outside the `for` loop. Before starting to plough through the events, we set up a Boolean flag variable called `any_luck`, initialized to `false`. If we find even one event where the month and day match the target, we will set the flag to `true`. After the loop, we check the flag, and if it is not `true`, we print a message about not finding any events (because we only set the flag to `true` if we have printed at least one event).

There is one more thing here that has been left unexplained. The calls to the `parse` method are followed by a call to `unwrap`. This method is related to the error handling mechanism of Rust. Since Rust has no exceptions, error conditions are dealt with using the `Result`.

The `parse` method returns `std::result::Result`, which is an enumeration, with two values: `Ok` and `Err`. Dealing with these values explicitly, like we should, is beyond what we know about Rust at this point, so we will defer the discussion, and use the `unwrap` method, which simply panics on error. Since the data we use is coming from inside our own program, unwrapping is an acceptable compromise here. When we eventually get data from outside the program, we will definitely do some proper error handling.

Chapter summary

The `bool` data type is used to store truth values. The `if` expression can be used to decide which statements to execute, with an optional `else` part. Both parts must produce a value of the same type.

We can convert between strings and numbers, but error conditions are not handled properly yet.

Chapter 10. Functions

Learn about

- How to define functions in Rust
- How to use function arguments
- How to return a result from a function

Defining and using functions

Every Rust program starts from a function called `main`, so we have already seen how to define a function. Let's dig deeper and make some useful functions so that we can call them from `main`.

In the previous chapter we did some string and number juggling, taking slices from a string that was made out of an integer, and converting them back into numbers. The program got a bit repetitive, because we had to do the same thing twice (we aim for DRY, or Don't Repeat Yourself).

Let's make a function that handles the steps of extracting the year, month, and day from a date expressed as an `i32` value. This function will return a tuple with three members. Here is the function definition, using the `fn` keyword:

Example 10.1. A function to extract year, month, and day

```
fn get_year_month_day(date: i32) -> (i32, i32, i32) {
    let date_string = date.to_string();
    assert!(date_string.len() == 8);

    let year_string = &date_string[..4];
    let year = year_string.parse().unwrap();

    let month_string = &date_string[4..6];
    let month = month_string.parse().unwrap();
```

```
    let day_string = &date_string[6..8];
    let day = day_string.parse().unwrap();

    (year, month, day)
}
```

The function is called get_year_month_day, and it takes one argument of type i32 called date. The -> points to the return type of the function, namely a tuple with three i32 members, representing the year, the month and the day of month, as extracted from the i32 once it has been converted to a string.

This function does almost exactly the same thing as the duplicated code in the previous chapter. We've made the function return also the year, because even if we don't need it to compare the month-day values, we do need it for printing out the year of the event.

A function can return a value at any time using the return keyword with a value that conforms to the return type, but in the absence of an explicit return, the last expression in the function is taken to be the return value. Here, the last line of the function is

```
(year, month, day)
```

It collects the three i32 values computed earlier into a tuple, which then becomes the return value of the function. There is no semicolon after it, because it is an expression, not a statement.

Of course, a function does not need to have a return value at all. The main function, for example, has been defined without a return type (it actually has one, but let's not go there now). The vocabulary in Rust is the same as in C, C++ and Python: all subprograms are called functions, and those that do not return a value are still called functions and not procedures.

In main, the get_year_month_day function is called twice, and the return value is assigned to the variables date_parts (computed before the loop) and event_date_parts (computed for each event inside the loop). Before the month-day values can be compared, the relevant components are extracted into pairs to make the program easier to understand. If they match, the year and description of the current event in the loop are printed.

If there are no matching events, nothing is printed from inside the loop, but the `any_luck` flag variable is checked after the loop to see if we should print out a message about it.

Here is the relevant, revised source code of the `main` function that calls the `get_year_month_day` function:

Example 10.2. Using the `get_year_month_day` function

```
fn main() {
    let events = [
        (1996_01_23, "JDK 1.0 released"),
        (2008_12_03, "Python 3.0 released"),
        (2015_05_15, "Rust 1.0.0 released"),
        (2025_09_16, "Java 25 released"),
        (2025_10_07, "Python 3.14 released"),
        (2025_12_11, "Rust 1.92.0 released"),
    ];

    // Get the month and day from our target date:
    let date = 2015_05_15;
    let date_parts = get_year_month_day(date);
    let month_day = (date_parts.1, date_parts.2);

    let mut any_luck = false;  // Boolean flag

    for event in events {
        // Get the month and day from the event's date:
        let event_date_parts = get_year_month_day(event.0);

        // Make the month-day pairs, compare them, and print
        // event year and description if they are equal:
        let event_month_day = (event_date_parts.1, event_date_parts.2);
        if event_month_day == month_day {
            println!("{}: {}", event_date_parts.0, event.1);
            any_luck = true;
        }
    }

    if !any_luck {
        println!("No events for {date}");
```

```
    }
}
```

The order of the functions in the main.rs source file does not matter. It is a matter of personal preference and team coding conventions, or a style guide issue, whether we put the main function first, last, or in the middle. This author puts main last in the source file out of habit, due to a history with languages that need to have functions defined before they are invoked, but it seems that many Rust developers actually prefer it at the start of the source file.

The get_year_month_day function uses the assert! macro to establish a runtime condition. If, for some reason, the length of the date as string is not exactly eight numeric digits (four plus two plus two), the program will panic. We can try this by changing the value of the date variable to something illegal for our purposes, like 2015515 that we discussed earlier. The program execution will be stopped with the following message:

```
thread 'main' (2585204) panicked at src/main.rs:39:5:
assertion failed: date_string.len() == 8
note: run with `RUST_BACKTRACE=1` environment variable to display a backtrace
```

If we want a more detailed trace of the functions that were called before the panic, we'll set the RUST_BACKTRACE environment variable as suggested, and run the program again.

The assert! macro is a handy way of catching situations that really should never occur. We could also use the assert_eq! macro:

```
assert_eq!(date_string.len(), 8);
```

The assertion can also have a custom message as its last argument:

```
assert_eq!(
    date_string.len(), 8,
    "Date string should be exactly eight characters");
```

Chapter summary

Functions let you group statements together and call them by name, possibly with arguments. If there is no explicit return statement, the last expression in the function becomes its return value. A function does not need to specify a return type, however.

We can use the `assert!` and `assert_eq!` macros to catch conditions that shouldn't occur. An assertion that fails will cause the program to panic.

Chapter 11. Structs

Learn about

- How to use structs to make new, composite data types
- How to implement operations for structs

Grouping values into structs

So far we have dealt mostly with primitive types like integers, floating-point values, and Boolean values, although we have also seen strings (the true nature of which still remains mostly hidden), and we have made tuples and arrays out of values of various types.

One of the most flexible ways of creating heterogeneous data structures as named data types is by using a *struct*. The term "struct" is short for "structure", a holdover from the C and C++ languages. (In the Pascal family of languages, structs are usually called records.)

By any name, structs in Rust are something like *classes* in object-oriented languages, because they not only store data, but they can also have associated functions, much like methods in Java or member functions in C++. Additionally, structs can implement *traits*, a major feature of Rust that still awaits full disclosure in a later chapter. However, Rust is not an object-oriented language, and it has been argued that it is actually beyond[1].

Our events program handles historical events with a date and a description. The event itself is a good candidate for turning into a struct, but we'll start with something more rudimentary: the date when the event occurred.

Rust has a fairly light standard library compared to many other languages, and one of the things not covered by it is date handling. This is, in itself, a rather complicated subject, to be approached with caution, but a limited subset is easier to deal with. Since we are interested only in dates, we can get by with a simple struct, defined using the `struct` keyword, like this:

[1]https://www.thecodedmessage.com/posts/oop-1-encapsulation/

Example 11.1. The `Date` struct

```
struct Date {
    year: i16,
    month: u8,
    day: u8,
}
```

Since that was so easy, let's make a struct for the event too, so that we can get rid of the tuples, and their rather inconvenient way of specifying a numeric index for the tuple members:

Example 11.2. The `Event` struct

```
struct Event {
    date: Date,
    description: String,
}
```

That is even simpler, but you may still wonder what `String`, the type of the `description`, actually is. The placeholder answer is that `String` is the dynamic string type of Rust, whose contents can be modified by adding or removing characters. The memory for the text in a `String` is allocated dynamically from heap memory instead of stack memory.

To use our new structs we need to transition the events program from tuples to structs, like this:

Example 11.3. Replacing tuples with structs

```
fn main() {
    let events = [
        Event {
            date: Date { year: 1996, month: 1, day: 23 },
            description: String::from("JDK 1.0 released")
        },
        Event {
            date: Date { year: 2008, month: 12, day: 3 },
            description: String::from("Python 3.0 released")
```

```
        },
        Event {
            date: Date { year: 2015, month: 5, day: 15 },
            description: String::from("Rust 1.0.0 released")
        },
        Event {
            date: Date { year: 2025, month: 9, day: 16 },
            description: String::from("Java 25 released")
        },
        Event {
            date: Date { year: 2025, month: 10, day: 7 },
            description: String::from("Python 3.14 released")
        },
        Event {
            date: Date { year: 2025, month: 12, day: 11 },
            description: String::from("Rust 1.92.0 released")
        },
    ];

    let date = Date { year: 2015, month: 5, day: 15 };

    let mut any_luck = false;  // Boolean flag

    let month_day = (date.month, date.day);
    for event in events {
        let event_month_day = (event.date.month, event.date.day);
        if event_month_day == month_day {
            println!("{}: {}", event.date.year, event.description);
            any_luck = true;
        }
    }

    if !any_luck {
        println!("No events for {}-{}", date.month, date.day);
    }
}
```

Initializing structs

Structs can be initialized by specifying a value for all their fields inside curly brackets { and }. The declaration of the array seems a bit long-winded, because the initialization of the `Date` and `Event` structs is quite verbose. We can improve on this, but let's make a few points first.

- We don't need the `get_year_month_day` function anymore, since we are not making conversions from numbers to strings, extracting substrings, and converting them back to numbers again; instead we are dealing with separate integer values for year, month, and day all the time.
- We are not using tuples anymore. There is nothing wrong with tuples as such, but structs do this particular thing better. You can use named fields instead of numeric indices when initializing structs and referring to their members.
- We can put structs into an array, just like we put tuples there earlier.
- The members of the `Date` struct have data types that don't waste memory with 32-bit integers, when a smaller ones are enough to store all the possible values (year is typically in the low thousands, either side of zero, while month and day both fit in a byte).
- We can access the fields of the struct with the dot notation. In the case of nested structs we just continue dotting until we reach the field we need.
- Structs can be initialized by specifying their members, if we use them in the context that they were declared in. If we were making a library, we would need to either make the fields public, or provide constructors and accessors as associated functions or methods, as we will see later.

Struct implementations

Instead of specifying each member individually, structs can be created using free functions that return values of the appropriate struct. They could take all the struct fields as parameters, or use default values for some. Rust does not have function overloading, so we will need to come up with distinct names if we want to have multiple constructor functions.

Let's now define some handy functions to create `Date` and `Event` structs:

Example 11.4. Utility functions to make dates and events

```
fn make_date(year: i16, month: u8, day: u8) -> Date {
    Date {
        year: year,
        month: month,
        day: day,
    }
}

fn make_event(date: Date, description: String) -> Event {
    Event {
        date: date,
        description: description,
    }
}
```

With these functions, an `Event` could be initialized like this, using the `make_event` function with a nested call to the `make_date` function:

```
make_event(make_date(1996, 1, 23), String::from("JDK 1.0 released"))
```

This is slightly better, since we don't need to keep repeating the names of the struct fields. They serve well as reminders about what the fields are, but when repeated like earlier they can become unwieldy.

There is some unnecessary repetition inside the functions themselves, since the function parameters have the same names as the struct fields. This can be fixed with *field init shorthand*; if a variable has the same name as a struct field, you only need to mention it once, like this:

Example 11.5. Using the field init shorthand

```
fn make_date(year: i16, month: u8, day: u8) -> Date {
    Date { year, month, day }
}

fn make_event(date: Date, description: String) -> Event {
    Event { date, description }
}
```

That is much more compact and involves less typing.

Free functions to initialize structs are fine, but nearly all the Rust library structs define *associated functions* that belong to the struct. We'll want to do the same, so that our own structs work the same way as existing Rust data types. This brings us to *implementations*, or *impls* for short.

Let's give the `Date` struct an associated function that makes a new struct with fields initialized using the values we specify. The implementation is not that much different from the free function we saw earlier, but the associated function literally belongs to the struct type. We can achieve this with an `impl` block, delimited by curly brackets:

Example 11.6. An `impl` block for the `Date` struct

```
impl Date {
    fn new(year: i16, month: u8, day: u8) -> Self {
        Self { year, month, day }
    }
}
```

The function is called `new`, or more properly, `Date::new`. The function definition is inside the curly brackets of the `impl` block, which can also have more than one function inside it. Those functions will then all belong to the type mentioned after the `impl` keyword.

The `Self` data type here is an alias for the type mentioned after the `impl` keyword. This is an ergonomic feature of Rust; if we later change the name of the type, we don't need to hunt for the old type name among the associated functions in the `impl` block if we used `Self` instead of the actual type name.

The `Event` struct also gets its own `impl` block, and an associated function `Event::new` to make a new value of this type:

Example 11.7. An `impl` block for the `Event` struct

```
impl Event {
    fn new(date: Date, description: String) -> Self {
        Self { date, description }
    }
}
```

This allows us to declare the array elements like this in the main program:

```
Event::new(
    Date::new(2025, 12, 11),
    String::from("Rust 1.92.0 released"))
```

Less curly brackets, less boilerplate, more Rust-like, and also makes it possible to guard the initialization of the struct fields in the constructor.

Methods

Associated functions are all about the actual type, whereas *methods* work on the values of the type. Methods need a *reference* to distinguish which value is being worked on. This reference is similar to `this` in Java or C++, or the traditional name `self` used in Python.

Let's make a method that returns just the month and the day of an event. For convenience, we'll also define a struct that represents just the month and the day, and return a value of that type.

The most important thing here is the parameter of the `month_day` method. It is `&self`, or a reference to `self`. The `self` reference is also used in the method body to pick out the `month` and `day` fields to initialize the `MonthDay` struct that is returned from the method.

Example 11.8. A helper struct and a related accessor function

```
#[derive(Debug, PartialEq)]
struct MonthDay {
    month: u8,
    day: u8,
}
```

```
impl Event {
    fn month_day(&self) -> MonthDay {
        MonthDay { month: self.date.month, day: self.date.day }
    }
}
```

Just before the MonthDay struct definition there is a line:

```
#[derive(Debug, PartialEq)]
```

This is a Rust *annotation*, which is used here to automatically define an implementation of the Debug and PartialEq traits.

Since MonthDay does not implement the Display, we need the Debug trait, to be able to print a MonthDay value using the debug placeholder {:#?} of the println! macro. Also, we need the PartialEq trait in order to compare two MonthDay values. You can comment this line out and try to compile the program to look at the lengthy but helpful error message in detail.

Let's have a look at the whole program at this point, to get a better idea of where we are going:

Example 11.9. The complete events program

```
struct Date {
    year: i16,
    month: u8,
    day: u8,
}

impl Date {
    fn new(year: i16, month: u8, day: u8) -> Self {
        Self { year, month, day }
    }
}

#[derive(Debug, PartialEq)]
struct MonthDay {
    month: u8,
    day: u8,
}
```

```
struct Event {
    date: Date,
    description: String,
}

impl Event {
    fn new(date: Date, description: String) -> Self {
        Self { date, description }
    }

    fn month_day(&self) -> MonthDay {
        MonthDay { month: self.date.month, day: self.date.day }
    }
}

fn main() {
    let events = [
        Event::new(Date::new(2025, 12, 11),
                   String::from("Rust 1.92.0 released")),
        Event::new(Date::new(1996, 1, 23),
                   String::from("JDK 1.0 released")),
        Event::new(Date::new(2008, 12, 3),
                   String::from("Python 3.0 released")),
        Event::new(Date::new(2015, 5, 15),
                   String::from("Rust 1.0.0 released")),
        Event::new(Date::new(2025, 9, 16),
                   String::from("Java 25 released")),
        Event::new(Date::new(2025, 10, 7),
                   String::from("Python 3.14 released")),
        Event::new(Date::new(2025, 12, 11),
                   String::from("Rust 1.92.0 released")),
    ];

    let month_day = MonthDay { month: 5, day: 15 };

    let mut any_luck = false;  // Boolean flag

    for event in events {
        if event.month_day() == month_day {
            println!("{}: {}", event.date.year, event.description);
            any_luck = true;
        }
```

```
    }

    if !any_luck {
        println!("No events for {:#?}", month_day);
    }
}
```

The program can be compiled and run, and it displays the same result as earlier: the one event that occurs on May 15th. However, now we manipulate structs and their fields instead of tuples and plain integers.

Chapter summary

Structs let us compose new data types from primitive types or other structs, and also add behavior to them using implementation blocks. Struct members and methods are referred to using the dot notation.

Methods use a `self` reference to target a specific instance of a struct. This corresponds to some specific variable declared in the calling program.

Annotations are used to add implementations generated by the Rust compiler. The Rust standard library defines many annotations related to traits like `Debug`.

Chapter 12. Enums and pattern matching

Learn about

- How to define enumerated types or *enums* in Rust
- How to use enums as struct members
- How to use pattern matching with the `match` expression

Using enums for alternative values

Enumerated types or *enums* are one of the most loved features of Rust, but for reasons that you might not think about at first. In many other languages, enums are basically just numeric constants that are somehow related, although Java got a more powerful `enum` type back in version 5. When fully utilized, Rust enums are more like sum types, or *algebraic data types* found in functional languages like Haskell or OCaml, and that is what makes them so powerful. Let's learn about enums, first with some easy examples.

In Chapter 11, *Structs* we defined a `Date` struct with fields for year, month, and day. However, we had no way of checking that the values actually make sense. For example, February always has 28 days, except in a leap year, when it has 29. We could make a bogus date like

```
Date {
    year: 2026,
    month: 2,
    day: 30    // oops!
}
```

and nobody would notice until the error came back to bite us. The `MonthDay` struct isn't any different in this respect. Although it isn't a complete solution to the potential problem, using an enum for the month at least gives us partial correctness:

Example 12.1. An enum representing the months

```
#[derive(Debug, PartialEq, Copy, Clone)]
enum Month {
    January, February, March,
    April, May, June,
    July, August, September,
    October, November, December,
}
```

We use the `enum` keyword, give the type a name (here it is `Month`), and list the members. The convention here is to use `CamelCase`. We have not defined any means to get the conventional month number from this enum, each member does not necessarily even have a corresponding integer. Instead, we are just using the enum values as symbolic names for the months.

Typically, you would put each enum variant on its own line, but here they have been combined into four lines, matching the quarters of the year, and saving some vertical space in the book.

There is also a `derive` attribute to avoid compiler errors that relate to the Rust concept of ownership, which warrants its own discussion later.

Let's now update our `Date` and `MonthDay` structs to use the new `Month` enum instead of the `u8` type. Also the way that we initialize the events and the target date will need to change (again):

Example 12.2. Date struct using the `Month` enum

```
struct Date {
    year: i16,
    month: Month,
    day: u8,
}

impl Date {
    fn new(year: i16, month: Month, day: u8) -> Self {
        Self { year, month, day }
    }
```

```
}

#[derive(Debug, PartialEq)]
struct MonthDay {
    month: Month,
    day: u8,
}

fn main() {
    let events = [
        Event::new(Date::new(1996, Month::January, 23),
                   String::from("JDK 1.0 released")),
        Event::new(Date::new(2008, Month::December, 3),
                   String::from("Python 3.0 released")),
        Event::new(Date::new(2015, Month::May, 15),
                   String::from("Rust 1.0.0 released")),
        Event::new(Date::new(2025, Month::September, 16),
                   String::from("Java 25 released")),
        Event::new(Date::new(2025, Month::October, 7),
                   String::from("Python 3.14 released")),
        Event::new(Date::new(2025, Month::December, 11),
                   String::from("Rust 1.92.0 released")),
    ];

    // ...rest of main appears below
}
```

Now we are using the enum values instead of bare numbers, so that we avoid accidentally specifying something like `13` or `0` as the month.

Now that we have the `MonthDay` struct, we can use that to define the target date, since we don't need the year for that. Because we have derived the necessary traits for `MonthDay`, we can compare the target month-day with the event's month-day:

```
let month_day = MonthDay { month: Month::May, day: 15 };
for event in events {
    if event.month_day() == month_day {
        println!("{}: {}", event.date.year, event.description);
        any_luck = true;
    }
```

```
}
```

When you compile the program, you will get warnings because some of the variants of the `Month` enum are never used. However, the program compiles and runs fine. Here is the full program so far:

Example 12.3. The `events` program updated to use the `Month` enum

```
#[derive(Debug, PartialEq, Copy, Clone)]
enum Month {
    January, February, March,
    April, May, June,
    July, August, September,
    October, November, December,
}

struct Date {
    year: i16,
    month: Month,
    day: u8,
}

impl Date {
    fn new(year: i16, month: Month, day: u8) -> Self {
        Self { year, month, day }
    }
}

#[derive(Debug, PartialEq)]
struct MonthDay {
    month: Month,
    day: u8,
}

struct Event {
    date: Date,
    description: String,
}

impl Event {
    fn new(date: Date, description: String) -> Self {
```

```
        Event { date, description }
    }

    fn month_day(&self) -> MonthDay {
        MonthDay { month: self.date.month, day: self.date.day }
    }
}

fn main() {
    let events = [
        Event::new(Date::new(2025, Month::December, 11),
                   String::from("Rust 1.92.0 released")),
        Event::new(Date::new(1996, Month::January, 23),
                   String::from("JDK 1.0 released")),
        Event::new(Date::new(2008, Month::December, 3),
                   String::from("Python 3.0 released")),
        Event::new(Date::new(2015, Month::May, 15),
                   String::from("Rust 1.0.0 released")),
        Event::new(Date::new(2025, Month::September, 16),
                   String::from("Java 25 released")),
        Event::new(Date::new(2025, Month::October, 7),
                   String::from("Python 3.14 released")),
        Event::new(Date::new(2025, Month::December, 11),
                   String::from("Rust 1.92.0 released")),
    ];

    let month_day = MonthDay { month: Month::May, day: 15 };

    let mut any_luck = false;  // Boolean flag

    for event in events {
        if event.month_day() == month_day {
            println!("{}: {}", event.date.year, event.description);
            any_luck = true;
        }
    }

    if !any_luck {
        println!("No events for {:#?}", month_day);
    }
}
```

Enums with associated values

The feature that separates Rust enums from the less expressive alternatives of many other languages is the ability to have associated values for some or all of the enum variants. This essentially turns enums into sum types, which are a powerful way of representing data structures.

The most frequent examples of associated values are the `Option` and `Result` types, and we will have a look at both in upcoming chapters.

We will see an extended example of an enum with associated values in Chapter 39, *Refactoring the Event struct*.

Pattern matching

One of the distinguishing features of Rust is *pattern matching*, which replaces the traditional `switch` statement of C-style languages with a much more flexible alternative. Like the `if` conditional, `match` is also an expression that produces a value. Matches consist of match *arms* that distinguish various alternatives. Each arm must produce a value of the same type.

In order to get an idea of what a typical `match` expression looks like, let's define a function called `day_count` to find out the number of days in a month, given a value of the enum type `Month` at the start of this chapter. The function takes one argument of type `Month` and returns a `u8`, the smallest integer type that will fit the maximum number of days in a month. (To keep things simple, we could just use `i32` for everything, since that is the inferred integer type unless otherwise specified.) We'll develop a couple of versions of the function using a `match` expression, and end up with a concise and clear result.

The first version just uses a match expression to get a value that is one of 28, 30, or 31, depending on the month. This version does not take into account the fact that there could be 29 days in February instead of 28 if there is a leap year. This is just to have a look at the match expression syntax.

Example 12.4. Day count without leap year checking

```
// First version, leap year not accounted for
fn day_count(month: Month) -> u8 {
    match month {
        Month::January => 31, Month::February => 28, Month::March => 31,
        Month::April => 30, Month::May => 31, Month::June => 30,
        Month::July => 31, Month::August => 31, Month::September => 30,
        Month::October => 31, Month::November => 30, Month::December => 31,
    }
}
```

The thick arrow => leads to the expression belonging to the particular match arm. It can also be a block delimited with curly brackets. The match arms are separated with a comma.

To test the function separately from the events program, just copy the definition of the `Month` enum and the `day_count` function to the Rust Playground, and add some relevant code in the main function:

```
fn main() {
    println!("There are {} days in January", day_count(Month::January));
}
```

You will get some warnings about unused enum variants, but in the Standard Output section of the Playground you should see:

```
There are 31 days in January
```

This version of the function has some unnecessary repetition, as many of the match arms produce the same value. We can fix this by grouping the values separated with a vertical bar `|`:

Example 12.5. Day count with less match arms

```
// Second version with grouped matches
fn day_count(month: Month) -> u8 {
```

```
    match month {
        Month::April | Month::June | Month::September | Month::November => 30,
        Month::February => 28,
        _ => 31
    }
}
```

The last match arm is _, which marks the catch-all arm; if none of the other arms match, this one will be used. This is based on the fact that all of the months not specifically mentioned have 31 days. The Rust compiler will flag an error if all enum variants are not handled by the `match` expression.

Finally, we can fix the February/leap year issue by adding a `year` parameter, defining a new function called `is_leap_year`, and changing the `Month::February` arm to use it:

Example 12.6. Day count with leap year check

```
// Third version, with leap year accounted for
fn day_count(month: Month, year: i32) -> u8 {
    match month {
        Month::April | Month::June | Month::September | Month::November => 30,
        Month::February => if is_leap_year(year) { 29 } else { 28 },
        _ => 31
    }
}

fn is_leap_year(year: i32) -> bool {
    (year % 4 == 0 && year % 100 != 0) || (year % 400 == 0)
}
```

The leap year calculation is based on the classic formula: to be a leap year, a year number must be divisible by four, except for end-of-century years, which must be divisible by 400. So, the year 2000 was a leap year, but 1900 was not.

It is also possible to define methods on enums, like for structs. In the previous example the `day_count` function seems to "belong" to the enum, so by implementing it as a method of the `Month` we get better cohesion, and also one less parameter at the call site. Here is a complete program with the required changes applied, and tested using the year 2020 (a leap year) as an example:

Example 12.7. Implementing a method for an enum

```
#[derive(Debug, PartialEq, Copy, Clone)]
enum Month {
    January, February, March,
    April, May, June,
    July, August, September,
    October, November, December,
}

impl Month {
    fn day_count(&self, year: i32) -> u8 {
        match self {
            Month::April | Month::June | Month::September | Month::November => 30,
            Month::February => if is_leap_year(year) { 29 } else { 28 },
            _ => 31
        }
    }
}

fn is_leap_year(year: i32) -> bool {
    (year % 4 == 0 && year % 100 != 0) || (year % 400 == 0)
}

fn main() {
    let year = 2020;
    let month = Month::February;
    let count = month.day_count(year);

    println!("In {year}, February had {count} days.");
}
```

This will result in the following output:

```
In 2020, February had 29 days.
```

There is much more to pattern matching. For a more extensive treatment, see *The Rust Programming Language* [Kla2026] and *Programming Rust* [Bla2021].

Chapter summary

Enumerated types or enums collect alternative values together. Like structs, enums can have method implementations.

The `match` expression is used to test for various alternatives of an enum. This is a distinguishing feature of Rust known as *pattern matching*.

Chapter 13. Optional values

Learn about

- The Rust Option type
- How to handle the Some and None variants

Option instead of nullable

Null or missing values have been causing trouble for application programmers and database operators alike for a long time[1]. Java has the ubiquitous NullPointerException if you forget to check for null, but has gained an optional type in version 8 called java.util.Optional<T>. C# now has nullable types, Swift has optionals, and Rust has the Option type.

In Rust, the Option<T> type is used to express a situation where there may or may not be a value. Even in the case of there being no actual value, there will always be the Option value, and you can examine it to find out if an actual value is present or not. This is a clever idea that may take a while to sink in unless it is already familiar, but the bottom line is that there is no null value in Rust, so there can never be a null pointer exception either (of course, there are no exceptions in Rust either, but there are pointers—we'll get to that)[2].

Option is a *generic type*, meaning that the type of the actual value inside an Option (if any) can be anything that is specified in the definition. The type is expressed with a *type parameter*. The definition of the Option type actually looks like this:

```
enum Option<T> {
    None,
    Some(T),
}
```

[1]https://www.infoq.com/presentations/Null-References-The-Billion-Dollar-Mistake-Tony-Hoare/
[2]There is such a thing as unsafe Rust, which has raw pointers that can be null, but we won't go there in this book.

So, it is an enum with two variants. Here `T` is the generic type parameter.

Let's see how this fits into our example domain. Say that we want to add a category to the events, so that we can group them by topic. We'll have a two-level categorization, with a primary category and a secondary category, but the secondary category is optional. In other words, there must always be a primary category, but there doesn't have to be a secondary category. We can use the `Option` type in a struct field to achieve this:

Example 13.1. Category struct with optional field

```
#[derive(Debug)]
struct Category {
    primary: String,
    secondary: Option<String>,
}
```

We'll also define two associated functions to make categories of different flavors:

Example 13.2. The `impl` block for the `Category` struct

```
impl Category {
    fn new(primary: &str, secondary: &str) -> Self {
        Self {
            primary: primary.to_string(),
            secondary: Some(secondary.to_string())
        }
    }

    fn from_primary(primary: &str) -> Self {
        Self {
            primary: primary.to_string(),
            secondary: None
        }
    }
}
```

The new function takes both primary and secondary values, and makes a Category value out of them. Since the secondary category is optional, it is wrapped into Some to construct the right variant of the Option<String> type.

The from_primary function only has one argument, the primary category value, so it sets the secondary category to None.

The parameters of the functions are expressed as references to strings, and the functions make owned String values out of them using the to_string() method.

Now that we have a new Category type, let's update the Event struct to include a category, so that every event must have one:

Example 13.3. Event struct with a category field

```
struct Event {
    date: Date,
    description: String,
    category: Category,
}

impl Event {
    fn new(date: Date, description: String, category: Category) -> Self {
        Event { date, description, category }
    }
}
```

Of course, we also need to update the declaration of the events array (again...):

Example 13.4. Event declarations updated to include category

```
    let events = [
        Event::new(
            Date::new(2025, Month::December, 11),
            String::from("Rust 1.92.0 released"),
            Category::new("programming", "rust")),
        Event::new(
            Date::new(1996, Month::January, 23),
```

```
        String::from("JDK 1.0 released"),
        Category::new("programming", "java")),
    Event::new(
        Date::new(2008, Month::December, 3),
        String::from("Python 3.0 released"),
        Category::new("programming", "python")),
    Event::new(
        Date::new(2015, Month::May, 15),
        String::from("Rust 1.0.0 released"),
        Category::new("programming", "rust")),
    Event::new(
        Date::new(2025, Month::September, 16),
        String::from("Java 25 released"),
        Category::new("programming", "java")),
    Event::new(
        Date::new(2025, Month::October, 7),
        String::from("Python 3.14 released"),
        Category::new("programming", "python")),
    Event::new(
        Date::new(2025, Month::December, 11),
        String::from("Rust 1.92.0 released"),
        Category::new("programming", "rust")),
];
```

We'll also update the way we print the matching events to include the category. We use the debug printing for now, even though it doesn't look very nice. (Eventually we will cave in and implement the `Display` trait.)

```
println!(
    "{}: {} ({:#?})",
    event.date.year,
    event.description,
    event.category);
```

Now the output does indeed include the category:

```
2015: Rust 1.0.0 released (Category {
    primary: "programming",
    secondary: Some(
        "rust",
    ),
```

```
})
```

Handling optional values

If we want to create an instance of an optional type, we have two choices: to create the variant that includes the wrapped value, or create the variant with no value at all. For example, the secondary category in the `Category` struct is an `Option<String>`. If it has a value, it will be given as something like `Some("rust")`. To indicate a missing secondary category we just use `None`. These are the ways used in the constructor functions of `Category`.

When we want to find out if there is an optional value or not, the most complete way is to use a `match` expression to handle both variants. Suppose we want to regenerate the category string from a `Category` instance, so that we get a result like `"programming/rust"` or just `"programming"` in the absence of a secondary category. This is how we would handle it using the `match` expression:

Example 13.5. Handling the optional second category component

```
let category = Category::from_primary("programming");
let mut result = String::new();
match category.secondary {
    Some(secondary) => {
        result.push_str(&category.primary);
        result.push('/');
        result.push_str(&secondary);
    },
    None => {
        result.push_str(&category.primary);
    }
};
```

This works, but is needlessly wordy. We can do better; since `match` is an expression, we can assign the result of that expression directly to the result, without using a mutable variable:

```
let result = match category.secondary {
    Some(secondary) => &format!("{}/{}", &category.primary, secondary),
```

```
    None => &format!("{}", &category.primary)
};
```

Note that we need to take the reference of what the format! macro returns. In both cases we end up with a string, and it either has just one part, or it has two parts with a slash between them.

Another way of handling this is to use the if let syntax. We handle the primary case first, and then do anything else as necessary:

```
let category = Category::new("programming", "rust");
let mut result = category.primary.to_string();
if let Some(secondary) = category.secondary {
    result.push_str(&format!("/{}", secondary));
}
```

Here we have used the fact that a category always has a primary field, so that we can prepare it in advance. If there is no secondary category, we are done. Otherwise we append a slash and the secondary category to the existing result.

Note

The full "events" program developed so far can be found in the GitHub repository of this book, in the ch-option directory.

Chapter summary

Rust has no null value, making Rust programs immune to null pointer references. Instead, Rust has the Option<T> enum type, with two variants: Some(T) with an associated value, or None to indicate no value.

To handle optional values, we use the match expression or the if let construction.

To make values of the Option<T>, we wrap any existing value with Some, or we just use None when there is no value.

Chapter 14. Ownership, references and borrowing

Learn about

- Rust memory management and the concept of ownership
- How to use references in Rust
- Borrowing, or using data owned by others in a controlled manner

Memory safety

The feature that distinguishes Rust from most other programming languages is *memory safety*, which kicks in already when the program is being compiled. This sometimes results in a longer development time because the Rust compiler is very strict regarding the rules of memory safety.

Three fundamental concepts are central to memory safety in Rust:

- Ownership
- References
- Borrowing

These concepts influence how you design data structures, how functions accept values as parameters and return their results, and how multiple parts of your program interact with the same piece of data. While it can sometimes feel that the rules are too restrictive, they actually eliminate entire classes of program errors before your program even runs.

Ownership

Some of the most common errors related to memory usage in other programming languages stem from manual memory management, including:

- Accessing memory after it has been freed

- Freeing the same memory twice
- Modifying data concurrenctly without synchronization

While there are solutions to these problems, they often involve a lot of additional work for the programmer. Rust attempts to shift this burden to the compiler, and the primary concept making this possible is *ownership*.

Ownership is a central concept in Rust, but it is something that most likely is not familiar to programmers coming from other programming languages, especially those that have automatic memory management (including "garbage collection").

At any point in time, the Rust compiler needs to know:

- Who owns a piece of data;
- How long that data is valid;
- Who is allowed to access it.

The part of the Rust compiler that tracks this information is called the *borrow checker*, and the error messages it emits will become very familiar to any beginning (but also seasoned) Rust programmers.

Based on personal experience, this author has identified three phases in a programmer's relationship with the borrow checker:

1. Why the #&% am I not allowed to do X in Rust?
2. OK, I kind of see why doing X wouldn't make sense.
3. Thank you, Borrow Checker, for looking after my code!

Of course, your experience may be different, but the end result often is increased confidence in both the borrow checker and the code you have written.

Every value in Rust has a single *owner*, a variable that is responsible for that value. There can be only one owner at a time. When the owner goes out of *scope*, the value is automatically *dropped*, and the memory allocated for it is freed. There is no need to manually free memory. The Rust compiler inserts the appropriate cleanup code automatically when needed.

Memory for the values of variables is allocated either from *stack* memory or *heap* memory. Stack memory is usually associated with function parameters and local variables, while heap memory is intended for dynamic allocation.

Rust strongly prefers stack memory allocation, and uses it for all values that have a *fixed size* known at compile time. When stack memory is being used, the values are pushed onto the stack when a scope begins, and popped off the stack when the scope ends.

Memory for data structures that can grow or shrink at runtime is allocated on the heap, but a pointer to that memory can and will be stored in stack memory.

Scope

Scope is a region of the program where a given variable is accessible. It is central to the Rust memory model, because it determined when values are created, when they can be accessed, and when they are destroyed.

Usually a scope is introduced by a *block*, delimited by curly brackets `{` and `}`. For example, the body of a function is a scope, and the `if` and `match` expressions also introduce scopes. You can create a scope whenever you need one using curly brackets.

When the execution the program leaves a block, the variables in its scope are no longer accessible. If you attempt to use them outside the block, it results in a compiler error.

In Rust, scope determines *lifetime*. When a value is bound to a variable, it becomes valid and remains so until the end of the scope of the variable. When the variable goes out of scope, Rust automatically releases any values owned by the value by calling `drop` on it.

Examples of ownership and scope

Let's look at some examples of ownership and scope. In the next example, we declare a variable `day`, and then create a new scope where we assign it to another variable `next_day` so that we can add one to it and print it out:

Example 14.1. Trying to use a variable that is out of scope

```
fn main() {
    let day = 11;

    {
        let mut next_day = day;
        next_day += 1;
    }

    println!("day = {}  next_day = {}", day, next_day);
}
```

If we try to compile this program in the Rust Playground, the compiler will stop with an error message:

```
Compiling playground v0.0.1 (/playground)
error[E0425]: cannot find value `next_day` in this scope
 --> src/main.rs:9:46
  |
9 |     println!("day = {}  next_day = {}", day, next_day);
  |                                              ^^^^^^^^
  |
help: the binding `next_day` is available in a different scope in the same function
 --> src/main.rs:5:17
  |
5 |         let mut next_day = day;
  |                 ^^^^^^^^

For more information about this error, try `rustc --explain E0425`.
error: could not compile `playground` (bin "playground") due to 1 previous error
```

The `next_day` variable is not accessible outside the scope it was declared in. However, if we declare the variables in the same scope, as in the next example, all is good.

Simple stack-only types, like the primitive integer types, floating-point types, Boolean, and characters, can be copied, so there is usually no need to be concerned about ownership. Here we do the same as in the previous example, but this time both variables are in the same scope, and the assignment succeeds:

Example 14.2. Using a variable in the current scope

```
fn main() {
    let day = 11;
    let mut next_day = day;
    next_day += 1;
    println!("day = {}  next_day = {}", day, next_day);
}
```

The Rust compiler sees no problem with this; the value is copied to the other variable, but the original variable is left intact.

However, if we use the `Date` struct we defined earlier to represent calendar dates (as a simplified version), the situation becomes rather different:

Example 14.3. Trying to assign a type that does not implement the `Copy` trait

```
#[derive(Debug)]
struct Date {
    year: i16,
    month: u8,
    day: u8,
}

fn main() {
    let today = Date { year: 2026, month: 2, day: 11 };
    let mut tomorrow = today;
    tomorrow.day += 1;
    println!("today = {:#?}  tomorrow = {:#?}", today, tomorrow);
}
```

If we try to compile this program, the Rust compiler will stop with an error message:

```
Compiling playground v0.0.1 (/playground)
error[E0382]: borrow of moved value: `today`
  --> src/main.rs:12:49
```

```
   |
 9 |     let today = Date { year: 2026, month: 2, day: 11 };
   |         ----- move occurs because `today` has type `Date`, which does not
implement the `Copy` trait
10 |     let mut tomorrow = today;
   |                        ----- value moved here
11 |     tomorrow.day += 1;
12 |     println!("today = {:#?}  tomorrow = {:#?}", today, tomorrow);
   |                                                 ^^^^^ value borrowed here after
move
```

This is the ownership mechanism in action. Simple types implement the Copy trait (see Chapter 18, *Traits* for details), so they can be copied, but our Date struct does not.

Here, the value of the today has been *moved* to the tomorrow variable, who has now become the new owner of the value. This makes the today variable invalid, and the Rust compiler notices the error.

Since the Date struct only has primitive types as members, we may think we can fix this by deriving the Copy trait implementation:

Example 14.4. Deriving the Copy trait

```
#[derive(Debug, Copy)]
struct Date {
    year: i16,
    month: u8,
    day: u8,
}
```

However, the Rust compiler still isn't happy:

```
Compiling playground v0.0.1 (/playground)
error[E0277]: the trait bound `Date: Clone` is not satisfied
   --> src/main.rs:1:17
    |
  1 | #[derive(Debug, Copy)]
    |                 ^^^^ the trait `Clone` is not implemented for `Date`
```

```
    |
note: required by a bound in `Copy`
   --> /playground/.rustup/toolchains/stable-x86_64-unknown-linux-gnu/lib/rustlib/src/
rust/library/core/src/marker.rs:462:17
    |
462 | pub trait Copy: Clone {
    |                 ^^^^^ required by this bound in `Copy`
help: consider annotating `Date` with `#[derive(Clone)]`
    |
  2 + #[derive(Clone)]
  3 | struct Date {
    |

For more information about this error, try `rustc --explain E0277`.
error: could not compile `playground` (bin "playground") due to 1 previous error
```

Now the compiler is suggesting that we also need to implement the `Clone` trait. This was actually already suggested by the previous error message, but there is a good chance that we did not read all of it. The messages from the Rust compiler can be long, but they often contain very useful suggestions, so it pays to read them thoroughly.

What did the previous error message suggest, again? Let's go back and find out.

```
note: if `Date` implemented `Clone`, you could clone the value
  --> src/main.rs:2:1
   |
 2 | struct Date {
   | ^^^^^^^^^^^ consider implementing `Clone` for this type
...
10 |     let mut tomorrow = today;
   |                        ----- you could clone this value
   = note: this error originates in the macro `$crate::format_args_nl` which comes from
 the
     expansion of the macro `println` (in Nightly builds, run with -Z macro-backtrace
 for more info)

For more information about this error, try `rustc --explain E0382`.
error: could not compile `playground` (bin "playground") due to 1 previous error
```

So the correct fix for this problem seems to be to implement both the `Copy` and `Clone` traits:

Example 14.5. Deriving both `Copy` and `Clone` along with `Debug`

```
#[derive(Debug, Copy, Clone)]
struct Date {
    year: i16,
    month: u8,
    day: u8,
}
```

You will see some warnings from the Rust compiler about unused members, but now the value in the `today` variable can be copied to `tomorrow`.

Types like `String` and `Vec<T>` follow move semantics by default. If we need to make copies of them, we will have to use the `clone` method. More often than that, however, you will just want to use the value for a while. This is where you need *borrowing*, which is done using *references*.

References

A *reference* in Rust is essentially a pointer to a value that is owned by someone else. There are both *immutable* and *mutable* references for different situations.

As per the ownership rules, Rust allows any number of immutable references to the same value, as long as no mutable references exist at the same time. This means that you could have a situation like this where you have multiple immutable references to the same date, and then proceed to work on them (without mutating them, of course):

Example 14.6. Multiple immutable references

```
fn main() {
    let today = Date { year: 2026, month: 2, day: 11 };
    let maybe_tomorrow = &today;
    println!("today = {:#?}", today);
    println!("maybe_tomorrow = {:#?}", maybe_tomorrow);
}
```

The ampersand character & marks a reference, as in `&today` above.

Mutable references are more interesting. The original variable being referred to must be declared as `mut`, and only one mutable reference to a value can exist at a time. The mutable reference is specified as `&mut` instead of just `&`. To change the value of the `today` variable we can get a mutable reference to it and change the value of the `day` field:

Example 14.7. Mutable references to a variable

```
fn main() {
    let mut today = Date { year: 2026, month: 2, day: 11 };
    println!("today = {:?}", today);

    let tomorrow = &mut today;
    tomorrow.day += 1;
    println!("tomorrow = {:?}", today);  // note what is being printed
}
```

The output from the program is:

```
today = Date { year: 2026, month: 2, day: 11 }
tomorrow = Date { year: 2026, month: 2, day: 12 }
```

After the change we printed out the value of the `today` variable, so the original value was indeed changed through the mutable reference.

Borrowing

Borrowing happens when you use a reference to access a value that is owned by someone else. At any given time, you may have *either* any number of immutable references, *or* exactly one mutable reference, but not both.

Borrowing is most useful when you're defining a function that needs to use a value, but the value should not be moved, because you want to use it again later in the same scope. Instead the ownership needs to be retained by whoever calls the function. This is particularly common when you want to pass a `String` or a `Vec<T>` to a function.

Chapter summary

Rust achieves memory safety by controlling memory usage through the concept of *ownership*. You can have many read-only references to a value, but only one mutable reference at a time. You can *borrow* memory owned by other parts of the program if you follow the rules administered by the *borrow checker*, a major subsystem of the Rust compiler. For very thorough explanations of the topics in this chapter, see *The Rust Programming Language* [Kla2026] and *Rust in Action* [McN2021].

Chapter 15. Vectors

Learn about

- How to store a varying number of elements in a vector
- How to find out the number of elements in a vector

Storing elements in a dynamic vector

Until now we have used an array to store the events, since we had just a small number of events, and they were all initialized inside the program from static data. In the long term, an array is not the most suitable option for this kind of data. In this chapter we will take a look at the most common collection type in Rust, the *vector*, or more accurately the `std::vec::Vec<T>` type.

Like the `Option<T>` type we saw in Chapter 13, *Optional values*, `Vec<T>` is a generic type, and the `T` is the type parameter. The elements in the vector will be values of type `T`.

To put our events in a vector instead of an array, we first declare the vector to contain `Event` values, and then use the `push` method to add some events, all in our `main` function:

Example 15.1. Declaring a vector and adding elements

```
let mut events: Vec<Event> = Vec::new();

events.push(Event::new(
        Date::new(2025, Month::December, 11),
        String::from("Rust 1.92.0 released"),
        Category::new("programming", "rust")));
events.push(Event::new(
        Date::new(1996, Month::January, 23),
        String::from("JDK 1.0 released"),
        Category::new("programming", "java")));
events.push(Event::new(
```

```
        Date::new(2008, Month::December, 3),
        String::from("Python 3.0 released"),
        Category::new("programming", "python")));

// ...and so on.
```

The vector has been declared as mutable so that we can "push" the elements into it. Separately pushing each value into the vector gets tedious quickly, so Rust has a handy `vec!` macro to initialize the whole vector at the same time, with the elements in square brackets and separated by commas:

Example 15.2. Using the `vec!` macro to initialize a vector

```
let events = vec![
    Event::new(
        Date::new(2025, Month::December, 11),
        String::from("Rust 1.92.0 released"),
        Category::new("programming", "rust")),
    Event::new(
        Date::new(1996, Month::January, 23),
        String::from("JDK 1.0 released"),
        Category::new("programming", "java")),
    Event::new(
        Date::new(2008, Month::December, 3),
        String::from("Python 3.0 released"),
        Category::new("programming", "python")),
];
```

This is almost identical to the array initialization we saw earlier in Chapter 7, *Tuples and arrays*. The compiler will infer the values that are going in the vector, so in most cases you don't even need to specify the actual type of the vector. Here the vector is immutable, because it is initialized all at once.

The advantages of using a vector come from being able to add and remove values later, provided that you have declared the vector with the `let mut` statement. Also, the memory required for the elements is allocated dynamically on the heap, and the vector itself stores only pointers to the values, so if you have truly huge lists of things, they may not fit in stack memory if you put them in an array.

Iterating through a vector is the same as with an array, so that part of the program does not need any changes. Vectors do also have many additional facilities for flexible iteration. For all the various methods of iterating through a vector, or finding values in one, see the `Vec<T>` documentation.

In many respects, vectors and arrays are similar. The main difference is that while arrays are static, vectors are dynamic. However, the current number of elements in a vector can be queried with its `len` method. You can also index the elements in a vector using the same notation as arrays, with square brackets. Vectors allocate more memory as needed, but they can also be initialized with the desired capacity, to ensure that allocations of additional memory are not needed frequently as elements are added.

Sorting a vector

Sorting a vector requires that the elements implement the `std::cmp::Ord` trait. This is going to require lots of derived traits for all the types concerned, so we'll deal with this properly in the Today program, developed in Part III, "Programming Today".

Chapter summary

Vectors can grow and shrink dynamically, and they can be initialized as empty or all elements can be provided at once using the `vec!` macro.

Vectors can be iterated like arrays, and individual elements can be accessed with an index. Out of bounds index values cause a panic.

Chapter 16. Command-line arguments

Learn about

- Getting information from a command-line argument
- Making a struct from a string

Getting at the arguments

Among its many features the Rust standard library, or the `std` module, contains utilities to get the command-line arguments of an executable program. To use these utilities and other facilities of the standard library we need to learn how to bring types into scope.

Certain standard library types are automatically brought into scope by the *prelude*. Others will need to be mentioned explicitly with the `use` keyword.

The command-line argument handling is found in the `std::env` module. Instead of hard-coding our target date for events into the program, we can get it from a command-line argument.

Converting a string to a `MonthDay`

We first need a method to make a `MonthDay` from a string. The following example shows the associated function `MonthDay::from_str`:

Example 16.1. Making a `MonthDay` value from a string

```
#[derive(Debug, PartialEq)]
struct MonthDay {
    month: Month,
    day: u8,
}
```

```
impl MonthDay {
    fn from_str(s: &str) -> Self {
        assert!(s.len() == 4);
        let month_string = &s[..2];
        let month = Month::from_i32(month_string.parse().unwrap());
        let day: u8 = s[2..].parse().unwrap();
        MonthDay { month, day }
    }
}
```

This method takes slices of the string argument (first two and last two digits) and parses them as numbers.

We also need a way to make a `Month` enum from an `i32`, so we'll make another associated function, `Month::from_i32`:

Example 16.2. Making a `MonthDay` value from an integer

```
impl Month {
    fn from_i32(number: i32) -> Self {
        match number {
            1 => Month::January,
            2 => Month::February,
            3 => Month::March,
            4 => Month::April,
            5 => Month::May,
            6 => Month::June,
            7 => Month::July,
            8 => Month::August,
            9 => Month::September,
            10 => Month::October,
            11 => Month::November,
            12 => Month::December,
            _ => panic!("Invalid month number: {}", number),
        }
    }
}
```

If the month number is not one of 1 to 12, the program intentionally causes a panic by using the `panic!` macro. This is the easiest way out of trouble, as far as we know at this point.

The following prints out the `MonthDay` value using the debug representation:

```
let month_day = MonthDay::from_str("0515");
println!("{:#?}", month_day);
```

The value is printed in a format that closely resembles the `struct` definition:

```
MonthDay {
    month: May,
    day: 15,
}
```

Handling the month-day argument

We need to replace the hard-coded string with the actual value of a command-line argument. Rust provides the arguments in a vector, so we bring the `std::env` module into scope and pick the second command-line argument (the one with index 1), if any, because the first one is the name of the executable. Here we have first brought the `std::env` module into scope with the `use` statement:

Example 16.3. Handling the month-day argument

```
use std::env;

fn main() {
    let args: Vec<String> = env::args().collect();
    let month_day = MonthDay::from_str(&args[1]);  // note: 1, not 0
    println!("{:#?}", month_day);

    // ... rest of the main program
}
```

We can supply the program with one or more command-line arguments using Cargo. To do that, we separate the `cargo` from the arguments with `--` (two consecutive dashes):

```
% cargo run -- 0515
MonthDay {
    month: May,
    day: 15,
}
2015: Rust 1.0.0 released (Category {
    primary: "programming",
    secondary: Some(
        "rust",
    ),
})
% cargo run -- 1211
MonthDay {
    month: December,
    day: 11,
}
2025: Rust 1.92.0 released (Category {
    primary: "programming",
    secondary: Some(
        "rust",
    ),
})
```

The program seems to work as intended; when we give it a month-day string like `0515` or `1211` as a command-line argument, it is correctly parsed and can be used to find matching events. Of course, if the command-line argument is malformed, the program will panic, just like it was designed to do:

```
% cargo run -- xyz
thread 'main' (2857491) panicked at src/main.rs:145:9:
assertion failed: s.len() == 4
note: run with `RUST_BACKTRACE=1` environment variable to display a backtrace
% cargo run -- 0000
thread 'main' (2858053) panicked at src/main.rs:34:18:
Invalid month number: 0
note: run with `RUST_BACKTRACE=1` environment variable to display a backtrace
```

If we wanted to test the program on the current date, we could use the Unix `date` utility (available on Linux and macOS) to generate the command-line parameter as part of the `cargo` command:

```
% date +%m%d
0525
% cargo run -- `date +%m%d`
```

However, we won't get any results printed unless we add an event with a month-day of the current date, then build and run again.

Chapter summary

Command-line argument handling is in the `std::env`, which needs to be brought into scope with the `use` statement.

Arguments are stored in a vector, and the first one is the name of the executable program.

We can run the program with the `cargo run`. Those command-line arguments that want to pass to the program need to be separated from the Cargo arguments with two dashes.

Chapter 17. Errors

Learn about

- How to use the `Result` to handle error conditions
- How to propagate errors

No panic, but a result

Errors happen, no matter what. We have already seen a rather dramatic way of handling an error, namely the "panic". It can occur as a result of something going badly wrong in the program, or because the programmer purposefully invoked the `panic!` macro.

Fortunately, not all errors are something to panic about. Rust also has *recoverable* errors, so that the program can find out if something went wrong and make any necessary corrections that apply, at runtime. This is made possible by the `Result<T, E>` type.

Like `Option`, `Result` is a generic type, but instead of just one type parameter, it has two. This is how `Result` is defined in the standard library:

```
enum Result<T, E> {
    Ok(T),
    Err(E),
}
```

It has two generic type parameters, `T` and `E`. Both are used as the types of associated values. `T` is the type of the value for the case where everything went OK, and `E` is the type of the error value for when something went wrong. Any function or method can use `Result` to return a result to the caller. The Rust standard library has a number of predefined generic `Result` variants, and you can also make your own.

Using `Result` is the Rust way of handling errors, because the language has no exception-handling mechanism. The idiomatic way is to use a `match` expression to cover both variants of the Result, just as we did with the Option type in Chapter 13, *Optional values*.

For example, say that we want to open a text file with information about historical events, but the file might not exist. This is how we would handle the situation:

Example 17.1. Trying to open a file

```
use std::fs::File;

fn main() {
    let file_result = File::open("events.txt");

    let file = match file_result {
        Ok(f) => f,
        Err(e) => {
            panic!("Error opening file: {:?}", e);
        }
    };

    // If we make it here, we can start reading from `file`
}
```

If the file called events.txt is not found, the program intentionally panics. Inside the Err arm of the match expression we could check for the actual error type with another match expression on the result of the kind method of the error. The actual error type here is std::io::Error, as can be seen from the documentation of the std::fs::File::open.

Using the unwrap and expect methods

If we're going to panic on error anyway, we might as well skip the match expression altogether, and use the unwrap method, like we have done before, when we parsed slices of string in order to convert them to integers. The previous example would then look like this:

Example 17.2. Using the `unwrap` method to handle the error

```
use std::fs::File;

fn main() {
    let file = File::open("events.txt").unwrap();

    // If we make it here, we can start reading from `file`
}
```

That is not very user friendly, though, so instead of `unwrap` we might want to consider the `expect` method, which lets us specify the error message to show when panicking:

Example 17.3. Using the `expect` method to handle the error

```
use std::fs::File;

fn main() {
    let file = File::open("events.txt")
        .expect("Text file with events should be available");

    // If we make it here, we can start reading from `file`
}
```

Using the `expect` method gives more context to the problem, so that we can fix any errors if possible, and run the program again.

Propagating errors

Not all errors need to be handled on the spot. Sometimes the caller of a function or method knows more about how to handle the error in their particular situation. Rust also allows us to pass the error upwards or *propagate* it.

If we were to separate the reading of the file into its own function, we should define the return type of the function as a `Result`. The `Ok` variant could be the contents of the file, while the `Err` variant contains the error if any occurred.

In the case of reading a file the error is some variant of `std::io::Error`, so our function would look something like this:

Example 17.4. Propagating errors from a function

```
use std::fs::File;
use std::io::{self, Read};

fn read_events(filename: &str) -> Result<String, io::Error> {
    let file_result = File::open(filename);

    let mut file = match file_result {
        Ok(file) => file,
        Err(e) => return Err(e),  ❶
    };

    // OK, we have a file, let's read its content:

    let mut text = String::new();
    match file.read_to_string(&mut text) {
        Ok(_) => Ok(text),
        Err(e) => Err(e),  ❷
    }
}

fn main() {
    let filename = "events.txt";
    match read_events(&filename) {
        Ok(text) => {
            println!("{}", text);
        },
        Err(e) => {
            eprintln!("Unable to read from file '{}', error: {}",
                filename, e);
        }
    }
}
```

In the previous example there are two places, marked ❶ and ❷, where the error is propagated back to the caller.

Note

You can also use the ? operator (question mark) to make error handling a little more compact. It does mostly the same as the error propagation, but it also automatically converts errors to custom error types. For more information about this handy operator see the excellent explanation in *The Rust Programming Language* [Kla2026].

Chapter summary

Errors in Rust programs are handled either by an explicit panic (not very user-friendly) or dealing with `Result<T, E>` types, either using the `match` expression or calling the `unwrap` or `expect` methods. Errors can also be propagated from functions up to their caller, who may be in a better position to handle the error.

Chapter 18. Traits

Learn about

- How traits specify behavior for types
- How to implement a trait for a type
- Useful standard traits like `Display` and `Default`

Traits specify behavior

Traits are a way of specifying behavior that can be shared by various types. If you are familiar with Java, traits are somewhat like interfaces in that language. We can define a trait and then implement it for any type.

Traits can be implemented either by providing an `impl` block, or using the `#[derive]` attribute. We can easily derive common traits like `Debug` or `Clone` using `#[derive]`, which takes one or more traits (separated by commas) to derive:

Example 18.1. Using the `derive` attribute

```
#[derive(Debug, Clone)]
struct Category {
    primary: String,
    secondary: Option<String>,
}
```

In this case, deriving the `Debug` causes the Rust compiler to automatically generate an implementation for the `fmt` method, described in the `Debug` trait documentation. Also, deriving the `Clone` trait adds another method, `clone`. You could implement these methods yourself, but in most situations it is much easier to derive them.

Implementing the Display trait

Earlier in this book there has been a recurring theme of printing out some values using the debug placeholder {:#?} because the type of the value did not "implement the Display trait". Well, this chapter is where we finally get rid of that disclaimer, because we will now implement the Display trait for the domain types we have made.

The full name of the Display trait is std::fmt::Display, so we need to bring std::fmt into scope before we start. Let's begin with the Category struct:

Example 18.2. Implementing the Display trait for Category

```
use std::fmt;

impl fmt::Display for Category {
    fn fmt(&self, f: &mut fmt::Formatter) -> fmt::Result {
        match &self.secondary {
            Some(sec) => write!(f, "{}/{}", self.primary, sec),
            None => write!(f, "{}", self.primary),
        }
    }
}
```

The Display trait defines just one method, fmt, which takes a reference to the value being formatted for display, and a reference to a fmt::Formatter value, supplied by the caller (in practice usually the println! macro or similar). The return value is a fmt::Result value, but we don't need to handle the variants, because that is the responsibility of the caller.

With that, we are able to display any Category value with the println! macro using the normal placeholder {}:

Example 18.3. Printing out struct values normally

```
let rust_cat = Category::new("programming", "rust");
println!("{}", rust_cat);
// displays "programming/rust"

let prog_cat = Category::from_primary("programming");
println!("{}", prog_cat);
// displays "programming" because there is no secondary category
```

There are a couple of things to note about the `Display` trait implementation. First, the `fmt` method uses the `write!` macro, which takes the formatter as its first argument. Second, the `write!` macro returns `fmt::Result`, and that will be the return value of the `fmt` method. That is why there is no semicolon here; the last expression in a function or method will be its return value.

Similarly, we can implement `std::fmt::Display` for the `Event` struct:

Example 18.4. `Display` trait for `Event`

```
impl fmt::Display for Event {
    fn fmt(&self, f: &mut fmt::Formatter) -> fmt::Result {
        write!(f, "{}: {} ({})",
            self.date.year, self.description, self.category)
    }
}
```

This allows us to whittle down the event printing in `main` to just `println!("{event}");`. The `println!` macro will call the `fmt` method of each type. Now, when the program prints out a matching event, it will look like this:

```
2015: Rust 1.0.0 released (programming/rust)
```

Tip

When you implement the `Display` trait for a type you automatically get an implementation of the `std::str::ToString` trait. (In fact, it is not recommended to implement `ToString` directly.) Then you can call the `to_string` method on the object:

```
let cat = Category::new("programming", "rust");
assert_eq!(cat.to_string(), "programming/rust");
```

The `Default` trait

The Rust standard library has a potentially useful trait called `Default` that lets us specify a default value for a struct or enum, if there is a suitable one. The standard Rust types already implement the `Default` trait, and it is easy to do for our own types as well. The trait defines just one method called `default` that returns `Self`, which represents the type that is implementing the trait.

In Chapter 11, *Structs* we defined a `Date` struct that represents a calendar date. Even though we won't have much use for this type anymore after we take the `chrono` crate into use, it provides a good example of how to implement the `Default` trait.

For simplicity, the following is the definition of the `Date` struct, with the month specified as `u8` instead of the `Month` enum. To implement the `Default` trait we add an `impl Default` block for this struct.

Example 18.5. Implementing the `Default` trait

```
#[derive(Debug, Copy, Clone)]
struct Date {
    year: i16,
    month: u8,
    day: u8,
}

impl Default for Date {
    fn default() -> Self {
```

```
        Self { year: 1970, month: 1, day: 1 }
    }
}
```

The default value we use is the Unix epoch, or January 1st, 1970.

The following example contains the full `Date` struct that can be run in the Rust Playground. It also has an implementation of the `Display` trait for the `Date` struct thrown in for good measure, with a test program.

Example 18.6. Testing the `Display` and `Default` traits

```
use std::fmt;

struct Date {
    year: i16,
    month: u8,
    day: u8,
}

impl Date {
    fn new(year: i16, month: u8, day: u8) -> Self {
        Self { year, month, day }
    }
}

impl Default for Date {
    fn default() -> Self {
        Self { year: 1970, month: 1, day: 1 }
    }
}

impl fmt::Display for Date {
    fn fmt(&self, f: &mut fmt::Formatter) -> fmt::Result {
        write!(f, "{:04}-{:02}-{:02}",
            self.year, self.month, self.day)
    }
}

fn main() {
    let epoch: Date = Default::default();
```

```
    let rollover = Date::new(2038, 1, 19);

    println!(
        "Unix time started on {} and will end on {}. Well, not anymore.",
        epoch,
        rollover);
}
```

Now the epoch variable is initialized using the Default::default() method, and the dates are printed using the println! macro, which in turn uses the Display trait implementation of the Date struct.

> **Note**
>
> We could also use the #[derive(Default)] attribute if our struct or enum contains only members that already implement the Default trait. The derived implementation will then use the Default::default() methods of the respective types.

The FromStr trait

The std::str::FromStr trait is a useful counterpart to the std::fmt::Display trait we saw earlier. If we have in mind a string representation for a type, we can implement this trait to get a convenient way to convert the string to a value of our type.

Using the Category struct as an example, let's see how to implement the FromStr trait. In this context a category has a canonical string representation of the form primary[/secondary]. This notation means that there must always be a primary part, but the secondary part is optional. An implementation of the from_str function from the FromStr trait should take this into account.

The from_str function returns a Result, so we need an error type, which can be just String, but it could also be an enum with more detailed variants of error situations. We declare the error type in the FromStr trait implementation.

We pass the canonical string representation of the category to the from_str function, and proceed to do some rudimentary error checking. If the category string is empty even after trimming, we return an error. Otherwise we try to split the string on a slash like before, to get either one or two parts.

Example 18.7. Implementing the FromStr trait

```
use std::str::FromStr;

impl FromStr for Category {
    type Err = String;

    fn from_str(s: &str) -> Result<Self, Self::Err> {
        let s = s.trim();
        if s.is_empty() {
            return Err(String::from("empty category"));
        }

        let parts: Vec<&str> = s.split("/").collect();
        if parts.len() < 2 {
            Ok(Self {
                primary: parts[0].to_string(),
                secondary: None
            })
        } else {
            Ok(Self {
                primary: parts[0].to_string(),
                secondary: Some(parts[1].to_string())
            })
        }
    }
}
```

Since the `from_str` function returns `Result`, any code that tries to convert a string to a `Category` value must handle the potential error, either with a `match` expression or by just calling the `unwrap` method.

With the `FromStr` trait implementation in place it is now possible to create a category from a single string of the canonical format:

```
let cat = Category::from_str("programming/rust").unwrap();
assert_eq!(format!("{}", cat), "programming/rust");
```

Because the output from the `Display` is identical to the string passed to the `from_str` function, the round trip is complete.

In Chapter 16, *Command-line arguments* we defined a function called `from_str` for the `MonthDay` struct. Now that we know more about traits, we can see that it is exactly what we need for a `FromStr` trait implementation, so let's make it official:

Example 18.8. Implementing `FromStr` for `MonthDay`

```
impl FromStr for MonthDay {
    type Err = String;

    fn from_str(s: &str) -> Result<Self, Self::Err> {
        if s.len() != 4 {
            return Err(String::from("invalid length for string"));
        }

        let month_string = &s[..2];
        let month: Month;
        match month_string.parse() {
            Ok(m) => month = Month::from_i32(m),
            Err(_) => {
                return Err(String::from("invalid month"));
            }
        };

        let day: u8;
        match s[2..].parse() {
            Ok(d) => day = d,
            Err(_) => {
                return Err(String::from("invalid day"));
            }
        };

        Ok(MonthDay { month, day })
    }
}
```

This gives us the chance to introduce better error handling, although the `Month::from_i32` function will still panic if the month number is not between 1 and 12 inclusive, and the month-day extracted from the command-line argument is not validated.

Now that `MonthDay::from_str` returns `Result` we need to fix the main program. Here we also have an opportunity to handle some error conditions:

Example 18.9. Dealing with `Result` when parsing `MonthDay`

```
fn main() {
    let args: Vec<String> = env::args().collect();
    if args.len() < 2 {
        eprintln!("usage: events mmdd");
        return;
    }

    let md_arg = &args[1];  // note: 1, not 0
    let month_day = match MonthDay::from_str(md_arg) {
        Ok(m) => m,
        Err(_) => {
            eprintln!("Bad month-day: {}", md_arg);
            return;
        }
    };

    // ...and so on
```

Defining traits

To *define* a trait of our own design we use the `trait` keyword followed by the name of the trait, and then specify the method headers, but no actual method bodies. They will be supplied by the types that actually implement the trait.

The methods of a trait are implicitly public, so there is no need to use the `pub` keyword with them. In fact, the Rust compiler will flag an error if you do that:

```
% cargo build
   Compiling events v0.1.0 (/Users/me/Projects/Rust/learn-rust/ch-traits/events)
error[E0449]: visibility qualifiers are not permitted here
   --> src/main.rs:124:5
```

```
    |
124 |     pub fn fmt(&self, f: &mut fmt::Formatter) -> fmt::Result {
    |     ^^^ help: remove the qualifier
    |
    = note: trait items always share the visibility of their trait

For more information about this error, try `rustc --explain E0449`.
error: could not compile `events` (bin "events") due to 1 previous error
```

We will see a practical example of defining a trait in Part III when we implement some features of the Today program.

Chapter summary

Traits define functionality that can be shared among types. Many structs and enums can implement the same trait, each in its own way. We can implement many of the useful traits in the Rust standard library with the `#[derive]` attribute or an explicit `impl` block that mentions the trait and the type, like `impl Default for Date`. Methods in traits are implicitly public.

Chapter 19. Crates

Learn about

- Crates, the ecosystem libraries of Rust
- How to extend programs with crates
- How to generate random events for our program

Beyond the standard library

The scope of the Rust standard library is not quite as wide as that of many other languages. This is on purpose. It gives developers the flexibility to implement features that work across platforms and hardware arhitectures separately from the main Rust tools.

In Rust, a lot of the functionality often found in the standard library of a language is implemented with *crates*, which are libraries that can be easily taken into use in applications. They contain Rust source code and other data which is combined with the host application using Cargo.

Cargo, the tool that we have used earlier for building and running our Rust application, is also the package manager for Rust. It lets you add, update, and remove crates used by your application. You can also do these tasks manually by editing the `Cargo.toml` configuration file.

Typically the crates you use come from crates.io[1], the Rust crate registry. You can also use crates that are locally on your computer, or in a Git code repository. If you want your crate to have a wider distribution in the Rust community, you can publish it on crates.io. Cargo can handle the publishing (for requirements and details, see The Cargo Book[2]).

It is very common for Rust programs to rely on a fairly large number of external crates, downloaded from crates.io or GitHub. The crates are versioned,

[1] https://crates.io
[2] https://doc.rust-lang.org/cargo/

and you can choose to pin any crates you use to a specific version, only updating until you are sure that some new version of a crate is compatible with your application. The crate versions adhere to the Semantic Versioning specification, or SemVer[3] for short.

Making random dates with some crates

We have previously defined a `Date` struct to represent dates for historical events. For testing purposes, it could be useful to be able to quickly make lots of events, with dates that are distributed over the calendar year, on years that span a desired range. We could make dates that have random year, month, and date components.

The Rust standard library does not have facilities for generating random numbers, but there is a crate for that, called `rand` . We will use this crate in our events program, but first we need to add a utility method to the `Date` struct to test that the date is valid.

If we create dates where all the components are randomly generated, we may end up with dates that are not valid. For example, we could end up with a date like 31st of November, or 30th of February. However, these situations are easy to check, so the next example is a method called `is_valid` to handle the checking. It returns `true` if the date is valid, and `false` if not.

This method should go in the `impl` block of the `Date` struct. For printing out the dates, we also derive the `Debug` trait:

Example 19.1. Method for checking the validity of a date

```
#[derive(Debug)]
struct Date {
    year: i16,
    month: Month,
    day: u8,
}
```

[3]https://semver.org

```
impl Date {
    fn is_valid(&self) -> bool {
        self.day >= 1 && self.day <= day_count(self.month, self.year)
    }
}

fn day_count(month: Month, year: i16) -> u8 {
    match month {
        Month::April | Month::June | Month::September | Month::November => 30,
        Month::February => if is_leap_year(year) { 29 } else { 28 },
        _ => 31
    }
}

fn is_leap_year(year: i32) -> bool {
    (year % 4 == 0 && year % 100 != 0) || (year % 400 == 0)
}
```

The `is_valid` method also relies on the `day_count` and `is_leap_year` functions developed in Chapter 12, *Enums and pattern matching*, slightly modified as shown above.

We can test the `is_valid` method with a couple of dates, both valid and invalid:

Example 19.2. Checking some good and bad dates

```
    let dates = [
        // OK - 2000 was a leap year, so February has 29 days
        Date { year: 2000, month: Month::February, day: 29 },

        // bogus - April never has 31 days
        Date { year: 2026, month: Month::April, day: 31 },

        // OK - May has 31 days
        Date { year: 2012, month: Month::May, day: 31 },

        // bogus - day zero is never valid
        Date { year: 2026, month: Month::January, day: 0 },
    ];

    for date in dates {
```

```
        if date.is_valid() {
            println!("{:?} is valid", date);
        } else {
            println!("{:?} is bad", date);
        }
    }
```

The program correctly reports the status of the various dates using the debug display:

```
Date { year: 2000, month: February, day: 29 } is valid
Date { year: 2026, month: April, day: 31 } is bad
Date { year: 2012, month: May, day: 31 } is valid
Date { year: 2026, month: January, day: 0 } is bad
```

Now that we can test if a date is usable, we can start generating them randomly, and discard any invalid dates.

Add the `rand` crate to the program with the command `cargo add rand`:

```
% cargo add rand
    Updating crates.io index
      Adding rand v0.10.1 to dependencies
    [...]
```

Cargo adds the `rand` crate and its dependencies, and updates the `Cargo.toml` file with a reference to the crate in the `[dependencies]` section:

```
% cat Cargo.toml
[package]
name = "events"
version = "0.19.0"
edition = "2024"

[dependencies]
rand = "0.10.1"
```

The latest version of the `rand` crate at the time of this writing was 0.10.1, but you can also use a specific version, or some variation of SemVer (there are some differences, though, so see The Cargo Book for details on versioning).

To make use of the `rand` crate we need to bring the `rand::RngExt` trait into scope at the start of our program. Then we add an associated function to the `Date` struct for generating a random date with year, month, and date components in specified ranges:

Example 19.3. Generating random dates

```
use rand::RngExt;

impl Date {
    fn random() -> Self {
        let mut rng = rand::rng();
        Self {
            year: rng.random_range(1900..2099),
            month: Month::from_i32(rng.random_range(1..=12)),
            day: rng.random_range(1..=31),
        }
    }
}
```

Finally, we'll add some test code to `main` for generating a vector of valid random dates, with some statistics collected and printed just out of interest:

Example 19.4. Testing random date generation

```
    let mut random_dates = Vec::<Date>::new();
    let mut total_count = 0;
    let mut valid_count = 0;
    const MAX_COUNT: i32 = 100_000;
    while valid_count < MAX_COUNT {
        let candidate = Date::random();
        total_count += 1;
        if candidate.is_valid() {
            random_dates.push(candidate);
            valid_count += 1;
        }
    }
    println!("Generated {} random date candidates to get {} valid dates",
```

```
    total_count, random_dates.len());
```

Here we use the newly created `Date::random` function to generate a random `Date` values. A sample run of the program looks like this (of course, with randomness involved, the actual number of candidates will be different on successive runs):

```
Generated 101892 random date candidates to get 100000 valid dates
```

Making random descriptions

We can also generate random event descriptions, but without some effort their quality will not be as good as that of the random dates, unless we are happy with unreadable alphabet soup. Still, it is easier at this stage to generate some substandard test material than to collect a significant number of actual historical events.

Let's use the `cgisf_lib` crate from crates.io to generate some random sentences to be used as event descriptions. This crate got its name from the famous example phrase *"colorless green ideas sleep furiously"*, created by the linguist Noam Chomsky in 1957 to demonstrate a sentence that is syntactically valid, but semantically nonsensical.

Add the `cgisf_lib` crate to the project with the command `cargo add cgisf_lib`:

```
% cargo add cgisf_lib
    Updating crates.io index
      Adding cgisf_lib v0.2.1 to dependencies
    Updating crates.io index
     Locking 11 packages to latest Rust 1.92.0 compatible versions
      Adding cgisf_lib v0.2.1
      Adding const_format v0.2.35
      Adding const_format_proc_macros v0.2.34
      Adding getrandom v0.2.16
      Adding konst v0.2.19
      Adding konst_macro_rules v0.2.19
      Adding rand v0.8.5
      Adding rand_chacha v0.3.1
      Adding rand_core v0.6.4
```

```
    Adding unicode-xid v0.2.6
    Adding wasi v0.11.1+wasi-snapshot-preview1
```

If you now take a look at `Cargo.toml`, you will find that Cargo has added the crate:

```
% cat Cargo.toml
[package]
name = "events"
version = "0.1.0"
edition = "2024"

[dependencies]
cgisf_lib = "0.2.1"
rand = "0.9.2"
```

To generate sentences with the `cgisf_lib` crate, we first bring some of it into scope. The next example also shows how to bring several identifiers into scope with one `use` statement; we put a comma-separated list of them in curly brackets.

Let's generate ten example sentences and print them out:

Example 19.5. Generating random sentences

```
use cgisf_lib::{gen_sentence, SentenceConfigBuilder};

fn main() {
    for _ in 1..=10 {
        println!("{}",
            gen_sentence(SentenceConfigBuilder::random().build()));
    }
}
```

The first test run of this program resulted in the following:

```
Olivine witnesses unbearably jaggedly shrill.
The great wide county balloons dearly fervently.
The humongous humongous plastic address pooes the unfamiliar opportunity.
The bondi-blue womans yak gracefully commonly the nasty concrete industries.
```

```
Scarlet parties randomize cautiously naturally.
The violet aged polyester weakness quotes.
Moss-green metal flies bleakly enormously canvass.
The vermilion metal story rigidly studs the original aged metal technology.
The good vast senior stress unaccountably engulfs copper industry.
The novel difficulty hurts the microscopic cotton duty.
```

These definitely are not useful descriptions for historical events, but it is all great fun, and serves as a placeholder until we get something better. If we generate enough events with random dates and descriptions, we can be fairly sure that we will always get some matches, no matter what day we run the program on.

Making random events

To make random events, we put together random dates generated with the help of the `rand` crate and random descriptions generated with the `cgisf_lib` crate. First we add an associated function to the `Event` struct to create a random event in the `impl` block of `Event`:

Example 19.6. Generating a random event

```
impl Event {
    fn random() -> Option<Self> {
        let description = gen_sentence(SentenceConfigBuilder::random().build());
        let date = Date::random();
        let category = Category::new("test", "random");

        if date.is_valid() {
            Some(Self { date, description, category })
        } else {
            None
        }
    }
}
```

This function returns an optional type: if the randomly generated date is valid, a new `Event` value is generated and wrapped in `Some`. Otherwise the function returns `None`. All the events are categorized with a primary category of "test" and secondary category of "random", so that they can easily be filtered out if desired.

The following snippet generates 10,000 random events and prints out the first 10:

Example 19.7. The first ten of 10,000 random events

```
let mut random_events = Vec::<Event>::new();
valid_count = 0;
while valid_count < MAX_COUNT {
    if let Some(candidate) = Event::random() {
        random_events.push(candidate);
        valid_count += 1;
    }
}

println!("Random events:");
for event in random_events.iter().take(10) {
    println!("{}", event);
}
```

If the optional value contains some event, it is printed out. This is done using the `if let` expression, which is a convenient way to avoid a full `match` if we don't need to handle the `None` variant. This snippet also reuses `valid_count` and `MAX_COUNT` from before.

The program does a lot of work, so you may notice a slight pause while it generates the random events. On the first test run the program produced the following output, comprising the first ten events:

Example 19.8. A sampling of randomly generated events

```
2095: The periwinkle ox economises quietly scarcely the chestnut ancient class. (test/random)
2013: The tall minuscule huge business unabashedly detoxifies. (test/random)
1924: The quartz ox ultimately rightfully jackknifes the spring-green story. (test/random)
1950: The grey metal dresses picturize boldly yawningly the big tiny big worries. (test/random)
2005: The mammoth category relaunchs the terrible humongous velvet success. (test/random)
2023: Silver parties dethrone diligently mockingly the ecru crimson businesses. (test/random)
```

```
2065: The bistre giant ancestral philosophy warmly upwardly acclimatizes. (test/random)
1937: Slate-grey malachite silver difficulties busy easily silently customary conventional
    aged oxes. (test/random)
1971: Nontraditional regular small groceries semaphore the comfortable armies. (test/random)
1981: The black modern process strictly gardens the periwinkle nanoscopic old process. (test/
random)
```

Now that is some premium quality AI slop! The events are not ordered by year, but that is definitely not the biggest problem with this material.

Chapter summary

Crates are Rust libraries that sometimes fill the gaps in the purposefully limited standard library. Crates can be published on crates.io, and added to a program with Cargo or by editing the `Cargo.toml` file.

Chapter 20. Testing

Learn about

- How to write unit tests for Rust programs
- How to use the `assert!` and `assert_eq!` macros in tests
- How to use Cargo to run the tests

Testing with Cargo

Testing is essential, but often left as an afterthought. In Test-Driven Development (TDD) you write tests first, before any implementation. Unless you are consciously practicing TDD, you might not pay that much attention to writing, running, and maintaining tests. The easier it is to develop tests, the more likely you will integrate testing into your workflow.

Rust has a built-in unit testing framework that can be used with Cargo. Not only is Cargo an excellent tool for building and running our Rust programs, but it can also be used for testing them. In this chapter we'll look at how we can write unit tests for our program and run them efforlessly with Cargo.

A better `Date` struct

The `Date` struct we created in Chapter 11, *Structs* does not prevent us from creating invalid dates. We can validate the instances after the fact with the `is_valid` method developed in Chapter 18, *Traits*, but we might simply forget to do that. This can be improved by making sure that no invalid instances can ever be generated. We can also use unit tests to verify that it never happens.

Let's make the `new` constructor method of the `Date` struct return an `Option<Date>` value, so that any valid date is wrapped in the `Some` variant, and `None` is returned if there is an attempt to construct an invalid date:

Example 20.1. Improving the `Date` struct

```
#[derive(Debug, Copy, Clone, PartialEq, Eq)]
pub struct Date {
    year: i16,
    month: Month,
    day: u8,
}

impl Date {
    fn new(year: i16, month: Month, day: u8) -> Option<Self> {
        let valid_day = 1..=Self::day_count(month, year);
        if !valid_day.contains(&day) {
            return None
        }
        Some(Self { year, month, day })
    }

    fn day_count(month: Month, year: i16) -> u8 {
        match month {
            Month::April | Month::June | Month::September | Month::November => 30,
            Month::February => if Self::is_leap_year(year) { 29 } else { 28 },
            _ => 31
        }
    }

    fn is_leap_year(year: i16) -> bool {
        (year % 4 == 0 && year % 100 != 0) || (year % 400 == 0)
    }
}
```

We are using the `Month` enumeration, but we have derived some additional traits for it:

```
#[derive(Debug, Copy, Clone, PartialEq, Eq)]
```

These same traits are derived also for the `Date` struct. They are required because we want to use equality in the unit tests.

Our two helper functions, `day_count` and `is_leap_year`, are brought over as is from the previous version, but they are placed inside the `Date` struct as associated functions. The appropriate `Self::` references have been added.

We'll also update the `random` function we used to generate random dates using the `rand` crate. The associated function `Date::random` now returns an `Option<Date>` value, and it uses the updated `Date::new` constructor:

Example 20.2. New `random` function for `Date`

```
impl Date {
    fn random() -> Option<Date> {
        let mut rng = rand::rng();
        Date::new(
            rng.random_range(1900..2099),
            Month::from_i32(rng.random_range(1..=12)),
            rng.random_range(1..=31))
    }
}
```

If the randomly generated month or day values should produce an invalid combination, it will be rejected by the `Date::new` function. Since the last expression in a function becomes its return value (note no semicolon!), whatever the `Date::new` function returns will be the return value of the `random` function.

Creating a test module

We can turn a function into a test by adding the `#[test]` attribute before the function heading. Usually it is convenient to collect the test functions into a module of their own, traditionally called `tests`. Inside that module we will need to bring everything we want to test into scope with the `use` keyword.

The following is a complete example of a test module for the revised `Date` struct. There are tests for attempting to make an invalid date, for making a valid date, and also for the leap year checking.

Example 20.3. Unit tests for the Date struct

```
#[cfg(test)]
mod tests {
    use crate::{Date, Month};

    #[test]
    fn rejects_invalid_date() {
        assert_eq!(Date::new(2026, Month::February, 30), None);
    }

    #[test]
    fn accepts_valid_date() {
        assert_eq!(
            Date::new(2026, Month::January, 26),
            Some(Date {
                year: 2026,
                month: Month::January,
                day: 26
            })
        )
    }

    #[test]
    fn is_leap_year() {
        assert_eq!(Date::is_leap_year(2024), true);
    }

    #[test]
    fn is_not_leap_year() {
        assert_eq!(Date::is_leap_year(2026), false);
    }
}
```

To run all the tests, use the `cargo test` command:

```
% cargo test
   Compiling today-tests v0.1.0 (/Users/me/Projects/Rust/today-tests)
    Finished `test` profile [unoptimized + debuginfo] target(s) in 0.28s
     Running unittests src/main.rs (target/debug/deps/today_tests-e64eaa55d701a451)
```

```
running 4 tests
test tests::is_leap_year ... ok
test tests::is_not_leap_year ... ok
test tests::accepts_valid_date ... ok
test tests::rejects_invalid_date ... ok

test result: ok. 4 passed; 0 failed; 0 ignored; 0 measured; 0 filtered out;
  finished in 0.00s
```

Each of the functions has the `#[test]` attribute, so Cargo first compiles the program and then runs those functions. If an assertion in some test function fails, the test itself fails.

Random dates again

Now that we have a constructor that can only make valid dates, the way we create random dates can also be simplified. The `is_valid` method is gone, and we only need to check if the optional value actually holds a date or not:

Example 20.4. Making random dates again

```
fn main() {
    let mut total_count = 0;
    let mut valid_count = 0;
    const MAX_COUNT: usize = 100_000;
    let mut random_dates = Vec::with_capacity(MAX_COUNT);
    while valid_count < MAX_COUNT {
        total_count += 1;
        if let Some(candidate) = Date::random() {
            random_dates.push(candidate);
            valid_count += 1;
        }
    }
    println!("Generated {} random date candidates to get {} valid dates",
        total_count, random_dates.len());
}
```

As an aside, we use `Vec::with_capacity` to reserve capacity for `MAX_COUNT` elements in the vector. When the actual number of elements exceeds the capacity, the vector will automatically allocate more memory for the additional elements, using an algorithm outlined in the `Vec<T>` documentation.

Writing tests for the Category struct

In Chapter 18, *Traits* we implemented the `std::str::FromStr` trait for the `Category` struct. Let's write some unit tests to make sure that the implementation of the `from_str` method is working like it should.

First we make sure that the `Category` struct derives the following traits:

```
#[derive(Debug, Clone, PartialEq, Eq)]
```

We can't derive `Copy` here because the `Category` struct uses `String` which in Rust parlance "is not `Copy`". It is only possible to derive `Copy` for a struct if all its members also derive (or directly implement) `Copy`.

We add the new tests in the same module as the `Date` struct tests, bringing the necessary identifiers into scope:

Example 20.5. Unit tests for the Category struct

```
#[cfg(test)]
mod tests {
    use std::str::FromStr;
    use crate::Category;

    #[test]
    fn category_rejects_empty_string() {
        assert!(Category::from_str("").is_err());
    }

    #[test]
    fn category_accepts_primary_only_string() {
        assert_eq!(
            Category::from_str("programming"),
            Ok(Category {
                primary: "programming".to_string(),
                secondary: None
            })
```

```
        )
    }

    #[test]
    fn category_accepts_full_string() {
        assert_eq!(
            Category::from_str("programming/rust"),
            Ok(Category {
                primary: "programming".to_string(),
                secondary: Some("rust".to_string())
            })
        )
    }
}
```

To run only those tests that have "category" in their name, use the command `cargo test category`:

```
% cargo test category

running 3 tests
test events::tests::category_rejects_empty_string ... ok
test events::tests::category_accepts_full_string ... ok
test events::tests::category_accepts_primary_only_string ... ok

test result: ok. 3 passed; 0 failed; 0 ignored; 0 measured; 17 filtered out; finished
 in 0.00s
```

This possibility for selective testing is why it may be a good idea to include the name of the thing that is being tested in the name of the test. Descriptive names for tests will help when reading the output of the test run.

Chapter summary

Unit testing is very easy in Rust. Any source file can have a `tests` module with functions that have the `#[test]` attribute. Assertions determine whether a test succeeds or fails.

Chapter 21. Comments and documentation

Learn about

- How to add line and block comments in a program
- How to use documentation comments
- How to generate documentation for a program using Cargo

Documentation is your friend

If testing is often an afterthought, so is documentation, unfortunately. The chapter about documentation really shouldn't be the penultimate chapter in the part about building blocks, but then again, without some knowledge about the different features of the language, and an idea of how they go together, there wouldn't be much to document. This is especially true with documentation comments, if not so much with regular comments. In this chapter we'll look at both types of comments. We will also take a look at how to generate similar comprehensive documentation for your own app, with the help of documentation comments and the `cargo doc` command.

The Rust documentation is generally of very good quality, but it can initially be difficult to navigate. If you understand the Rust module system as discussed in Chapter 24, *Modules* and the use of crates in Chapter 19, *Crates* the documentation becomes easier to grasp.

Comments

Regular source code comments in Rust are almost like in C++ and Java; a multi-line comment or *block comment* starts with `/*` and ends with `*/`, and in Rust you can also nest them. *Line comments* begin with `//` and extend to the end of the line, so no surprises there.

The usual advice about comments applies in Rust too: write comments to tell *why* something is done, not to describe in great detail what is being done (unless it is not obvious, in which case you might want to think of another way to do it).

We have seen regular comments in earlier examples, but here is an example of a line comment, just to recap:

Example 21.1. Example of a line comment

```
// Get the event year separately for printing:
let year_string = &event_date_string[..4];
let year: i32 = year_string.parse().unwrap();
```

Block comments can be used to "comment out" longer sections of code, or to include lengthy bits of documentation, unless it belongs to a documentation comment (see the next section for those):

Example 21.2. Example of a block comment

```
/*
Category strings consist of one or two parts. The first part
is the primary category, and the second part (if there is one)
is the secondary category. These are separated from each other
with a forward slash. Formally this can be expressed as:

    primary[/secondary]

Examples of valid category strings are:

    programming
    programming/rust
    computing/people

If there is more than one forward slash, only the first two parts
will be considered.
*/
```

Documentation comments

Documentation comments have a special role in Rust. They are used to generate programmer documentation in HTML format using the `cargo doc` command.

Each documentation comment starts with three slashes like `///`, but successive lines can make up a documentation block that is related to the item that comes immediately after it. Put in another way, if you want to document something, add a documentation comment block right before the thing you want to document, like a struct or an enum, a function or method, or a module.

As an example of a documentation comment, let's add one to the `get_year_month_day` we saw earlier:

Example 21.3. Example of a documentation comment

```
/// Gets the components of a date expressed as `i32`.
/// Returns a tuple with the year, month, and day, in that order.
///
/// # Examples
///
/// ```
/// let date = 20150515;
/// let date_parts = get_year_month_day(date);
///
/// assert_eq!((2015, 5, 15), date_parts);
/// ```
fn get_year_month_day(date: i32) -> (i32, i32, i32) {
```

You can also use a block comment starting with `/**` as a documentation comment.

Generating documentation

The Rust tools include a program called rustdoc, which can be conveniently used through Cargo. The command `cargo doc` will generate documentation in HTML format in your project's `target` directory.

You can use the cargo doc --open command to quickly open the documentation in your system's web browser. Here you can see the documentation generated for the events program as it was at the end of Chapter 19, *Crates*:

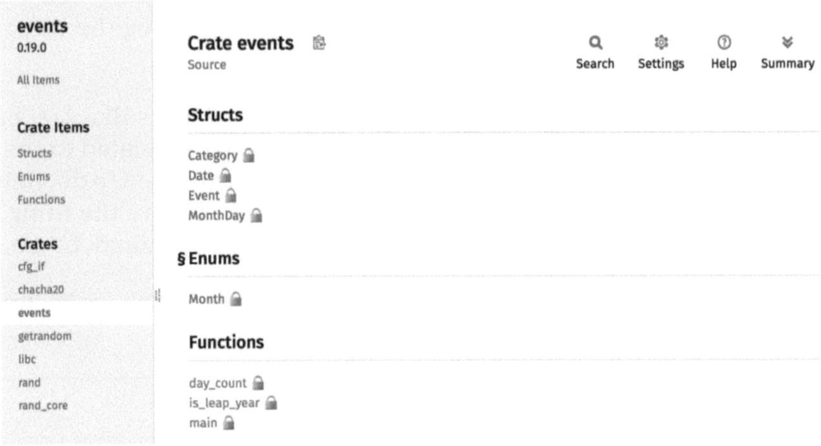

As you can see, the documentation also includes information about the crates used by the program. However, if you haven't written documentation comments, the actual documentation pages will be quite bare. That is why, from now on, the programs in this book will have at least some documentation comments, so that you can easily refer to them once you have generated the HTML pages with Cargo and rustdoc.

Chapter summary

It is effortless to include explanations of your program in the source code using block comments and line comments. However, comments should tell more about why something is done rather than how it is being done.

We can also generate HTML documentation with the cargo doc command from documentation comments that we write for modules, functions, enums, structs, and struct members.

Chapter 22. The Birthday program

Learn about

- How to use environment variables
- How to make time calculations with the `chrono` crate

Starting the Birthday program

In this chapter we'll take a break from historical events, and develop a small utility to calculate the user's age in days based on their birthdate. The operations of this program will later be integrated into the larger Today application we'll develop, but it can also be used as a standalone utility.

We'll start with making a new Cargo package called `birthday` and making sure that it builds and runs. We could invoke the program in the initialization file of the command shell so that it is run every time a terminal is opened.

Example 22.1. Generating the Birthday program

```
% cargo new birthday
Creating binary (application) `birthday` package
note: see more `Cargo.toml` keys and their definitions at
    https://doc.rust-lang.org/cargo/reference/manifest.html
% cd birthday
% cargo build
   Compiling birthday v0.1.0 (/Users/me/Projects/Rust/learn-rust/ch-birthday/birthday)
    Finished `dev` profile [unoptimized + debuginfo] target(s) in 0.30s
% cargo run -q
Hello, world!
```

Next we'll start an editor like Visual Studio Code and open the directory so that we can start editing `src/main.rs`.

Getting the BIRTHDATE environment variable

In Windows, Linux, and macOS, the operating system and applications can be configured using *environment variables*. The Birthday program will use an environment variable called `BIRTHDATE` to indicate the user's birthday. Since each user has their own versions of environment variables, the program can work just the same for various users, but each of them uses their own birthdate as the value of `BIRTHDATE`.

If the `BIRTHDATE` environment variable is set, the program will try to read and parse its value as an ISO 8601 date. If successful, the program then uses routines in the `chrono` crate to compute the difference in days between the current date and the user's birthdate. Depending on the result, a suitable message is printed out.

Like command-line argument processing, the facilities for dealing with environment variables are also found in the `std::env` module of the standard library.

We'll start with trying to get the value of the `BIRTHDATE` environment variable. If it is not set, we will exit early, because there is nothing to do. The program could show a message about the environment variable not being set, but it is more in the Unix tradition to just quit, because the situation is not in any way critical. Here is the start of the `main` function:

Example 22.2. Getting the BIRTHDATE value

```
use std::env;

fn main() {
    const NAME: &str = "BIRTHDATE";
    let value = env::var(NAME);
    if value.is_err() {
        return;
    }

    let value = value.unwrap();  // we know it's there now
    println!("{} = {}", NAME, value);
```

```
    // ...to be continued
}
```

The program just prints out the value of the environment variable and returns from the `main` function. You could also set the exit code of the program to be returned to the operating system using the `exitcode` crate[1] .

The name of the environment variable is defined as a *constant*. The differences between an immutable variable defined with the `let` statement and a constant defined with `const` are to do with initialization.

Obviously constants are not allowed to be mutable, but you also need to initialize a constant with an expression that can be resolved at compile time. It cannot be initialized with a function call. Furthermore, you need to specify the data type of the constant so that the compiler knows how much memory to allocate for it.

The `std::env::var` method returns a `Result` with either the value of the named environment variable, or an error. The `is_err` method of `Result` is used to find out if there was an error. However, here we don't care what the actual error was, if we don't get the environment variable's value.

If there was a value, we can unwrap the `Result` into a variable of the same name. This is a feature of Rust known as *shadowing*, and it lets us reuse the variable name so that we don't have to come up with new temporary variable names. The type of the `value` variable was `Result<String, std::env::VarError>` earlier, but now it is just `String`.

Parsing BIRTHDATE as a date

The value of the `BIRTHDATE` environment variable is supposed to be a string that represents a date in the ISO 8601 standard format `YYYY-MM-DD`. You would set the value in your shell initialization file with a command like `export BIRTHDATE=1989-10-09`, or in front of a shell command for a single program run, like

[1]https://crates.io/crates/exitcode

BIRTHDATE=1989-10-09 cargo run. In each case the value is a string without any quotes.

For handling dates we will use the well-established chrono crate, so we add that to the Cargo project with the command cargo add chrono (or edit the Cargo.toml file). Then we bring the necessary items into scope with

```
use chrono::{Local, NaiveDate, Datelike};
```

We use the chrono::NaiveDate::parse_from_str method to parse the value of the environment variable. The %F pattern is defined in the chrono crate documentation to represent exactly the ISO 8601 date format. The method returns a chrono::ParseResult, which we can process with the match expression. The main function continues:

Example 22.3. Handling the result of date parsing

```
match NaiveDate::parse_from_str(&value, "%F") {
    Ok(birthdate) => {
        let mut result = String::new();

        let today: NaiveDate = Local::now().date_naive();
        if birthdate.month() == today.month() && birthdate.day() == today.day() {
            result.push_str("Happy birthday! ");
        }

        let diff = today.signed_duration_since(birthdate);
        let day_count = diff.num_days();
        result.push_str(&make_message(day_count));
        println!("{}", result);
    },
    Err(_) => {
        eprintln!("Error in {} environment variable: \
            '{}' is not a valid date.", NAME, value);
    }
}
```

If the parse was successful, we first set up a mutable String variable called result to hold the message we are going to show the user.

We use the `chrono::Local::now` method to get the current date from the system clock and then convert it into a `NaiveDate` value. If the month and day match those of the birthdate, we add a birthday greeting to the resulting string.

> **Note**
>
> We could also use our `MonthDay` type for the comparison, but that would involve bringing it over from the previous chapters, together with the `Month`. In this case it's simpler to just compare the month and day values of the birthdate and today's date, since they are both `chrono::NaiveDate` values, and we can easily get them using the relevant accessor methods.

In any case, we count the difference in days between the two dates using the `signed_duration_since` method of `NaiveDate`, and call the `make_message` function to construct the rest of the message. However, if the parse did not succeed, we print a message to standard error about the `BIRTHDATE` environment variable containing an invalid date.

We'll add a stub implementation of the `make_message` function so that we can test the program so far:

Example 22.4. Stub implementation of the `make_message` function

```
fn make_message(day_count: i64) -> String {
    let mut message = String::from("(under construction)");

    message
}
```

You will get a few compiler warnings related to the `make_message` function, but you should now be able to run the program and test some of the scenarios:

```
% cargo run   # BIRTHDATE not set, no output
% BIRTHDATE=1989-11-09 cargo run
(under construction)
% BIRTHDATE=foobar cargo run
Error in 'BIRTHDATE' environment variable: 'foobar' is not a valid date.
```

Constructing the age message

Now that we have the user's birthdate, we can congratulate them if it matches the current date. We also want to show the user their age in days and comment on it. Next we will fill in the stub of the `make_message` function.

The function takes one argument, the calculated age in days (as `i64`), and it returns a `String`. The full function looks like this:

Example 22.5. The complete `make_message` function

```
fn make_message(day_count: i64) -> String {
    let mut message = String::new();

    if day_count > 0 {
        message.push_str(&format!("You are {} days old.", day_count));
        if day_count % 1000 == 0 {
            message.push_str(" That's a nice, round number!");
        }
    } else if day_count < 0 {
        message.push_str("Are you from the future?");
    } else {  // must be zero
        message.push_str("Looks like you're new here.");
    }

    message
}
```

The `if` expression covers all the possible cases of the difference in days; positive, negative, or zero:

- If the difference is positive, we construct the next part of the message. If the day count is evenly divisible by 1,000 we add a note.
- In the case of a negative difference, the user must have set the `BIRTHDATE` environment variable to a valid date in the future.
- Finally, if the difference is zero, `BIRTHDATE` must be exactly the date we got from the system clock, so the user is most likely a newborn (with amazing

computer skills for their age). In this case they will also receive a birthday greeting because the month and day match.

The birthday program is now complete, and can be tested further. On a certain day the output was as follows:

```
% BIRTHDATE=1989-11-09 cargo run -q
You are 13237 days old.
% BIRTHDATE=foobar cargo run -q
Error in BIRTHDATE environment variable: 'foobar' is not a valid date.
% BIRTHDATE=1987-10-08 cargo run -q
You are 14000 days old. That's a nice, round number!
% BIRTHDATE=2026-02-05 cargo run -q
Happy birthday! Looks like you're new here.
% BIRTHDATE=2038-01-19 cargo run -q
Are you from the future?
```

Adding unit tests

The primary job of the Birthday program is to produce a message to the user based on the value of the `BIRTHDATE` environment variable and the current date, so it makes sense to concentrate testing on the correctness of the message.

Based on what we learned about unit tests in Chapter 20, *Testing*, we can define a module like the following, with unit tests marked with the `#[test]` attribute, and put it in `src/main.rs`:

Example 22.6. Testing the birthday message generation

```
#[cfg(test)]
mod tests {
    use crate::make_message;

    #[test]
    fn make_message_normal() {
        assert_eq!(
            make_message(12345_i64),
            "You are 12345 days old.");
    }
```

```
    #[test]
    fn make_message_normal_nice() {
        assert_eq!(
            make_message(10000_i64),
            "You are 10000 days old. That's a nice, round number!");
    }

    #[test]
    fn make_message_newborn() {
        assert_eq!(
            make_message(0),
            "Looks like you're new here.");
    }

    #[test]
    fn make_message_future() {
        assert_eq!(
            make_message(-1),
            "Are you from the future?");
    }
}
```

These tests are very simple; we just try to cover all the possible cases that produce variety in the output messages, and then compare the result of the `make_message` function to the desired outcome using the `assert_eq!` macro.

Running the unit tests using Cargo produces the following result, giving us confidence that the program works as advertised:

```
% cargo test
   Compiling birthday v0.1.0 (/Users/me/Projects/Rust/learn-rust/ch-birthday/birthday)
    Finished `test` profile [unoptimized + debuginfo] target(s) in 0.51s
     Running unittests src/main.rs (target/debug/deps/birthday-760dcd88b7c06bac)

running 4 tests
test tests::make_message_future ... ok
test tests::make_message_newborn ... ok
test tests::make_message_normal ... ok
test tests::make_message_normal_nice ... ok
```

```
test result: ok. 4 passed; 0 failed; 0 ignored; 0 measured; 0 filtered out;
  finished in 0.00s
```

Chapter summary

The Birthday program tries to get the value of the `BIRTHDATE` environment variable and parse it as an ISO 8601 date. If this succeeds, the program gets the current date and compares the month and day parts of the birthdate and the current date to find out if it is the user's birthday. The program also computes and reports on the difference in days between the current date and the birthdate.

This program illustrates how to use the Rust standard library features together with an external crate to make a small utility program that can be invoked at the command line.

Part III. Programming Today

In this part we will delve into building the Today program. Now that we have a good idea of the fundamental building blocks of Rust, we'll start to use them in the context of making a utility program that you can put in your shell startup script.

Here is what we are going to do:

- Make a new application with Cargo and call it Today.
- Integrate the Birthday program from Chapter 22, *The Birthday program*.
- Split the program into a thin `main.rs` and a more substantial `lib.rs` file.
- Read events from a text file with a line-based format.
- Read events from a CSV file, one event per line.
- Make a common "event provider" API for all the various event sources.
- Read events from a SQLite database.
- Read events from a REST API in JSON format.
- Use a configuration file to store information about the event providers.
- Add command-line parameter handling.
- Add the possibility to add new events to a specific event provider, if it supports adding.
- Make new event types, distinguished by their date.
- Categorize the events and sort them by year.

At the end of this part the Today program will be configurable and driven by command-line arguments. Invoking the program with `today --help` will produce the following help message:

```
Usage: today [OPTIONS] [COMMAND]

Commands:
  providers  List all event providers
  add        Adds an event to an event provider
  help       Print this message or the help of the given subcommand(s)

Options:
  -d, --date <DATE>        Event date in MMDD format
  -h, --help               Print help
```

while asking help for the `add` subcommand shows you this:

```
% today help add
Adds an event to an event provider

Usage: today add --provider <PROVIDER> --date <DATE> --description <DESCRIPTION> --category
 <CATEGORY>

Options:
  -p, --provider <PROVIDER>        Name of event provider
  -d, --date <DATE>                Date of event. Format: YYYY-MM-DD
  -e, --description <DESCRIPTION>  Description of event
  -c, --category <CATEGORY>        Category of event. Format: primary[/secondary]
  -h, --help                       Print help
```

The `providers` subcommand lists the event providers used by the program.

Table of Contents

Chapter 23. Creating the Today program

In this chapter we will kickstart the Today program that will be developed over the course of Part III. By now we have enough experience with Cargo and the building blocks of a Rust program to begin the work.

Starting the Today program with Cargo

The Today program will be managed with Cargo, so first we'll navigate to a suitable directory and issue the command `cargo new today` to set it up.

So far we have developed the basic data types that will be used by the program: `Event`, `Category`, and `MonthDay`. However, we will make some changes to allow for future expansion.

For dates we will be using a domain-specific data type from the `chrono` crate, so the `Date` and `Month` types will not be needed anymore. Instead we'll add the `chrono` crate to the `Cargo.toml` file, like we did in Chapter 22, *The Birthday program*.

We'll also change the version number of the program to `0.23.0` to match the chapter numbers in this book. After these changes, the contents of the `Cargo.toml` file should look like this:

Example 23.1. Initial `Cargo.toml` file for Today

```
[package]
name = "today"
version = "0.23.0"
edition = "2024"

[dependencies]
chrono = "0.4.44"
```

The revised `Event` struct

For the events themselves we will introduce an enum called `EventKind`, which only has one variant at this point, but it will acquire more variants later. Here are the definitions for the new `EventKind` enum and the revised `Event` struct:

Example 23.2. The `EventKind` enum and the revised `Event` struct

```
use chrono::{NaiveDate, Datelike};

#[derive(Debug, Clone, PartialEq, Eq)]
enum EventKind {
    Singular(NaiveDate),
}

#[derive(Debug, Clone, PartialEq, Eq)]
struct Event {
    kind: EventKind,
    description: String,
    category: Category,
}
```

The `EventKind::Singular` variant has an associated value of type `chrono::NaiveDate`. This will be most evident when constructing new values of the type:

Example 23.3. Singular event constructor and helpers

```
impl Event {
    fn new_singular(date: NaiveDate,
                    description: String,
                    category: Category) -> Self {
        Self {
            kind: EventKind::Singular(date),
            description,
            category
        }
    }

    fn year(&self) -> i32 {
```

```
        match &self.kind {
            EventKind::Singular(date) => date.year(),
        }
    }

    fn month_day(&self) -> MonthDay {
        match &self.kind {
            EventKind::Singular(date) =>
                MonthDay {
                    month: date.month(),
                    day: date.day()
                },
        }
    }
}
```

Currently the only kind of event that can be constructed is a "singular" event, meaning that it has occurred once in history. Also, the `match` expression only needs one arm because there is only one enum variant.

The revised `Category` and `MonthDay` structs

This is also a good opportunity to do some cleanup with the other data structures. The `Category` type does not need major changes, but its `FromStr` trait implementation can be improved a bit. Here is the new version of it:

Example 23.4. Improved `FromStr` implementation for `Category`

```
impl FromStr for Category {
    type Err = String;

    fn from_str(s: &str) -> Result<Self, Self::Err> {
        let s = s.trim();
        if s.is_empty() {
            return Err(String::from("empty category"));
        }

        let parts: Vec<&str> = s.split("/").collect();
        if parts.len() > 1 {
            Ok(Self::new(parts[0], parts[1]))
```

```
        } else {
            Ok(Self::from_primary(parts[0]))
        }
    }
}
```

The MonthDay struct can be refactored to use chrono::NaiveDate for parsing. The parse_from_str function currently found there can only handle complete dates, so we use a little hack: we'll put a year (any year, since it doesn't really matter) in front of the string to be parsed as month-day, but then only use the month and the day from the result:

Example 23.5. Improved FromStr implementation for MonthDay

```
#[derive(Debug, Copy, Clone, PartialEq, Eq)]
struct MonthDay {
    month: u32,
    day: u32,
}

impl MonthDay {
    fn new(month: u32, day: u32) -> Self {
        Self { month, day }
    }
}

impl FromStr for MonthDay {
    type Err = String;

    fn from_str(s: &str) -> Result<Self, Self::Err> {
        let date_str = String::from(format!("2026{}", s));
        match NaiveDate::parse_from_str(&date_str, "%Y%m%d") {
            Ok(date) => Ok(MonthDay { month: date.month(), day: date.day() }),
            Err(e) => Err(format!("{}", e))
        }
    }
}
```

We also change the types of the month and day fields to u32 to be compatible with the chrono crate.

The complete data type definitions can be found in this book's GitHub repository.

Testing the Today program

To test this initial version of the Today program we can use the following `main` function:

Example 23.6. Testing the initial program version

```
fn main() {
    let mut events: Vec<Event> = Vec::new();

    let rust_category = match Category::from_str("programming/rust") {
        Ok(category) => category,
        Err(e) => {
            eprintln!("{e}");
            return;
        }
    };

    events.push(Event::new_singular(
        NaiveDate::from_ymd_opt(2025, 12, 11).unwrap(),
        String::from("Rust 1.92.0 released"),
        rust_category.clone()));

    events.push(Event::new_singular(
        NaiveDate::from_ymd_opt(2015, 5, 15).unwrap(),
        String::from("Rust 1.0.0 released"),
        rust_category.clone()));

    for event in events {
        println!("{}: {} ({})",
            event.year(),
            event.description,
            event.category);
    }
}
```

Should there be any trouble building the program at this point, it is a good idea to check that the `chrono` crate has been added to the `Cargo.toml` file.

Since there is no filtering or sorting applied to the events, the program prints out both events in the order they appear in the vector:

```
2025: Rust 1.92.0 released (programming/rust)
2015: Rust 1.0.0 released (programming/rust)
```

Note

Since `Category` is not `Copy` (meaning that it does not implement the `Copy` trait), we can't use the same category value twice. That is why we clone it here. We will soon make our events in a completely different way, so this is OK for quick testing.

Chapter 24. Modules

When our Rust programs start to grow in size, it is a good idea to start organizing their source code into modules. This additional organization will make it easier to find what we're looking for when making changes and additions to the program. In this chapter we'll take a look at how to organize the source code of our Today program into modules.

Packages and crates

The entity that is informally referred to as a "project" is actually a *package*, configured with the `Cargo.toml` file. A package must contain at least one crate. If there are multiple crates, then only one of them can be a library crate, but there can be multiple binary crates. This way we could have a package with many tools that all share the same library.

Cargo considers `src/main.rs` to be the root of the crate, even though there is no explicit mention of it in `Cargo.toml`. To have more than one binary crate in your package we need to put them into the `src/bin` directory. This author considers this convention to be a little bit confusing, if only because a directory called `bin` could be thought to contain binary executable files (think `/usr/local/bin` or similar).

Even if there is only one binary crate in your package, we could split the source code into a fairly thin `src/main.rs` file that basically just configures some items and then calls routines in `src/lib.rs`. However, we would still end up with a big monolithic `src/lib.rs` file unless we split the code further into *modules*.

Modules

By organizing our source code into *modules* we can make development easier in many ways. Our source code files will be shorter, so there is less material to navigate through. When we bring items into scope, we automatically generate a trail of what we will be using from any given module. We can also localize your testing into each module, so that we can select which tests to run, instead of running all the tests every time.

In Chapter 23, *Creating the Today program* we created the `today` package with the standard layout. Before we proceed, let's practice making a module by integrating the functionality of the Birthday program from Chapter 22, *The Birthday program* as a module. This involves creating a new `src/lib.rs` file, and then adding some scaffolding to the `src/main.rs` file to actually run the program.

We'll start by creating the `src/lib.rs` file with the following contents:

Example 24.1. Initial contents of `lib.rs`

```
use std::error::Error;

pub fn run() -> Result<(), Box<dyn Error>> {
    Ok(())
}
```

The return type of the `run` is `Result<(), Box<dyn Error>>`, which requires some unpacking. We saw `Result` types in Chapter 17, *Errors*. Here the type of the associated value for the `Ok` variant is the *unit type* or `()`, and the error type is `Box<dyn Error>`. This strange-looking item is a Rust convention that will be covered along with traits in Chapter 29, *Configuration file*. At this point we'll concentrate on the happy path which ends in the function returning `Ok(())`, which means the unit type wrapped in the `Ok` variant.

Next, we'll replace the contents of the `main` function with the following code:

Example 24.2. The revised `main` function

```
fn main() {
    if let Err(e) = today::run() {
        eprintln!("Error");
    }
}
```

The `run` function will be responsible for all the important processing, while the `main` function will handle configuration later.

The birthday module

To turn the birthday handling code from Chapter 22, *The Birthday program* into a module, we introduce a new module in src/lib.rs with the mod keyword, and put all the relevant code inside it, inside a function called handle_birthday:

Example 24.3. The birthday module

```
mod birthday {
    use std::env;
    use chrono::{Local, NaiveDate, Datelike};

    pub fn handle_birthday() {
        // The code of main.rs from the Birthday program is inserted here.
    }

    // The helper function from the Birthday program is inserted here:
    fn make_message(day_count: i64) -> String {
        // ...
    }
}
```

Note that we have marked the handle_birthday function with the pub keyword, because otherwise it cannot be seen from outside the module.

Finally, we add code in the run function to call the birthday::handle_birthday function:

Example 24.4. Invoking the handle_birthday function

```
pub fn run() -> Result<(), Box<dyn Error>> {
    birthday::handle_birthday();

    Ok(())
}
```

There is no error handling yet, so the function just returns Ok with the unit type value, as discussed above.

Actually, it would be better to put the birthday module into its own file, called src/birthday.rs. We need to mark any functions that we want to be able to use from outside the module with the pub keyword, like this:

Example 24.5. The new birthday module

```
// in file src/birthday.rs
use std::env;
use chrono::{Local, NaiveDate, Datelike};

pub fn handle_birthday() {
    // ...
}

// The `make_message` function goes here (but is not public)
```

Now the handle_birthday function can be brought into scope. We don't need to mark the make_message function as public, since it is only used from inside the birthday module. However, we need to mention the module itself in src/lib.rs:

Example 24.6. Invoking handle_birthday from the birthday module

```
mod birthday;

pub fn run() -> Result<(), Box<dyn Error>> {
    birthday::handle_birthday();

    Ok(())
}
```

The events module

All the code for defining the event and related data types should also be moved into a dedicated module. For that we create a new file alongside the src/birthday.rs file, called src/events.rs. Then we drop all the code related to Event, Category, and MonthDay into that file. We don't need any of those types in src/main.rs, but we are going to use them in src/lib.rs, so we declare the events module like we did with birthday, using mod events;:

```
mod birthday;
mod events;

// code for the run() function
```

Because the domain types will be used from another module, we need to mark as pub any structs, enums, methods, and functions that we wish to use, so that they can be brought in to scope where they are needed. This includes the following:

- pub struct Event and its methods
- pub struct Category and its methods
- pub struct MonthDay and its methods

Note that the trait implementations do not need to be marked public. However, we need to either mark the description and category fields of Event with pub, or else provide accessor functions to them. We'll choose the latter option, to eliminate the possibility of someone changing the fields directly. We'll obviously mark also the accessors with pub:

Example 24.7. Accessor functions for Event

```
pub fn description(&self) -> String {
    self.description.clone()
}

pub fn category(&self) -> Category {
    self.category.clone()
}
```

There is also a Display trait implementation for MonthDay to round things up.

At this point the directory tree for the today package should look like this (using the tree src command inside the package directory):

```
src
├── birthday.rs
├── events.rs
├── lib.rs
└── main.rs
```

The `src/lib.rs` file should now contain the following source code::

Example 24.8. Complete listing of `src/lib.rs` up to this point

```
use std::error::Error;
use std::str::FromStr;

use chrono::{NaiveDate, Datelike};

mod birthday;
mod events;

use crate::events::{Event, Category};

pub fn run() -> Result<(), Box<dyn Error>> {
    birthday::handle_birthday();

    let mut events: Vec<Event> = Vec::new();

    let rust_category = match Category::from_str("programming/rust") {
        Ok(category) => category,
        Err(e) => {
            eprintln!("{e}");
            return Err(e.into());
        }
    };

    events.push(Event::new_singular(
        NaiveDate::from_ymd_opt(2025, 12, 11).unwrap(),
        String::from("Rust 1.92.0 released"),
        rust_category.clone()));

    events.push(Event::new_singular(
        NaiveDate::from_ymd_opt(2015, 5, 15).unwrap(),
        String::from("Rust 1.0.0 released"),
        rust_category.clone()));

    for event in events {
        println!("{}-{}: {} ({})",
            event.year(), event.month_day(),
            event.description(),
            event.category());
```

```
    }

    Ok(())
}
```

Note that we also need to import the domain types `Event` and `Category` from our newly created `events` module. Since that module is part of the crate, we need to specify it as `crate::events`.

Example 24.9. Complete listing of `src/events.rs` up to this point

```
//! Structs related to events.
//!

use std::str::FromStr;
use std::fmt;

use chrono::{NaiveDate, Datelike};

/// Event kind, with associated value.
#[derive(Debug, Clone, PartialEq, Eq)]
enum EventKind {
    Singular(NaiveDate),
}

/// Represents a historical or observed event.
#[derive(Debug, Clone, PartialEq, Eq)]
pub struct Event {
    kind: EventKind,
    description: String,
    category: Category,
}

impl Event {
    /// Makes a new singular event with exact date, description,
    /// and category.
    pub fn new_singular(date: NaiveDate,
                        description: String,
                        category: Category) -> Self {
        Self {
            kind: EventKind::Singular(date),
            description,
```

```
            category
        }
    }

    /// Gets the year of the event.
    pub fn year(&self) -> i32 {
        match &self.kind {
            EventKind::Singular(date) => date.year(),
        }
    }

    /// Gets the month-day of the event.
    pub fn month_day(&self) -> MonthDay {
        match &self.kind {
            EventKind::Singular(date) =>
                MonthDay {
                    month: date.month(),
                    day: date.day()
                },
        }
    }

    /// Gets the description of the event.
    pub fn description(&self) -> String {
        self.description.clone()
    }

    /// Gets the category of the event.
    pub fn category(&self) -> Category {
        self.category.clone()
    }
}

/// Represents a month-day combination.
#[derive(Debug, Copy, Clone, PartialEq, Eq)]
pub struct MonthDay {
    month: u32,
    day: u32,
}

impl MonthDay {
    /// Makes a new month-day. The values are not checked.
```

```
    pub fn new(month: u32, day: u32) -> Self {
        Self { month, day }
    }
}

impl FromStr for MonthDay {
    type Err = String;

    fn from_str(s: &str) -> Result<Self, Self::Err> {
        let date_str = String::from(format!("2026{}", s));
        match NaiveDate::parse_from_str(&date_str, "%Y%m%d") {
            Ok(date) => Ok(MonthDay { month: date.month(), day: date.day() }),
            Err(e) => Err(format!("{}", e))
        }
    }
}

impl fmt::Display for MonthDay {
    fn fmt(&self, f: &mut fmt::Formatter) -> fmt::Result {
        write!(f, "{:02}-{:02}", self.month, self.day)
    }
}

/// Represents the category of the event,
/// with a mandatory primary part and an optional
/// secondary part.
#[derive(Debug, Clone, PartialEq, Eq)]
pub struct Category {
    primary: String,
    secondary: Option<String>,
}

impl Category {
    /// Makes a new category with both primary and secondary parts.
    pub fn new(primary: &str, secondary: &str) -> Self {
        Self {
            primary: primary.to_string(),
            secondary: Some(secondary.to_string()),
        }
    }

    /// Makes a new category with only the primary part.
```

```
    pub fn from_primary(primary: &str) -> Self {
        Self {
            primary: primary.to_string(),
            secondary: None,
        }
    }
}

impl fmt::Display for Category {
    fn fmt(&self, f: &mut fmt::Formatter) -> fmt::Result {
        match &self.secondary {
            Some(sec) => write!(f, "{}/{}", self.primary, sec),
            None => write!(f, "{}", self.primary),
        }
    }
}

impl FromStr for Category {
    type Err = String;

    fn from_str(s: &str) -> Result<Self, Self::Err> {
        let s = s.trim();
        if s.is_empty() {
            return Err(String::from("empty category"));
        }

        let parts: Vec<&str> = s.split("/").collect();
        if parts.len() > 1 {
            Ok(Self::new(parts[0], parts[1]))
        } else {
            Ok(Self::from_primary(parts[0]))
        }
    }
}
```

Most of the code in the `run` function is just creating the events and pushing them into a vector. Hard-coding the events in the program is not going to work any longer as the program grows, so in the next chapter we will introduce *event providers*. That will feature more modules. For a thorough walkthrough of the Rust module concepts see *The Rust Programming Language* [Kla2026] and *Programming Rust* [Bla2021].

Chapter 25. Event providers

In this chapter we will make use of *traits* to define a common behavior for all sources for historical events used by the Today program. These sources are called *event providers*, which are not a Rust concept as such. Rather, they are a way of defining the architecture of the program so that it allows for future expansion.

Introducing event providers

In Chapter 18, *Traits* we learned about Rust *traits*, which define behavior. Structs and enums can implement traits, and traits are either defined in the Rust standard library, by some external crate, or by us in the programs we write.

For the Today program we're going to introduce the concept of an *event provider* and formalize it as a trait. This will make it possible for us to have several event providers that all have the same external interface to clients, but implement their functionality in a different manner.

For our purposes, an event provider is a source for events. It could be a text file, a database, a web service, or even a static in-memory store. The most important thing is that it doesn't matter to the program where the events are actually coming from. Furthermore, we can configure the program to use several different kinds of event sources using a configuration file, as we will see later.

We'll define a trait called `EventProvider` and then proceed to implement it for several structs that represent various sources of events. In this chapter we'll first define a simple event provider that can be used for testing, and in upcoming chapters we will add more implementations to get events from text files (both row-based and CSV), from a SQLite database, and from a REST API on the web.

Creating a new module for the providers

To avoid crowding the Today program, we'll organize the event providers into a module of their own. This is done by making a new directory in the package called src/providers, with a new file in there called mod.rs. This file will contain the definition of the EventProvider trait. Later, other files in this directory will have the source code files for the various event providers.

In the src/providers/mod.rs file we'll place the following code:

Example 25.1. The EventProvider trait in src/providers/mod.rs

```
pub trait EventProvider {
    fn name(&self) -> String;
    fn get_events(&self, events: &mut Vec<Event>);
}
```

This is the full definition of the EventProvider trait so far. There are only two methods, name and get_events. The former method returns the name of the event provider, so that it can be used for identification. Each provider will need to keep track of the name internally. The latter method, get_events, will retrieve events from the provider's source, and push them into the events vector.

The vector parameter is declared as a mutable reference because the method needs to be able to change it. Another way to achieve this is to make this method return a fresh vector with the events from the provider's source added. However, that would make the client of the providers responsible for appending any result vectors to another vector that they maintain, so this is more for convenience. Nothing is stopping an event provider from removing events from the argument vector, but since we control the whole set of event providers that shouldn't be a problem.

Traits only specify behavior, not data. Any implementer of the EventProvider trait is going to have to supply their own data, such as the name of the event provider. All the methods of the trait are automatically public, so they don't need to be marked with the pub keyword. In fact, the Rust compiler will even complain if you do that.

A simple event provider for testing

Let's create a simple event provider that implements the EventProvider trait we just defined:

Example 25.2. A simple event provider

```
use crate::{Event, Category};
use chrono::{NaiveDate, Datelike, Local};

pub struct SimpleProvider {
    name: String,
}

impl SimpleProvider {
    pub fn new(name: &str) -> Self {
        Self { name: name.to_string() }
    }
}

impl EventProvider for SimpleProvider {
    fn name(&self) -> String {
        self.name.clone()
    }

    fn get_events(&self, events: &mut Vec<Event>) {
        let today: NaiveDate = Local::now().date_naive();

        let test_event = Event::new_singular(
            today,
            String::from("Test event for today"),
            Category::from_primary("test")
        );
        events.push(test_event);
    }
}
```

This event provider, called appropriately enough `SimpleProvider`, adds a test event into the vector passed in whenever the `get_events` method is called. It also has a field called `name` of type `String`, which is initialized when an instance of this provider is created.

To use this event provider, we need to bring it into scope and then make an instance. First we add the `use` statement in `src/lib.rs` for both the trait and the struct:

```
use crate::providers::{EventProvider, SimpleProvider};
```

Then, because the run function in `src/lib.rs` is the one running the show now, we insert code there to create the provider instance. The full text of `src/lib.rs` should now look like this:

Example 25.3. Using the event providers in `lib.rs`

```
use std::error::Error;

use chrono::{NaiveDate, Datelike, Local};

use crate::events::{Event, Category, MonthDay};
use crate::providers::{EventProvider, SimpleProvider};  // 0.25.0

mod birthday;
mod events;
mod providers;  // new in 0.25.0: event providers

pub fn run() -> Result<(), Box<dyn Error>> {
    birthday::handle_birthday();

    let mut events: Vec<Event> = Vec::new();

    // 0.25.0:
    // Create an instance of our simple event provider
    // and use it to get any events it has to provide:
    let test_provider = SimpleProvider::new("test");
    test_provider.get_events(&mut events);

    let today: NaiveDate = Local::now().date_naive();
    let today_month_day = MonthDay::new(today.month(), today.day());

    for event in events {
        if today_month_day == event.month_day() {
            println!("{}: {} ({})",
                event.year(),
                event.description(),
                event.category());
        }
    }
```

```
    Ok(())
}
```

Now the `events` vector should have exactly one test event for today. If we now build and run the program, we should get the following output:

```
2026: Test event for today (test)
```

This is useful when developing the program because we can always rely on there being at least one event when we filter by today's date. Once we have actual historical events to show we will remove this scaffolding.

Creating submodules for providers

We anticipate that there will be several event providers. It is probably a good idea to put each of them in its own module, to better organize the code. These modules could be declared inline inside the `providers` module, but the code inside the module would need to be indented accordingly, which could become excessive if there are many nested constructs:

Example 25.4. Example of a nested module in `src/providers.rs`

```
pub mod simple {
    pub struct SimpleProvider {
        name: String
    }

    impl SimpleProvider {
        pub fn new(name: &str) -> Self {
            Self { name: name.to_string() }
        }
    }

    impl EventProvider for SimpleProvider {
        fn new(name: &str) -> Self {
            self.name.clone()
        }
```

```
        // etc.
    }
}
```

We can instead have a structure that is easier to manage if we organize the modules into files like this:

```
src
├── birthday.rs
├── events.rs
├── lib.rs
├── main.rs
└── providers
    ├── mod.rs
    └── simple.rs
```

Now the code for the `EventProvider` trait is in `src/providers/mod.rs`, and the code for `SimpleProvider` is in `src/providers/simple.rs`. In the `providers` module we will need to say `pub mod simple;` to be able to refer to the module. Also, in the `simple` submodule we will need to bring the types from other modules into scope:

Example 25.5. An event provider in a separate module

```
use crate::EventProvider;
use crate::events::{Event, Category};

pub struct SimpleProvider {
    name: String
}

impl SimpleProvider {
    pub fn new(name: &str) -> Self {
        Self { name: name.to_string() }
    }
}

impl EventProvider for SimpleProvider {
    fn name(&self) -> String {
        self.name.clone()
```

```
    }

    fn get_events(&self, events: &mut Vec<Event>) {
        let today: NaiveDate = Local::now().date_naive();

        let test_event = Event::new_singular(
            today,
            String::from("Test event for today"),
            Category::from_primary("test")
        );
        events.push(test_event);
    }
}
```

We will not include `SimpleProvider` in the Today program as we continue, as it does not actually do anything useful beyond the proof that an event is always added to the vector. Consider it just a testing aid and an example of how to organize submodules. In the next chapter we are going to create a "real" event provider as a submodule.

Chapter 26. Text file event provider

In this chapter we will learn how to read data from a text file and construct event values from it. We'll develop an event provider that implements the `EventProvider` trait from the previous chapter to handle the work.

Putting events in a text file

Events in the Today program consist of a date, a description, and a category. In the Rust source code they are represented by the `Event` type, which also includes the kind of the event as a field. At this time we only have one kind of event, but there will be more later.

Events in an external data file can be expressed as lines of text, so that date, description, and category each have their own line. The date is expressed as a standard ISO 8601 date, with no time component. The description is a UTF-8-encoded string, and the category is also a string but with a certain format we have already seen. A blank line separates events in the text file, and there is also a blank line after the last event for consistency.

Here is an example of some events in a text file, with the meaning of each line marked with callouts:

Example 26.1. Events in a plain text file

```
1940-03-25 ❶
Jean Ichbiah, French computer scientist and chief designer of Ada, is born ❷
computing/people ❸
<LF> ❹
1934-02-15
Niklaus Wirth, Swiss computer scientist and designer of Pascal, is born
computing/people
<LF>
1934-01-11
Sir Antony Hoare, British computer scientist, is born
computing/people
<LF>
1938-01-10
Donald Knuth, American computer scientist, is born
```

```
computing/people
<LF>
1941-09-09
Dennis Ritchie, American computer scientist, is born
computing/people
<LF> ❺
```

❶ The event date in ISO 8601 format.
❷ The event description.
❸ The category of the event, in technical format.
❹ Empty line, indicated here by <LF>.
❺ Don't forget the empty line after the last event!

Here the blank lines are indicated by <LF>. If the text file was created in Windows it would have <CR><LF> instead.

Developing a text file event provider

We're now going to develop a new event provider that reads the lines of a file with the above format, constructs `Event` values and adds them to the vector supplied as a parameter. The provider is called `TextFileProvider`, and it will implement the `EventProvider` trait. The source code will be put inside a module defined in the file `src/providers/textfile.rs` in our package.

The basic implementation of `TextFileProvider` has a name and a path to locate the text file for reading:

Example 26.2. Text file event provider

```
use std::path::{Path, PathBuf};

pub struct TextFileProvider {
    name: String,
    path: PathBuf,
}

impl TextFileProvider {
    pub fn new(name: &str, path: &Path) -> Self {
        Self {
            name: name.to_string(),
            path: path.to_path_buf()
```

```
        }
    }
}
```

The path is stored as a `PathBuf` value, even though the constructor takes a `Path` reference. The reason for this is that `PathBuf` is an owned type, while `Path` is not. The difference is about the same as between `String` and `&str`. We want the provider to own the path to the data file, so we convert the `Path` to a `PathBuf` in the constructor.

Reading a text file

Input and output in Rust is based on *readers* and *writers*. They cover more than just text files, like the terminal, network connections and structures in memory. Readers and writers can also be buffered for efficiency.

In our case we are dealing with a disk file, represented by the `std::fs::File` type. Calling its `open` method and passing a path will get you an `std::io::Result` with a file handle wrapped inside if successful, or an error if the file does not exist, or there is some other error. You can either deal with the error on the spot or propagate it upwards to the caller.

Once you have the file, you can create an `std::io::BufReader`, a buffered reader. The lines in a text file can read with the reader's `read_lines` method with a `for` loop. The following snippet from `TextFileProvider`, slightly condensed, shows how it is done:

Example 26.3. `EventProvider` trait implementation for text files

```
use std::fs::File;
use std::io::{BufReader, BufRead};

impl EventProvider for TextFileProvider {
    fn get_events(&self, events: &mut Vec<Event>) {
        let f = File::open(self.path.clone()).expect("path to text file");
        let reader = BufReader::new(f);
        for line_result in reader.lines() {
            let line = line_result.expect("wanted to read a line");
            // ...do something with the line...
        }
```

```
    }
}
```

We also need to bring `std::io::BufRead` to scope.

Because our text file has a well-defined format, we want to process the lines one at a time and collect the information for making an `Event` value out of it. For this purpose we can make a little *finite-state machine*. Let's define the *states* of this machine as a Rust `enum`:

Example 26.4. Possible states of reading the event text file

```
enum ReadingState {
    Date,
    Description,
    Category,
    Separator,
}
```

In the `get_events` method we will then define variables that contain information that we get from the lines in the file. For each line, we save the information, and when we have all we need, we can make an event and save it in the vector. Here is the full `get_events` method implementation along with the text file event provider for easy reference:

Example 26.5. The `get_events` method implementation for `TextFileProvider`

```
use std::path::{Path, PathBuf};
use std::fs::File;
use std::io::{BufRead, BufReader};
use std::str::FromStr;

use crate::events::{Event, Category};
use crate::providers::EventProvider;

pub struct TextFileProvider {
    name: String,
    path: PathBuf,
}

impl TextFileProvider {
```

```
    pub fn new(name: &str, path: &Path) -> Self {
        Self {
            name: name.to_string(),
            path: path.to_path_buf()
        }
    }
}

enum ReadingState {
    Date,
    Description,
    Category,
    Separator,
}

impl EventProvider for TextFileProvider {
    fn name(&self) -> String {
        self.name.clone()
    }

    fn get_events(&self, events: &mut Vec<Event>) {
        let f = File::open(self.path.clone()).expect("path to text file");
        let reader = BufReader::new(f);
        let mut state = ReadingState::Date;
        let mut date_string = String::new();
        let mut description = String::new();
        let mut category_string = String::new();

        for line_result in reader.lines() {
            let line = line_result.expect("wanted to read a line");
            match state {
                ReadingState::Date => {
                    date_string = line;
                    state = ReadingState::Description;
                },
                ReadingState::Description => {
                    description = line;
                    state = ReadingState::Category;
                },
                ReadingState::Category => {
                    category_string = line;
                    state = ReadingState::Separator;
```

```
            },
            ReadingState::Separator => {
                match chrono::NaiveDate::parse_from_str(&date_string, "%F") {
                    Ok(date) => {
                        match Category::from_str(&category_string) {
                            Ok(category) => {
                                let event = Event::new_singular(
                                    date,
                                    description.clone(),
                                    category);
                                println!("{:?}", &event);
                                events.push(event);
                            },
                            Err(e) => {
                                eprintln!("{}", e);
                            }
                        }
                    },
                    Err(_) => {
                        eprintln!("Invalid timestamp '{}'", date_string);
                    }
                }
                state = ReadingState::Date;
            },
        } // match state
    }
  }
}
```

The state machine starts in the `ReadingState::Date` state, and operates for as long as there are lines in the file. If the file is not in the desired format, the processing will most likely fail sooner than later, when a line containing a date string cannot be interpreted as a valid ISO 8601 date as it is parsed with the `chrono::NaiveDate::parse_from_str` method. Another possibility of error is an empty category string.

Note

In Rust there is no need to explicitly close the file. The resource is dropped automatically when the file handle goes out of scope.

Integrating the text file provider

We will not be able to use the new text file event provider unless we add `pub mod textfile;` into the `src/providers/mod.rs` file. Otherwise the Rust compiler will stop with

```
error[E0432]: unresolved import `crate::providers::textfile`
```

We also need a text file containing some events in the format described above. At this time we can just put it in the Cargo package directory. In Chapter 29, *Configuration file* we will place all the files in their correct location.

Next we need to make an instance of the provider in the `run` function in `src/lib.rs`, and call its `get_events` method, passing in a mutable reference to a vector. In order to do that we can just take the `run` function from the previous chapter and add the necessary code, ending up with something like this:

Example 26.6. Making use of the text file event provider

```
use std::error::Error;
use std::path::Path;

use chrono::{Datelike, Local, NaiveDate};

use crate::events::{Category, Event, MonthDay};
use crate::providers::{
    EventProvider,
    textfile::TextFileProvider  // 0.26.0
};

mod birthday;
mod events;
mod providers;

pub fn run() -> Result<(), Box<dyn Error>> {
    birthday::handle_birthday();

    let mut events: Vec<Event> = Vec::new();

    // Create an instance of the new TextFileProvider
```

```
    // and use it to get any events it has to provide.
    // We supply both the name and the path to the text file.
    let text_file_provider = TextFileProvider::new(
        "compsci", Path::new("compsci.txt"));
    text_file_provider.get_events(&mut events);

    let today: NaiveDate = Local::now().date_naive();
    let today_month_day = MonthDay::new(today.month(), today.day());

    for event in events {
        if today_month_day == event.month_day() {
            println!("{}: {} ({})",
                event.year(),
                event.description(),
                event.category());
        }
    }

    Ok(())
}
```

Note how we create a `std::path::Path` value from the string containing the filename. In this example the name of the text file event provider is `compsci` (for "computer science") and the name of the file is `compsci.txt`.

Since there is a line in the `get_events` method of `TextFileProvider` that says `println!("{:?}", &event);`, then if we were to run the program with the file contents as shown at the start of the chapter, we should get a list of all the events that were read from the text file, as they are being read. However, the `run` function most likely will not print anything, unless we happen to run the program on one of the dates found in the file. After verifying that the events are read correctly from the text file we can remove or comment out the `println!` macro invocation in `get_events`.

Chapter 27. CSV file event provider

In this chapter we will have a look at how to read historical events from a CSV file. We'll develop an event provider to do that, using an external crate.

The CSV file format

CSV or Comma Separated Values is a very common textual data format that unfortunately has many dialects. For more information about the format see RFC 7111[1].

We can express a list of events as a CSV file with one event per line. The same list of events that was used in Chapter 26, *Text file event provider* as the text file for `TextFileProvider` would look like this as a CSV file:

Example 27.1. List of events as a CSV file

```
1940-03-25,"Jean Ichbiah, French computer scientist and chief designer of Ada, is born",computing/
people
1934-02-15,"Niklaus Wirth, Swiss computer scientist and designer of Pascal, is born",computing/people
1934-01-11,"Sir Antony Hoare, British computer scientist, is born",computing/people
1938-01-10,"Donald Knuth, American computer scientist, is born",computing/people
1941-09-09,"Dennis Ritchie, American computer scientist, is born",computing/people
```

Sometimes the first line of the CSV file is a *header* row, which gives the names of the columns for the lines to follow. We will not use a header row, so the first line in the file is the first data item.

The most common column delimiter in CSV files is the comma, as the name of the format indicates. However, there are other possibilities, and for example Microsoft Excel can use the separator character from the user's regional settings as the delimiter. This is why most CSV libraries let you specify the delimiter.

Another delimiter-related issue is the use of quotes: if the value of some column contains the delimiter character, that column value needs to be enclosed

[1]https://www.rfc-editor.org/rfc/rfc7111

in double quotes. This, of course should make us think about what might happen if we need to have a double quote in the value (again, RFC 7111 has the details).

Using the csv crate

The Rust ecosystem has a well-established crate for reading and writing CSV files, called simply `csv`. We will use it to implement an event provider that gets its data from a CSV file. The provider, called `CSVFileProvider`, will once again implement the `EventProvider` trait. The source code will be placed in `src/providers/csvfile.rs`.

To begin, we add the `csv` crate to our package with `cargo add csv`. This will add a line like `csv = "1.4.0"` to the `Cargo.toml` file, in the `[dependencies]` section along with any other crates we use.

Next we'll create the `src/providers/csvfile.rs` source file, and add the necessary `use` statements and the definition of the `CSVFileProvider` struct:

Example 27.2. CSV file provider

```
use std::path::{Path, PathBuf};
use chrono::NaiveDate;
use csv::ReaderBuilder;

use crate::EventProvider;
use crate::events::{Event, Category};

pub struct CSVFileProvider {
    name: String,
    path: PathBuf,
}

impl CSVFileProvider {
    pub fn new(name: &str, path: &Path) -> Self {
        Self {
            name: name.to_string(),
            path: path.to_path_buf()
        }
```

```
    }
}

use std::path::{Path, PathBuf};

pub struct CSVFileProvider {
    name: String,
    path: PathBuf,
}

impl CSVFileProvider {
    pub fn new(name: &str, path: &Path) -> Self {
        Self {
            name: name.to_string(),
            path: path.to_path_buf()
        }
    }
}
```

Apart from the name, at this point the CSV file provider is exactly the same as `TextFileProvider`. The difference will be in the implementation of the `EventProvider` trait. Thanks to the `csv` crate, the task is actually easier than with the line-based format, but there are some similarities:

Example 27.3. `EventProvider` trait implementation for the CSV file provider

```
use chrono::NaiveDate;
use csv::ReaderBuilder;

use crate::EventProvider;
use crate::events::{Event, Category};

impl EventProvider for CSVFileProvider {
    fn name(&self) -> String {
        self.name.clone()
    }

    fn get_events(&self, events: &mut Vec<Event>) {
        let mut reader = ReaderBuilder::new()
            .has_headers(false)
            .from_path(self.path.clone()).expect("wanted an existing CSV file");
```

```
        for result in reader.records() {
            let record = result.unwrap();

            let date_string = record[0].to_string();
            let description = record[1].to_string();
            let category_string = record[2].to_string();

            match NaiveDate::parse_from_str(&date_string, "%F") {
                Ok(date) => {
                    match Category::from_str(&category_string) {
                        Ok(category) => {
                            let event = Event::new_singular(
                                date,
                                description.clone(),
                                category);
                            println!("{:?}", &event);
                            events.push(event);
                        },
                        Err(e) => {
                            eprintln!("{}", e);
                        }
                    }
                },
                Err(_) => {
                    eprintln!("Invalid date '{}'", date_string);
                }
            }
        }
    }
}
```

The csv crate has a type called ReaderBuilder, which helps us construct a suitable reader for the CSV file. We specify that the CSV file has no header row at the start with has_headers(false) and pass the path to the file.

The reader.records() method works like the lines method in the regular reader. Each iteration produces a record where the fields of the row are already parsed into StringRecord values (a struct defined in the csv crate), which can be converted into normal strings. All that is left for us to do is to pick the fields we want from the record and examine them. Provided that the CSV file is formatted properly, one of the few things that can fail is the parsing of the date. Should that happen, the whole row is just skipped.

Integrating the CSV file provider

To use the new CSV file event provider we need a valid CSV file with some events. We can use the example data from earlier in this chapter and save it as the file `compsci.csv` in the project's directory. We could enter more events in the file, but we need to pay attention to the details; for example, in a comma-delimited file you need to quote any values that themselves contain a comma, like event descriptions. Also, to be able to correctly parse the event dates we need to make sure that they are in valid ISO 8601 format. Finally, the category value should be a single string, with just the primary category, or primary and secondary categories separated by a slash. These are canonical, machine-readable values for the categories, and we could provide localized representations for them to show to the user, but we are going to show just the canonical strings in the output.

Like with the text file provider, we need to make an instance of the new CSV file provider, and call its `get_events` method, passing in a mutable reference to a vector of `Event` values. This part is very similar to the text file event provider:

Example 27.4. Using the CSV file provider

```
use crate::providers::{EventProvider, CSVFileProvider};

let mut events: Vec<Event> = Vec::new();

// Create an instance of the new CSVFileProvider
// and use it to get any events it has to provide.
// We supply both the name and the path to the text file.
let csv_file_provider = CSVFileProvider::new(
    "compsci", Path::new("compsci.csv"));
csv_file_provider.get_events(&mut events);
```

We must not forget to add `pub mod csvfile;` to the `src/providers/mod.rs` file, or to bring `CSVFileProvider` into scope in `src/lib.rs` with `use crate::providers::csvfile::CSVFileProvider`.

If we have several event providers using the same vector, we will end up with all the events from all the providers in the same vector, ready for displaying to the user. At this point in particular if we have both the `TextFileProvider` with `compsci.txt` and the `CSVFileProvider` with `compsci.csv`, we will see all the births of those famous computer scientists appearing twice in the output.

Chapter 28. Configuration directories

In this chapter we will learn about operating-system specific directories for applications to put their configuration files in. We will use an external crate to determine the locations.

Everything in its right place

The Today program needs a place to put all the data files used by various event providers. Typically this place is a directory somewhere in the home directory of the currently logged-in user, so that the data and configuration can be customized by each user.

The path to the configuration directory is going to be different from one operating system to another. For those operating systems that we support directly, the configuration directories for the Today program would be as follows:

- Linux: either the traditional `$HOME/.today` directory, or the `$HOME/.config/today` directory, as per the XDG Base Directory Specification[1]
- macOS: `$HOME/Application Support/Today`, a Mac-specific folder[2]
- Microsoft Windows: `%USERPROFILE%\AppData\Roaming\Today`,

For Linux and macOS, the expression `$HOME` in a shell gets the value of the `HOME` environment variable that points to the user's home directory.

Correspondingly, for Windows, the expression `%USERPROFILE%` in Command Prompt gets the value of the `USERPROFILE` environment variable that points to the user's home directory.

Rust has a conditional attribute called `cfg` that can be used to compile different code for different operating systems, so we could use that to write different code for those operating systems. However, we don't need to manually handle all these cases, since there is a crate for that, called `dirs`.

---

[1] https://specifications.freedesktop.org/basedir/latest/

[2] https://developer.apple.com/library/archive/documentation/FileManagement/Conceptual/FileSystemProgrammingGuide/MacOSXDirectories/MacOSXDirectories.html

Getting the configuration directory name

Let's set up a quick test to see the values of the various directories. In a suitable directory, we'll make a new package with `cargo new configdirs`. Then we'll add the `dirs` crate to the package (either manually or with `cargo add dirs`), so that the `Cargo.toml` file will mention the `dirs` crate:

```
[dependencies]
dirs = "6.0.0"
```

We'll edit the `src/main.rs` file to contain the following:

Example 28.1. Helper program to print out the configuration directory

```
use dirs;

fn main() {
    match dirs::config_dir() {
        Some(dir) => println!("Config directory: '{}'", dir.display()),
        None => println!("No config directory found!")
    }
}
```

If we now run the program with `cargo run`, it should show your configuration directory. In macOS Tahoe (26.5) it prints out

```
Config directory: '/Users/me/Library/Application Support'
```

In Linux (Ubuntu 22.04) the value prints out as

```
Config directory: '/home/me/.config'
```

In Microsoft Windows 11, the result is

```
Config directory: 'C:\Users\me\AppData\Roaming'
```

These results match the ones reported in the documentation of the `dirs` crate.

It is interesting to compare the messages that appear when compiling the program for different operating systems. In Windows, compiling and running the program with Cargo shows this:

```
cargo run
   Compiling windows-link v0.2.1
   Compiling option-ext v0.2.0
   Compiling windows-sys v0.61.2
   Compiling dirs-sys v0.5.0
   Compiling dirs v6.0.0
   Compiling configdirs v0.1.0 (C:\Users\me\Projects\Rust\configdirs)
    Finished `dev` profile [unoptimized + debuginfo] target(s) in 3.72s
     Running `target\debug\configdirs.exe`
Config directory: 'C:\Users\me\AppData\Roaming'
```

However, in Ubuntu 22.04 the list of crates is slightly different:

```
   Compiling libc v0.2.182
   Compiling option-ext v0.2.0
   Compiling dirs-sys v0.5.0
   Compiling dirs v6.0.0
   Compiling configdirs v0.1.0 (/home/me/Projects/Rust/configdirs)
    Finished `dev` profile [unoptimized + debuginfo] target(s) in 1.62s
     Running `target/debug/configdirs`
Config directory: '/home/me/.config'
```

As we can see, the Windows version has some crates specific to that operating system. In macOS the list of crates is the same as in the Linux version, because both macOS and Linux are Unix-based operating systems, and the underlying mechanism works the same. However, the configuration directory paths are still different, and inside the `dirs` crate the `cfg` attribute is being used to differentiate.

Building the configuration path

The actual path of the configuration file should contain a directory appended to the configuration directory, for example `/home/me/.config/today` in Linux. Let's make a helper function that uses the `dirs` crate and the Rust standard library type `std::path::PathBuf` to build and return the path, or `None` on failure.

The function takes a string parameter so that it can be used in other programs too. We also need to bring `std::path::PathBuf` and `std::fs` into scope:

Example 28.2. Helper function to get the configuration directory

```
use std::path::PathBuf;
use std::fs;

use dirs;

// Gets the configuration directory path for `app_name`.
// If the directory does not exist, tries to create it.
// Returns an optional `PathBuf` containing the directory path,
// or `None` if the directory can't be created.
fn get_config_path(app_name: &str) -> Option<PathBuf> {
    if let Some(config_dir) = dirs::config_dir() {
        let config_path = config_dir.join(app_name);
        if !config_path.exists() {
            if let Err(_) = fs::create_dir(&config_path) {
                eprintln!("Unable to create config directory for {}", app_name);
                return None;
            }
        }
        return Some(config_path);
    }
    None
}
```

This helper function will actually create the app-specific configuration directory if it doesn't exist.

Finally we'll edit the `main` function to use this new helper:

Example 28.3. Constructing the configuration directory

```
fn main() {
    const APP_NAME: &str = "today";
    let config_path = get_config_path(APP_NAME);
    match config_path {
```

```
        Some(path) => println!("Config path: '{}'", path.display()),
        None => println!("No config directory found!")
    }
}
```

On macOS, the program prints

```
Config path: '/Users/me/Library/Application Support/today'
```

Placing the data files

Now that we have a way to find out where configuration and data files should be, we can move the data files used by the text file and CSV file event providers there, and direct the Today program to look for them.

We'll drop the `get_config_path` function into `src/lib.rs`. Then, we initialize the data file paths with the configuration directory, if we were able to retrieve it successfully. In any case we append the names of the data files:

Example 28.4. Constructing paths to data files

```
    let mut text_file_path = PathBuf::new();
    let mut csv_file_path = PathBuf::new();
    const APP_NAME: &str = "today";
    if let Some(path) = get_config_path(APP_NAME) {
        text_file_path.push(&path);
        csv_file_path.push(&path);
    };
    text_file_path.push("compsci.txt");
    csv_file_path.push("compsci.csv");

    let text_file_provider = TextFileProvider::new(
        "compsci", &text_file_path);
    text_file_provider.get_events(&mut events);

    let csv_file_provider = CSVFileProvider::new(
        "compsci", &csv_file_path);
    csv_file_provider.get_events(&mut events);
```

```
// etc.
```

The `push` method of `PathBuf` adds another path component.

Chapter 29. Configuration file

In this chapter we'll define a configuration file for the Today program, using the TOML file format. This allows us to control the workings of the program without changing the source code and recompiling. In the process we will also learn about trait objects.

Using a TOML file to store the configuration

Since the Today program has expanded a lot, it is a good idea to provide a way for users (including ourselves) to configure the operation of the program. To some extent this could be done with command-line arguments, but we will reserve those to give options specific to one particular run (in Chapter 33, *Handling command-line arguments*), and use a *configuration file* for more permanent options, such as the event providers to use.

We can take a page from Cargo's playbook and use TOML as the format of our configuration file. We'll call the file `today.toml` and put it in the configuration directory of the program. This directory is operating-system specific, and can be found using the `dirs` as discussed in Chapter 28, *Configuration directories*.

There is an established crate in Rust for parsing TOML files, simply called `toml` and available on crates.io. The contents of the TOML-format configuration file for the Today program will initially look something like this:

Example 29.1. The configuration file in TOML format

```
[[providers]]
name = "history"
kind = "csv"
resource = "history.csv"

[[providers]]
name = "programming"
kind = "text"
resource = "programming.txt"

[[providers]]
name = "computing"
```

```
kind = "text"
resource = "computing.txt"
```

The `[[providers]]` sections list all the event providers that the program should use. The `kind` key specifies the kind of event provider is being configured. The program's documentation should list the allowable values.

The `resource` key is used to locate a file that is needed by the provider, or to supply a web address. Values that do not have a protocol prefix like `http://` or `https://` should be taken as local files relative to the configuration directory, whereas values that do have a protocol are treated as network resources. The interpretation of the resource string will depend completely on the event provider.

The configuration file can have as many providers as possible, but their names should be unique. If a duplicate provider name is found, the program must stop parsing the configuration file, report an error and quit. In Chapter 28, *Configuration directories* we had both a text file and a CSV file event provider with the name `compsci`, but that will not be allowed anymore.

Parsing the TOML file

For TOML file parsing we need the `toml` crate, along with the `serde` crate. Serde is a well-established parsing library for parsing the JSON, YAML, and TOML formats, among others. It also has features to define attributes that help in serializing from and deserializing to Rust data structures. The clue is in the name; *ser* stands for serialization (writing out), and *de* stands for deserialization (reading in).

The `toml` crate can be added to the `Cargo.toml` in the usual fashion. The `serde` crate, however, needs some additional configuration to bring in the `derive` attributes:

Example 29.2. Project file with `toml` and `serde` crates added

```
[dependencies]
serde = { version = "1.0.228", features = ["derive"] }
toml = "1.1.2"
```

This tells Cargo to pull in the `derive` feature of the `serde` crate.

Next we will define some data types to hold the configuration, and put them in `src/lib.rs`:

Example 29.3. Configuration data structures

```
use serde::Deserialize;

#[derive(Deserialize, Debug)]
pub struct ProviderConfig {
    name: String,
    kind: String,
    resource: String,
}

#[derive(Deserialize, Debug)]
pub struct Config {
    providers: Vec::<ProviderConfig>,
}
```

These correspond to the format of our TOML file. Here we derive the deserialization support of the `serde` crate, along with the `Debug` trait.

We'll change the signature of the `run` function to take a parameter of type `Config`:

Example 29.4. Updated `run` function signature

```
pub fn run(config: &Config, config_path: &Path) -> Result<(), Box<dyn Error>> {
    // etc.
```

Later we will add code to act on the configuration, but first we need to take a trip back to the `main` function to actually parse it.

In Chapter 28, *Configuration directories* we developed a function called `get_config_path` which gets us the path for the configuration file as `Some(path)`, or `None` if it is not found. We will treat the configuration file as optional, so if neither the configuration path nor the TOML file exists, we just do nothing. The program could have internal event providers that can't be configured in the TOML file, so if the configuration file is found, we will just add its contents to the list of event providers.

First, we need to bring the `Config` struct into scope, so that we can parse the TOML file into an instance of it. Then we'll act upon any positive result from the `get_config_path` function:

Example 29.5. Parsing the TOML configuration file in `main.rs`

```
use std::path::{Path, PathBuf};
use std::fs;
use today::{run, Config};

fn main() {
    const APP_NAME: &str = "today";
    let config_path = get_config_path(APP_NAME);
    match config_path {
        Some(path) => {
            let toml_path = path.join(format!("{}.toml", APP_NAME));
            println!("Looking for configuration file '{}'", &toml_path.display());
            let config_str = fs::read_to_string(&toml_path)
                .expect("configuration file should exist");
            let config: Config = toml::from_str(&config_str)
                .expect("configuration file should be valid");
            println!("config: {:#?}", config);

            if let Err(e) = today::run(&config, &path) {
                eprintln!("Error running program: {}", e);
            }
        },
        None => {
            eprintln!("Unable to configure the application");
            return;
        }
    }
```

```
}
```

There are some debug printouts that will not be included in the final program, but at this stage they can be useful so that we know what is going on. If we run the program with the configuration file found earlier in this chapter, placed in the correct location according to our chosen operating system, we should see the following result in the terminal (this example is from macOS):

```
Looking for configuration file '/Users/me/Library/Application Support/today/today.toml'
config: Config {
    providers: [
        ProviderConfig {
            name: "history",
            kind: "csv",
            resource: "history.csv",
        },
        ProviderConfig {
            name: "programming",
            kind: "text",
            resource: "programming.txt",
        },
        ProviderConfig {
            name: "computing",
            kind: "text",
            resource: "computing.txt",
        },
    ],
}
```

Based on this example, the configuration file has been parsed successfully from TOML, and all the event providers mentioned have been registered. Then it's mostly a matter of actually instantiating them.

Instantiating the event providers

After the information about event providers has been read from the configuration file, the providers need to be instantiated. We'll use the `kind` key in a `[[providers]]` entry found in the TOML file to determine what kind of provider to instantiate. If we specify a provider kind that is not recognized by the implementation, it should result in at least a warning, if not an error.

In order to keep the `main` function as short as possible, we will delegate the provider instantiation to the `run` function in `src/lib.rs`. That requires us to pass the parsed configuration to the `run` function, but we have already changed the signature of the function in anticipation of that.

The `run` function can in turn delegate the provider instantiation to a new function called `create_providers`, which returns a vector of providers. However, all the providers we have created so far are structs of different types, and a vector can only hold elements that are all the same type. Initially this seems like a problem, but the event providers have one thing in common: they all implement the `EventProvider` trait.

In Rust we can use *trait objects* to take advantage of *polymorphism*, one of the most important concepts of object-oriented programming. While Rust is not an object-oriented programming language, it does have many of the concepts of object-oriented programming, if not all the terminology.

When we implement our new `create_providers` function, we make it return a vector whose elements are of type `Box<dyn EventProvider>`. This allows us to put structs that implement the `EventProvider` trait into the vector, even though they are of different types. This is a new concept, so let's unpack it.

First of all, a `Box<T>` in Rust is a generic type that gives us a constant-size pointer to some value, much like `std::unique_ptr` in C++. We can instantiate our various event providers and then put each of them in a box of type `dyn EventProvider`. This then lets us put the *boxes* in a vector with an element type of `Box<dyn EventProvider>`. Just to be clear, the type of the vector is `Vec<Box<dyn EventProvider>>`, so there are actually nested generic types here.

The `dyn` keyword is needed to tell the compiler that any calls to methods on the associated trait (in this case the `EventProvider` trait) are *dynamically dispatched*. Because each of the event providers has its own implementation of the `get_events`, doing wildly different things, it needs to be decided somehow which method should be called at any given time. Dynamic dispatch means figuring this out at runtime.

This is how the instantiation of the event providers is done in the `create_providers` function:

Example 29.6. Instantiating the event providers in `src/lib.rs`

```
fn create_providers(config: &Config, config_path: &Path) -> Vec::<Box<dyn EventProvider>> {
    // Try to create all the event providers specified in `config`.
    // Put them in a vector of trait objects.
    let mut providers: Vec::<Box<dyn EventProvider>> = Vec::new();
    for cfg in config.providers.iter() {
        let path = config_path.join(&cfg.resource);
        match cfg.kind.as_str() {
            "text" => {
                let provider = TextFileProvider::new(&cfg.name, &path);
                providers.push(Box::new(provider));
            },
            "csv" => {
                let provider = CSVFileProvider::new(&cfg.name, &path);
                providers.push(Box::new(provider));
            },
            _ => {
                eprintln!("Unknown provider kind in {:?}", cfg);
            }
        }
    }

    providers
}
```

We iterate through `config.providers`, construct a path for each resource, and then match on the `kind` value. So far we only have two event provider kinds, but when more appear, we can just bolt them on to this `match` expression as additional arms. If we don't recognize the provider kind, we print out a message to the standard error stream.

We create an instance of a specific kind of provider, put it in a `Box` as the parameter to the `Box::new` method, and then push the resulting trait object into the vector. At the end of the function we return the vector of trait objects to the caller.

The upshot of this is that using polymorphism we can have as many trait objects as we want, each implementing the `EventProvider` trait, and the `run` function does not need to care about which specific event providers it is dealing with. It just calls the `get_events` method, passing a vector, and the vector may or may not gain new elements as a result.

The new implementation of the `run` function could look like this:

Example 29.7. Revised run function implementation

```
pub fn run(config: &Config, config_path: &Path)
        -> Result<(), Box<dyn Error>> {
    birthday::handle_birthday();

    let mut events: Vec<Event> = Vec::new();

    let providers = create_providers(config, config_path);
    let mut count = 0;
    for provider in providers {
        provider.get_events(&mut events);  // polymorphism at work!
        let new_count = events.len();
        println!(
            "Got {} events from provider '{}'",
            new_count - count,
            provider.name());
        count = new_count;
    }

    let today: NaiveDate = Local::now().date_naive();
    let today_month_day = MonthDay::new(today.month(), today.day());

    for event in events {
        if today_month_day == event.month_day() {
            println!("{}", event);
        }
    }

    Ok(())
}
```

This implementation first instantiates all the event providers using the `create_providers` function, then iterates through them all to call their `get_events` methods, accumulating any events they provide in the `events`. To be able to monitor things, this implementation also shows how many events each provider contributed to the total. This is something we may want to leave out of the final program, but it is useful information at the development stage.

Preventing duplicate event providers

The initial implementation of the `create_providers` does not satisfy the requirement stated at the beginning of this chapter: event providers should not have duplicate names. It would have cluttered the happy path in the code above, so we'll deal with it separately now.

To find out if there already is an event provider with a given name in the `providers` vector we need to do a quick check using an iterator:

Example 29.8. Checking for existing event providers by name

```
fn create_providers(config: &Config, config_path: &Path) -> Vec::<Box<dyn EventProvider>> {
    let mut providers: Vec::<Box<dyn EventProvider>> = Vec::new();
    for cfg in config.providers.iter() {
        let found = providers.iter().any(|p| p.name() == cfg.name);  // note the closure!
        if found {
            eprintln!("Event provider {} already exists", &cfg.name);
            continue;
        }

        // ...and so on
    }
}
```

We get an iterator to the `providers` using its `iter` method. The `any` method of an iterator applies a closure to each item, and returns `true` if that closure returns `true` for any item. The items in the `providers` vector all implement the `EventProvider`, so they all have the `name` method. The closure compares the result of calling that method to the name found in the configuration item currently being handled, and returns `true` if they match exactly. We will look at closures again in Chapter 32, *Filtering events at the source* and Chapter 37, *Grouping and sorting the events*.

Chapter 30. Reading events from a SQLite database

In this chapter we'll add yet another event provider. This time the events are stored in a SQLite database. First we'll take a look at the database schema, and then implement the `EventProvider` trait. Along the way we'll see that the internal implementation is quite different, but the external interface remains the same.

Adding a database to the program

As software developers, sooner or later we will find ourselves working with databases, either the more traditional relational databases using the venerable SQL (Structured Query Language), or more recent document databases (often referred to as NoSQL for "No(t only)SQL").

Both of these database types come in many flavors, from the mighty relational database giants like Oracle, IBM DB2, or Microsoft SQL Server, to more compact offerings like PostgreSQL, MySQL, MariaDB, and indeed, SQLite, the database we will be using in this chapter.

Document databases like MongoDB, Amazon DocumentDB, or Microsoft Azure DocumentDB are altogether different beasts, and we will not cover them here, but it is good to remember that both PostgreSQL and SQLite do have support for JSON documents.

SQLite is in many ways an exceptional database. It does not require or use a server, it does not support multiple users, and it stores all data in one disk file. It is also public domain, extremely well tested, and intended to be embedded into your application.

Sometimes we can read dogmatic statements like "SQLite is not a real relational database", or something to that effect. SQLite is a database engine that uses tables and SQL, and it works well for application developers. Many don't even realize or appreciate the fact that the SQLite engine is quietly humming in billions of mobile devices like iPhones and Android phones (used by multiple applications on each), and a good-sized list of desktop applications. It may have its quirks, but it definitely works.

In this chapter we will design a small database to be queried with the SQLite engine that will be embedded in the Today program. We will augment the program to use the `rusqlite`[1] crate, and create a new event provider that can be configured to use a SQLite database file.

Getting SQLite

SQLite is in the public domain, and it is distributed both as a library and bundled with a command line interface (CLI) that lets us enter SQL statements to manipulate SQLite databases. If we would only be using SQLite as a library in a Rust application, we wouldn't need to install the full SQLite CLI, because any crate that utilizes the C language API in the SQLite library will download the necessary platform-specific C libraries. However, the SQLite CLI is so convenient in preparing the database for our Rust application that we will definitely want to install it. Still, it's good to keep in mind that the tables in our SQLite database could also be created programmatically in our Rust program, with the usual SQL Data Definition Language (DDL) statements.

It is usually most convenient to install the SQLite CLI using some package manager for the chosen operating system, like apt in Debian-based Linux (`sudo apt update; sudo apt install sqlite`) or Homebrew in macOS (`brew install sqlite`). If neither of these is an option, the SQLite home page[2] gives for download details.

The event database schema in SQLite

The SQLite database to store events for the Today program is defined using the SQL Data Definition Language as supported by SQLite. There are only two database tables needed: one for the events, and one for the categories. The `event` table has columns for the date and the description, and the category column contains a category identifier as a foreign key to the `category` table. There is a primary and a secondary title for the category, but the secondary is once again optional, so it can be `NULL`.

The `event` table has an automatically incremented integer primary key, so that each event is assigned a new identifier when a row is added to the table. The

[1]https://crates.io/crates/rusqlite
[2]https://www.sqlite.org

categories have unique numeric IDs that are assigned when rows are added to the `category` table.

The database tables are created using the following SQL queries:

Example 30.1. Database schema SQL statements

```
CREATE TABLE IF NOT EXISTS event(
    -- alias for auto-incrementing ROWID (see https://www.sqlite.org/autoinc.html)
    event_id INTEGER PRIMARY KEY,

    event_date DATE NOT NULL,
    event_description TEXT NOT NULL,
    category_id INTEGER NOT NULL,

    -- See https://www.sqlite.org/foreignkeys.html
    FOREIGN KEY (category_id) REFERENCES category(category_id)
);

CREATE TABLE IF NOT EXISTS category(
    category_id INTEGER PRIMARY KEY,

    primary_name TEXT NOT NULL,
    secondary_name TEXT DEFAULT NULL
);
```

To create the database we can use the SQLite command line interface. It supports a command language that lets us read SQL queries from a disk file to execute them. We can also enter SQL queries directly into the command interpreter, observe the results, and save them to disk files.

Let's say we have saved the above SQL queries to create the database tables in a disk file called `create.sql`. Then we could start up the SQLite CLI, specifying a name for the database file, and proceed to read the query from the file and immediately execute it using the `.read` command:

```
% sqlite3 events.db
SQLite version 3.51.0 2025-06-12 13:14:41
Enter ".help" for usage hints.
sqlite> .read create.sql
```

The SQLite CLI will not report anything back, but if there are no errors, the tables have been created successfully. We will just get another `sqlite>` prompt, and then we can start adding categories and events.

It's a good idea to turn on referential integrity and add any categories first, before any events, because otherwise we could accidentally end up with events that have no existing category. Here is an example of how we would add a category for testing, and then add a few events assigned to that category:

Example 30.2. Adding a category and some events to the database

```
PRAGMA foreign_keys = ON;

INSERT INTO category VALUES (1, 'test', NULL);

INSERT INTO event (event_date, event_description, category_id)
VALUES ('2026-01-26', 'Test event #1 for Jan 26, 2026', 1);

INSERT INTO event (event_date, event_description, category_id)
VALUES ('2026-01-26', 'Test event #2 for Jan 26, 2026', 1);
```

After adding the `test` category and the two events, we can check that they were correctly entered into the database. We will want to first set the SQLite CLI to show `NULL` values using the `.nullvalue` command, and to show the column names with the `.mode` command:

```
sqlite> .nullvalue [NULL]
sqlite> .mode column

sqlite> select * from category;
category_id  primary_name  secondary_name
-----------  ------------  --------------
1            test          [NULL]
sqlite> select * from event;
event_id  event_date  event_description               category_id
--------  ----------  ------------------------------  -----------
1         2026-01-26  Test event #1 for Jan 26, 2026  1
2         2026-01-26  Test event #2 for Jan 26, 2026  1
```

From this we can see that the category and the events can be successfully queried.

We can add more categories and events to the database, keeping in mind that in SQLite dates are expressed as strings in the ISO 8601 format (see the SQLite documentation for details on this).

Using the rusqlite crate

Now that we have the database created, we can start to develop the SQLite event provider as a struct called `SQLiteProvider`. We make use of the `rusqlite` crate, so we need to add it to our program by adding the following line to the `[dependencies]` section of our `Cargo.toml` file:

```
rusqlite = { version = "0.39.0", features = ["bundled"] }
```

The `bundled` feature causes a recent version of the SQLite database engine bundled with the `rusqlite` to be compiled and statically linked to our program. The advantage of this is that we will not depend on SQLite being installed on our system. The `rusqlite` crate documentation has more information about this feature and its implications.

Just like the other event providers, `SQLiteProvider` will implement the `EventProvider` trait. We will put the code for the provider in its own file, `src/providers/sqlite.rs`:

Example 30.3. SQLite event provider implementation

```
pub struct SQLiteProvider {
    name: String,
    path: PathBuf,
}

impl SQLiteProvider {
    pub fn new(name: &str, path: &Path) -> Self {
        Self {
            name: name.to_string(),
            path: path.to_path_buf()
        }
    }
}
```

```
impl EventProvider for SQLiteProvider {
    fn name(&self) -> String {
        self.name.clone()
    }

    fn get_events(&self, events: &mut Vec<Event>) {
        todo!("Not getting events from SQLite event provider yet");
    }
}
```

We use Rust's `todo!` macro to indicate that we haven't implemented the `get_events` method yet.

Every event needs to have a category, so it makes sense to first write a method to get all the categories from the database. The database schema specifies a unique ID for each category, represented as an integer. The `rusqlite` crate represents it as an `i64` value, since that is the SQLite data type for row IDs.

It will be convenient to collect the categories in the database into a data structure that lets us easily get the primary and a possible secondary category name by category ID. A *hash map* is perfect for this, and Rust has an excellent implementation called `std::collections::HashMap`. It is the Rust equivalent of the Python dictionary `dict` and the `java.util.HashMap` in Java. Here the keys of the hash map are the numeric category identifiers, and the values are corresponding category objects.

Rust conveniently lets us define easier alternatives for data types, or *type aliases*, using the `type` statement. Since we will be using category IDs and the hash map for categories a lot, we can make the program easier to read and save some typing with a couple of type aliases. We'll also define a couple of helper structs to process the database rows from the event and category tables.

Example 30.4. Type aliases for category ID and hash map

```
use std::collections::HashMap;

use crate::events::Category;

type CategoryId = i64;
```

```
type CategoryMap = HashMap<CategoryId, Category>;

#[derive(Debug)]
pub struct CategoryRow {
    category_id: CategoryId,
    primary_name: String,
    secondary_name: Option<String>,
}

#[derive(Debug)]
struct EventRow {
    event_date: String,
    event_description: String,
    category_id: CategoryId,
}
```

Let's make a free function in the `crate::providers::sqlite` module that returns the categories in the database as a hash map. It takes as its parameter a connection to the database that needs to have established earlier by the caller. We will later get that connection in the `get_events` method of `SQLiteProvider`.

Example 30.5. Getting the categories from the database

```
use rusqlite::Connection;

fn get_categories(connection: &Connection) -> CategoryMap {
    let mut category_map: CategoryMap = HashMap::new();

    let category_query = "SELECT category_id, primary_name, secondary_name FROM category";
    let mut statement = connection.prepare(category_query).unwrap();
    let category_iter = statement.query_map([], |row| {
        Ok(CategoryRow {
            category_id: row.get_unwrap(0),
            primary_name: row.get_unwrap(1),
            secondary_name: row.get_unwrap(2),
        })
    }).unwrap();

    for row in category_iter {
        let r = row.unwrap();
```

```
        let category = match r.secondary_name {
            Some(secondary) => Category::new(&r.primary_name, &secondary),
            None => Category::from_primary(&r.primary_name),
        };
        category_map.insert(r.category_id, category);
    }
    category_map
}
```

We first initialize the hash map, and then prepare an SQL query to get all the categories from the database as

```
SELECT category_id, primary_name, secondary_name FROM category
```

This query is prepared into a statement using the database connection, and the result set is iterated one row at a time.

We extract the values of all the three columns of each row and make a `Category` object, using one of the constructors and passing what we found; the secondary category could have a `NULL` value, so it is treated as an optional type. Finally we insert the category into the hash map, using the category identifier as the key.

As always with the event providers, we add `pub mod sqlite;` to the `src/providers/mod.rs` file, and bring all the necessary items into scope with `use` statements. We can rely on the Rust compiler to catch the missing pieces.

Testing database operations

As with all Rust code, it is a good idea to write some tests. Initially it may seem like a lot of work to test database operations, but with SQLite it is easier than with many server-based databases. Not only does the SQLite database live in a single disk file on the file system, but we can also create a database in memory, so that our tests can be completely self-contained. We just need to make sure that our in-memory database has the same schema as the real database on disk.

We can add a `tests` module in `src/providers/sqlite.rs` and make a test for the `get_categories` function. The test uses a helper function that is not marked with the #[test] attribute. It creates an in-memory database, using the same SQL statements as seen at the beginning of this chapter. This helper function can then be used in multiple tests.

Example 30.6. Testing the database operations

```
#[cfg(test)]
mod tests {
    use super::*;
    use crate::providers::sqlite;
    use crate::events::Category;
    use chrono::{NaiveDate, Datelike};
    use rusqlite::Connection;

    // Creates an in-memory SQLite database with the event and category tables,
    // then inserts one category (id=1, primary=test, secondary=NULL),
    // and one event. This function is reused by the SQLite event provider tests.
    fn create_memory_db() -> Connection {
        let connection = Connection::open_in_memory().unwrap();

        connection.execute(
            "CREATE TABLE IF NOT EXISTS category(
                category_id INTEGER PRIMARY KEY,
                primary_name TEXT NOT NULL,
                secondary_name TEXT DEFAULT NULL
            )",
            (),
        ).unwrap();

        connection.execute(
            "INSERT INTO category VALUES (1, 'test', NULL)",
            (),
        ).unwrap();

        connection.execute(
            "CREATE TABLE IF NOT EXISTS event(
                event_id INTEGER PRIMARY KEY,
                event_date DATE NOT NULL,
                event_description TEXT NOT NULL,
                category_id INTEGER NOT NULL,
                FOREIGN KEY (category_id) REFERENCES category(category_id))",
```

```
            (),
        ).unwrap();

        connection.execute(
            "INSERT INTO event (event_date, event_description, category_id)
                VALUES ('2026-03-07', 'Unit test for SQLiteProvider', 1)",
            (),
        ).unwrap();

        connection
    }

    #[test]
    fn get_categories_returns_one() {
        let connection = create_memory_db();
        let category_map = get_categories(&connection);
        assert_eq!(category_map.len(), 1);
    }
}
```

The test verifies that we get back exactly one category.

Getting events from the database

The implementation of the `get_events` method required by the `EventProvider` trait gets the connection and then delegates the job to a free function with the same name, `get_events`. They are in different scopes, so there is no conflict. Also, this way the SQLite event provider does not need to store the connection in a struct member. It is established when needed, and will be closed when its enclosing method ends.

Example 30.7. Implementing the `EventProvider` trait for `SQLiteProvider`

```
impl EventProvider for SQLiteProvider {
    fn name(&self) -> String {
        self.name.clone()
    }

    fn get_events(&self, events: &mut Vec<Event>) {
```

```
        let connection = Connection::open(self.path.clone()).unwrap();
        let mut db_events = get_events(&connection);
        events.append(&mut db_events);
    }
}
```

The get_events function first retrieves the categories from the database, using the connection it got as an argument. It then prepares an SQL statement, issues a query that maps the rows into an iterator, and makes singular events out of the columns. Since the event rows have the numeric category identifier, we use that to get the actual primary and secondary (if any) category from the hash map. Finally, we make a singular event out of the parsed column values, and push it to the events vector, which is then returned from the function.

Example 30.8. Getting events from the SQLite database

```
fn get_events(connection: &Connection) -> Vec<Event> {
    let category_map = get_categories(&connection);

    let event_query
        = "SELECT event_date, event_description, category_id FROM event".to_string();
    let mut statement = connection.prepare(&event_query).unwrap();
    let event_iter = statement.query_map([], |row| {
        Ok(EventRow {
            event_date: row.get_unwrap(0),
            event_description: row.get_unwrap(1),
            category_id: row.get_unwrap(2),
        })
    }).unwrap();

    let mut events: Vec<Event> = Vec::new();
    for row in event_iter {
        let r = row.unwrap();
        let date = NaiveDate::parse_from_str(&r.event_date, "%F").unwrap();
        let category = category_map.get(&r.category_id).unwrap();
        events.push(
            Event::new_singular(
                date,
                r.event_description,
                category.clone()));
```

```
    }

    events
}
```

This behavior can also be verified with a unit test in the tests module:

Example 30.9. Testing the `get_events` method of `SQLiteProvider`

```
    #[test]
    fn get_events_returns_one() {
        let connection = create_memory_db();
        let db_events = get_events(&connection);
        assert_eq!(db_events.len(), 1);
    }
```

Since there is only one event in the in-memory test database created by the create_memory_db function, we don't need to loop over the results.

Integrating the SQLite event provider

Since a SQLite database is stored in one disk file, this goes along well with the configuration file format we devised in Chapter 29, *Configuration file*. To add a SQLite database event provider to the configuration, we will need to add a section like the following to the TOML configuration file:

Example 30.10. Adding an SQLite event provider to the configuration

```
[[providers]]
name = "events-db"
kind = "sqlite"
resource = "events.db"
```

The main program needs no changes, but the run function in src/lib.rs needs to recognize the sqlite provider type. We'll add a new arm to the match cfg.kind.as_str() expression:

```
            "sqlite" => {
                let provider = SQLiteProvider::new(&cfg.name, &path);
                providers.push(Box::new(provider));
            },
```

We'll also add the statement `use crate::providers::sqlite::SQLiteProvider` to the top of the file.

Once the SQLite provider is created and the corresponding trait object is pushed into the `providers` vector, it will be consulted along with the other event providers when they are all iterated and queried for events.

Chapter 31. Reading events from a web service

In this chapter we'll get familiar with the Rust way of connecting to a web service. We'll develop a new event provider that can read events from a REST API.

Reading data from the web

All of the event providers we have developed so far have used local data, either from a text file or a SQLite database file. Let's make an event provider that can download events from a web service, using the HTTP protocol (or, rather, HTTPS) and a REST API endpoint.

The web service and REST API

The web service we are going to use is available on the public web. It was developed in Python using the Flask framework, and the events are read from a PostgreSQL database. This kind of web service could also be written in Rust, but that is out of the scope of this book.

The service has a REST API that allows us to send an HTTP GET request to an endpoint and specify the date that we want events for, using a query parameter. The path to use is `/api/v1/events`, but it should not be hard-coded into the event provider. Instead, it should be read from the configuration file as the resource associated with the event provider. The entry for a web event provider in the configuration file looks like this:

```
[[providers]]
name = "todayserver"
kind = "web"
resource = "https://todayserver-89bb2a1b2e80.herokuapp.com/api/v1/events"
```

The event provider uses this resource to construct the final path for the GET request.

Testing the API with `curl`

Before implementing the web event provider we can have a look at what the web API returns. We'll use the venerable `curl` program, which needs to be installed on our system if it's not already there. (We could also use `wget`.)

To avoid repeating the server URL in every request we can set up an environment variable and then use it in subsequent `curl` invocations:

```
% export TODAY_SERVER_URL=https://todayserver-89bb2a1b2e80.herokuapp.com
```

The API endpoint requires the `date` query parameter. If we send an HTTP `GET` request to the API endpoint without it, we will get an error with the response code 400:

```
% curl $TODAY_SERVER_URL/api/v1/events
<!doctype html>
<html lang=en>
<title>400 Bad Request</title>
<h1>Bad Request</h1>
<p>Missing date parameter</p>
```

However, if we add the `date` query parameter with the value specified in the `MM-dd` format, we should get back a JSON response:

```
% curl "$TODAY_SERVER_URL/api/v1/events?date=01-28"
[{"category":"test/fake","date":"1998-01-28","description":"Intel debuts ultra-slim
processors for quantum devices"},{"category":"test/fake","date":"2008-01-28",
"description":"Google releases AI-driven search customization tools"},
```

and so on. The events returned by the API are fake test data generated by a large language model, to represent fictional technology-related events. There are 20,000 of such events in the database of the web service, evenly distributed over the calendar year. This helps in testing, because we can be almost certain that whatever date we specify, we will get something back. All the test events are categorized as `"test/fake"` so that they can be easily filtered out as necessary.

We can get a better view of the JSON response if we pipe the result to the `jq` utility:

```
% curl "$TODAY_SERVER_URL/api/v1/events?date=01-28" | jq '.'
[
  {
```

```
    "category": "test/fake",
    "date": "2008-01-28",
    "description": "Google releases AI-driven search customization tools"
  },
  {
    "category": "test/fake",
    "date": "1988-01-28",
    "description": "Sony debuts modular gaming devices with hot-swappable parts"
  },
  {
    "category": "test/fake",
    "date": "2017-01-28",
    "description": "Amazon launches AI-augmented shopping experience"
  }
]
```

Making the web event provider

A web provider needs a URL to specify the endpoint of the REST API. We get it as a string from the configuration file, but to avoid errors that are caused by malformed URLs we should parse into an actual URL struct. The `url` crate has one that we can use, so we'll add the crate to the project dependencies soon.

We need two major things to make the HTTP request to the server and handle the response: an HTTP client and a JSON handler. Both of these can be built with the help of two very popular Rust crates, called `reqwest` and `serde`, respectively.

The `reqwest` crate is the most popular HTTP client library for Rust. It can work both synchronously and asynchronously. The `serde` crate, which we have met earlier in Chapter 29, *Configuration file,* is a generic framework for *ser*ializing and *de*serializing Rust data structures (hence the name), and it can handle JSON among other formats.

To add all these crates to the Today program, we need to either edit the `Cargo.toml` file or use the `cargo add` subcommand. We want to use some optional features, so editing the configuration file may be easiest. However, the Carfgo documentation gives more information about the `add` subcommand. Either way, we should end up with the following new lines in the `Cargo.toml` file's `[dependencies]` section:

Example 31.1. The `Cargo.toml` entries for web-related crates

```
[dependencies]
reqwest = { version = "0.13.3", features = ["blocking", "json"] }
serde = { version = "1.0.228", features = ["derive"] }
serde_json = "1.0"
url = "2.5.8"
```

This file will most likely already have `serde` there after implementing the TOML configuration file processing in Chapter 29, *Configuration file*. The actual version numbers may differ, of course.

We'll make a new file, `src/providers/web.rs`, for the provider. Instead of a string for the URL, the definition of `WebProvider` has a field of type `Url`, and it also takes a reference to a `Url` as the second argument of its `new` constructor function:

Example 31.2. Web event provider implementation

```
use url::Url;

pub struct WebProvider {
    name: String,
    url: Url,
}

impl WebProvider {
    pub fn new(name: &str, url: &Url) -> Self {
        Self {
            name: name.to_string(),
            url: url.clone(),
        }
    }
}
```

Making an HTTP request with the `reqwest` crate

The `reqwest` crate has both asynchronous and synchronous HTTP clients. We will use the synchronous client to make a blocking request to the web service.

This means that the program will stop to wait for the response from the web service. In a command-line program like this it is acceptable, and making the program asynchronous would be a lot of work at this point for not so much profit.

First we bring into scope the necessary identifiers from the new crates, and then proceed to implement the `EventProvider` trait for `WebProvider`. Initially we use today's date to construct the `date` URL parameter for the request:

Example 31.3. `EventProvider` implementation for `WebProvider`

```
use reqwest::blocking::{Client, Response};
use serde::Deserialize;
use serde_json;
use url::Url;

impl EventProvider for WebProvider {
    fn name(&self) -> String {
        self.name.clone()
    }

    fn get_events(&self, events: &mut Vec<Event>) {
        let today: NaiveDate = Local::now().date_naive();
        let month_day = MonthDay::new(today.month(), today.day());

        let mut url = self.url.clone();
        url.set_query(Some(&format!("date={}", month_day)));

        let client = Client::new();
        let request = client.get(url).send();
        let response: Response;
        if request.is_err() {
            eprintln!("Error while retrieving data: {:#?}", request.err());
            return;
        } else {
            response = request.ok().unwrap();
        }

        // ...to be continued
```

We construct the URL for the request by cloning the base URL and adding a query parameter with the `set_query` method of `Url`. The query parameter will be in `MM-DD` format since we have implemented the `Display` trait for the `MonthDay` struct earlier.

Then we make a `reqwest::blocking::Client`, and use its `get` to make a `GET` request, sending it off with the `send` method. If there was an error, we report it and return from this method; on success, we unwrap the response.

The server response contains a JSON array with zero or more events, and we need to turn those into actual `Event` values. This is easy to do with a helper struct that can store the JSON values as strings for further processing:

Example 31.4. A helper for JSON parsing

```
#[derive(Deserialize, Debug)]
struct JSONEvent {
    category: String,
    date: String,
    description: String,
}
```

This struct has a `derive` attribute with `Deserialize` from the `serde` crate.

To process the `JSONEvent` values and turn them into actual `Event` values we continue to develop the `get_events` method:

Example 31.5. The rest of the `get_events` method

```
// ... get_events continues

        let json_events = response.json::<Vec<JSONEvent>>().unwrap();
        println!("Got {} events from JSON", json_events.len());
        for json_event in json_events {
            let date = NaiveDate::parse_from_str(&json_event.date, "%F").unwrap();
            let category = match Category::from_str(&json_event.category) {
                Ok(cat) => cat,
                Err(e) => {
                    eprintln!("{}", e);
```

```
                continue;
            }
        };
        let event = Event::new_singular(date, json_event.description, category);
        events.push(event);
    }
  }
}
```

We treat the JSON array as a vector of `JSONEvent` values, and use the `reqwest` crate's JSON support together with `serde_json` to parse them. Then we run through the vector and turn the string fields of each `JSONEvent` value into something appropriate for an `Event`, so that we can make a singular event out of them. When the event has been constructed, it is added to the `events` vector that was supplied as a parameter to the `get_events` method.

We could also look into deriving `Deserialize` for the `Event` struct, but in this case it would likely be more trouble than it is worth.

Preparing for the web event provider

Once again, the `main` function needs no changes, but the `run` function in `src/lib.rs` needs to recognize the `web` provider type. Also, we'll want to parse the resource string we got from the configuration file into an actual URL, if possible. If the URL is malformed, we skip adding the provider. For these we'll add a new arm to the `match cfg.kind.as_str()` expression:

```
"web" => {
    match Url::parse(&cfg.resource) {
        Ok(url) => {
            let provider = WebProvider::new(&cfg.name, &url);
            self.providers.push(Box::new(provider));
        },
        Err(e) => {
            eprintln!("Error in URL for provider '{}': {}",
                &cfg.name, e);
        }
    }
},
```

Obligatory reminder: we need to add `pub mod web;` to `src/providers/mod.rs`, and bring items into scope as needed in `src/lib.rs`.

If we now compile and run the program, we will notice that the `reqwest` crate pulls in many dependencies, because it is a large crate. We are only using a fraction of its capabilities here.

Chapter 32. Filtering events at the source

In this chapter we will develop a flexible mechanism to filter events out of a larger group based on criteria we specify. We will learn how to use the Builder design pattern in Rust to easily implement event filters.

Getting just the events we want

Currently we are reading all events from all event sources, except for the web service provider, where there already is a URL query parameter to specify an exact month-day value. The other providers should work this way too, to avoid processing events that will never be displayed because they do not fall on the day of interest. Additionally, we may wish to filter any found events by category, so that we retrieve the minimum number of events.

Introducing event filters

Any parameters used to filter events, such as month-day, category, or some text found in the event description, could be specified at the command line. However, they still need to be collected into some kind of structure that we can pass on to any event provider.

Let's first define a struct called `EventFilter` to collect the options, and place its source code in a new module by creating a new source file called `filters.rs`. Later we will use the Builder design pattern to implement a way of constructing filters with different options.

Filter options

We'll express the various filter options with three struct fields, which are all optional. There is no constructor function to make a new `EventFilter`, since there will be a filter builder that lets us configure a filter with the various options. However, there are accessor methods to get each of the various options for those clients that need them.

Example 32.1. The `EventFilter` struct with accessors

```
use crate::events::{Event, MonthDay, Category};

pub struct EventFilter {
    month_day: Option<MonthDay>,
    description_contains: Option<String>,
    category_matches: Option<Category>,
}

impl EventFilter {
    pub fn month_day(&self) -> Option<MonthDay> {
        self.month_day.clone()
    }

    pub fn description_contains(&self) -> Option<String> {
        self.description_contains.clone()
    }

    pub fn category_matches(&self) -> Option<Category> {
        self.category_matches.clone()
    }
}
```

The event filter owns the options, so when they are requested, we clone them. In the next section, where we determine whether to accept an event or not, we will see that internally we can just use the struct fields.

Accepting the event

An event filter needs a method that returns `true` or `false` depending on whether the filter accepts a given event or not, based on any options it is currently storing (if any). We'll call this method `accepts`, and specify one parameter, a reference to some `Event` being examined.

The `accepts` method needs to examine the options to find out what needs to be checked to determine the acceptance criteria for a particular event. The next example shows one possible implementation of this method:

Example 32.2. The `accepts` method of the event filter

```
impl EventFilter {
    pub fn accepts(&self, event: &Event) -> bool {
        if let Some(month_day) = &self.month_day {
            if event.month_day() != *month_day {
                return false;
            }
        }

        if let Some(ref text) = self.description_contains {
            if !event.description().to_lowercase().contains(text) {
                return false;
            }
        }

        if let Some(ref filter_cat) = self.category_matches {
            if event.category() != *filter_cat {
                return false;
            }
        }

        true
    }
}
```

This code is taking advantage of the `if let` pattern that we saw in Chapter 13, *Optional values*. If none of the filter criteria are present, the logic goes all the way down to the last expression, making `true` the return value of the method. All existing criteria are checked on the way down. If a criterion is present, it will be compared to what is in the event. If they differ, we short circuit and return immediately, because the filter can't possibly match if some specific option does not match. If a criterion is not present, it will not affect the return value.

Note that the category criterion requires an exact match, for example `programming/rust`. This could be made more flexible by allowing matches for just the primary category, accepting any secondary category (including none at all). Here is an opportunity to try one's hand at implementing this kind of wildcard category equality. We have already derived `PartialEq` and `Eq` for `Category`, so the exact comparison is easy.

Constructing filters with the Builder pattern

Constructing an event filter could be done with one single associated function, but keeping the options and their associated values in check quickly becomes a lot of work. The Builder pattern[1] can help in this kind of situation. It lets us chain together method calls, each of which returns a partially configured object that can be further configured as needed. At the end of the call chain we build the final object. As we get more familiar with the Rust standard library and external crates, we will see that the Builder pattern is quite common in Rust.

The `FilterBuilder` type maintains its own option fields, and the associated function `new` initializes them all to `None`. This corresponds to an "all-pass" filter. The builder also has methods to set the option fields, and they work in three stages:

- Take a `mut self` parameter;
- modify the specified option; and
- return the updated object (that is, `self`).

We'll note that the argument to the various methods is `mut self` and not `&mut self`. This means that the method takes ownership of the value, but then returns it back to the caller. By calling one of these methods we are signalling the intent to set that particular option in the filter.

Another notable thing is that the struct fields and the methods to set them have the same name: `month_day` sets the `month_day` field, and so on. This is perfectly acceptable, and also quite common in Rust.

Finally, the `build` method makes a new `EventFilter` with all the options as they were set by the earlier method calls, and returns it using the `self` keyword:

[1]See https://refactoring.guru/design-patterns/builder

Example 32.3. The filter builder

```
pub struct FilterBuilder {
    month_day: Option<MonthDay>,
    description_contains: Option<String>,
    category_matches: Option<Category>,
}

impl FilterBuilder {
    pub fn new() -> Self {
        Self {
            month_day: None,
            description_contains: None,
            category_matches: None,
        }
    }

    pub fn month_day(mut self, month_day: MonthDay) -> Self {
        self.month_day = Some(month_day);
        self
    }

    pub fn description_contains(mut self, text: impl Into<String>) -> Self {
        self.description_contains = Some(text.into().to_lowercase());
        self
    }

    pub fn category_matches(mut self, category: &Category) -> Self {
        self.category_matches = Some(category.clone());
        self
    }

    pub fn build(self) -> EventFilter {
        EventFilter {
            month_day: self.month_day,
            description_contains: self.description_contains,
            category_matches: self.category_matches,
        }
    }
}
```

Now, whenever we wish to construct an event filter, we can use the FilterBuilder struct like this:

Example 32.4. Using the filter builder

```
let today: NaiveDate = Local::now().date_naive();
let month_day = MonthDay::new(today.month(), today.day());

let filter: EventFilter = FilterBuilder::new()
    .month_day(month_day)
    .category_matches(Category::new("programming", "rust")))
    .description_contains("released".to_string())
    .build();
```

This filter would accept any events that fall on today where the category is programming/rust and the description contains the text "released".

The final build method call returns the actual object being configured. This filter has all the possible options set, but we could specify any combination of them (month-day and category, but not description, and so on).

Testing the filters and the builder

It is easy to test that the filters are working as intended, and that the filter builder is building the kind of filter we want, by writing some unit tests using the Rust unit testing facilities that we have seen in Chapter 20, *Testing*.

Here is an example of a unit test that verifies the operation of an "all-pass" filter, or a filter that has no options, so that it accepts any event. This test actually managed to find a bug in an earlier implementation of the filter; the test failed because the accept method erroneously returned false instead of true when there were no filter options.

Example 32.5. Testing the event filter

```
#[cfg(test)]
mod tests {
    use super::*;
    use chrono::NaiveDate;

    #[test]
    fn filter_accepts_anything() {
        let rust_category = Category::new("programming", "rust");
        let event = Event::new_singular(
            NaiveDate::from_ymd_opt(2026, 3, 5).unwrap(),
            "Rust 1.94.0 released".to_string(),
            rust_category.clone());
        let filter = FilterBuilder::new()
            .build();
        assert!(filter.accepts(&event));
    }
}
```

The test creates one singular event, and then builds an event filter with no options. The event should be accepted unconditionally, so the test succeeds if the `assert!` macro succeeds. We could write several of these kinds of tests for various filter options and combinations.

It is also easy to write some tests to verify that the filter *builder* works as advertised. For example, building a filter with no options should result in all the filter accessor methods returning `None`. The following test builds a tuple of the method results, and the assertion compares that to another tuple with all `None` values:

Example 32.6. Testing the filter builder

```
    #[test]
    fn build_filter_no_options() {
        let filter = FilterBuilder::new().build();
        let contains = (
```

```
        filter.month_day(),
        filter.category_matches(),
        filter.description_contains());
    assert_eq!(contains, (None, None, None));
}
```

Note

If we find the Builder pattern useful, we can streamline the making of builders with the bon crate[2]. It can generate builders for functions and structs using derive attributes:

```
use bon::Builder;

#[derive(Builder)]
pub struct EventFilter {
    // ...
}

let filter = EventFilter::builder()
    .description_contains("Rust".to_string())
    .build();
```

Refactoring the event providers

The EventProvider trait and the event providers implementing it need to be refactored slightly to support filtering. The get_events method needs a reference to an EventFilter as a parameter:

[2]https://bon-rs.com

Example 32.7. The refactored `EventFilter` trait

```
use crate::Event;
use crate::filters::EventFilter;

pub mod textfile;
pub mod csvfile;
pub mod sqlite;
pub mod web;

pub trait EventProvider {
    fn name(&self) -> String;
    fn get_events(&self, filter: &EventFilter, events: &mut Vec<Event>);
}
```

To refactor the event providers we also need to add `use crate::filters::EventFilter;` to each provider module, and change the `get_events` signature. That is easiest to do at the same time we're doing the actual implementation changes that refer to the filter. Refactoring typically introduces many small changes like this, but the Rust compiler is good at pointing them out, and rust-analyzer running in your editor can find them even before compiling.

The `get_events` method implementation is specific to each event provider, but there are similarities. For the text file and CSV file providers it can be as simple as this:

```
// original code
events.push(event);

// new code
if filter.accepts(&event) {
    events.push(event);
}
```

For the SQLite event provider the change is a bit more involved. We don't want to retrieve all the events from the database and filter them after the fact, because there could be thousands of events, and most of them probably wouldn't be needed, because they wouldn't fall on our target date. Instead we want to leverage the SQLite database engine and restrict the query to what is specified in the filter, using a `WHERE` clause in the SQL query.

Let's make a helper function to construct the `WHERE` clause in `src/providers/sqlite.rs`:

Example 32.8. Constructing the `WHERE` clause

```
fn make_where_clause(filter: &EventFilter, category_map: &CategoryMap) -> String {
    let mut parts: Vec<String> = Vec::new();

    if let Some(month_day) = filter.month_day() {
        let part = format!("strftime('%m-%d', event_date) = '{}'", month_day);
        parts.push(part);
    }

    if let Some(category) = filter.category_matches() {
        let mut filter_category_id: Option<CategoryId> = None;

        for (category_id, found_category) in category_map {
            if *found_category == category {
                filter_category_id = Some(*category_id);
                break;
            }
        }

        if let Some(id) = filter_category_id {
            parts.push(format!("category_id = {}", id))
        }
    }

    if let Some(text) = filter.description_contains() {
        parts.push(format!("event_description LIKE '%{}%'", text));
    }

    let mut result = "".to_string();
    if !parts.is_empty() {
        result.push_str("WHERE ");
        result.push_str(&parts.join(" AND "));
    }

    result
}
```

This function constructs an SQL WHERE clause from the filter options, so that it can be added to the database query if needed. We check all the possible filter options, and put them in the WHERE clause separated by AND. If the filter has no options, the WHERE clause ends up empty.

Since the SQLite event provider delegates the actual event query to a helper function, get_events, we modify that to pass the filter in so that it can be used to construct the WHERE clause:

Example 32.9. Adding the WHERE clause to the helper function

```
fn get_events(connection: &Connection, filter: &EventFilter) -> Vec<Event> {
    let category_map = get_categories(&connection);

    let mut event_query
        = "SELECT event_date, event_description, category_id FROM event".to_string();
    let where_clause = make_where_clause(filter, &category_map);
    if !where_clause.is_empty() {
        event_query.push(' ');
        event_query.push_str(&where_clause);
    }

    // rest of the function as before
```

Note that the query must now be made mutable. If the WHERE clause is not empty, it will be appended to the query. We can make some unit tests to verify that the clause is being constructed correctly:

Example 32.10. Testing the WHERE clause generation

```
    #[test]
    fn make_where_clause_empty() {
        let mut category_map = CategoryMap::new();
        category_map.insert(1, Category::from_primary("test"));
        let filter = FilterBuilder::new().build();
        let where_clause = make_where_clause(&filter, &category_map);
        assert_eq!(where_clause, "");
    }
```

```
    #[test]
    fn make_where_clause_month_day() {
        let mut category_map = CategoryMap::new();
        category_map.insert(1, Category::from_primary("test"));
        let today = NaiveDate::from_ymd_opt(2026, 3, 7).unwrap();
        let filter = FilterBuilder::new()
            .month_day(MonthDay::new(today.month(), today.day()))
            .build();
        let where_clause = make_where_clause(&filter, &category_map);
        assert_eq!(where_clause, "WHERE strftime('%m-%d', event_date) = '03-07'");
    }
}
```

Some other unit tests will need refactoring since the `filter` parameter has been added to the `get_events` function.

For the web provider the situation is a bit different. There REST API of the server has no query parameter for the category, so we can't restrict the results based on that. The same applies for matching some text in the event description. Still, we can let the filter decide at least partially what to do with the resulting events.

We'll refactor the `EventProvider` implementation of the web event provider in `src/providers/web.rs` to look like this:

Example 32.11. Web provider refactored for filtering

```
impl EventProvider for WebProvider {
    fn name(&self) -> String {
        self.name.clone()
    }

    fn get_events(&self, filter: &EventFilter, events: &mut Vec<Event>) {
        // We need a date query parameter for the URL, so if the filter
        // does not specify it, we are done.
        if filter.month_day().is_none() {
            eprintln!("No month-day in filter");
            return;
        }
```

```
        let month_day = filter.month_day().unwrap();

        let mut url = self.url.clone();
        url.set_query(Some(&format!("date={}", month_day)));

        let client = Client::new();
        let request = client.get(url).send();
        let response: Response;
        if request.is_err() {
            eprintln!("Error while retrieving data: {:#?}", request.err());
            return;
        } else {
            response = request.ok().unwrap();
        }

        let json_events = response.json::<Vec<JSONEvent>>().unwrap();
        println!("Got {} events from JSON", json_events.len());
        for json_event in json_events {
            let date = NaiveDate::parse_from_str(&json_event.date, "%F").unwrap();
            let category = Category::from_str(&json_event.category);
            let event = Event::new_singular(date, json_event.description, category);
            if filter.accepts(&event) {
                events.push(event);
            }
        }
    }
}
```

Now it becomes evident that we actually need to construct each event anyway, even if it ends up being rejected right away by the filter. This could be improved by adding another query parameter to specify the category, and maybe a third one for the description. However, that would require changes to the server implementation, and we might not always have that kind of control over the REST API you need to use, so here we do what we can.

Refactoring the run function

We still have some refactoring to do in order to make the new filter mechanism fit the existing framework. The `run` function in `lib.rs` needs a filter to pass to each event provider's `get_events` method. Since we have been using the current date, we can stick that in a filter. Also, we no longer need to iterate and filter the collected vector of events we received from the event providers since the filter has already done that. Here is the refactored `run` function:

Example 32.12. The new and improved `run` function

```
pub fn run(config: &Config, config_path: &Path) -> Result<(), Box<dyn Error>> {
    birthday::handle_birthday();

    // Make a new filter with today's date as the month-day:
    let today: NaiveDate = Local::now().date_naive();
    let today_month_day = MonthDay::new(today.month(), today.day());
    let filter = FilterBuilder::new()
        .month_day(today_month_day)
        .build();

    // Create the event providers and get events from them, filtered:
    let providers = create_providers(config, config_path);
    let mut count = 0;
    let mut events: Vec<Event> = Vec::new();
    for provider in providers {
        provider.get_events(&filter, &mut events);
        let new_count = events.len();
        println!(
            "Got {} events from provider '{}'",
            new_count - count,
            provider.name());
        count = new_count;
    }

    // Print out the filtered list of events (still in no particular order):
    for event in events {
        println!("{}: {} ({})",
            event.year(),
            event.description(),
            event.category());
    }

    Ok(())
}
```

We still need to add `mod filters;` and `use crate::filters::FilterBuilder` to this file.

Chapter 33. Handling command-line arguments

Command-line arguments are useful for controlling a single run of a program. In this chapter we will implement command-line argument handling for the Today program using the `clap` crate.

Controlling the program from the command line

The operation of the Today program is based mostly on the configuration file. By default, the program shows events from all registered event providers, filtered by an event filter that limites the events to those that fall on whatever date the real-time clock of the computer indicates. However, in some situations it is necessary to give the program some more guidance for a specific run. For example, we may want to see events of a specific date instead of the current, or show only events of one or more specific categories. This is achieved using *command-line arguments.*

All major operating systems have some mechanism of passing command-line arguments to a running program. Most often this is done using a command shell running in a terminal window. In Rust we can access the parameters passed to the program using the `std::env` module.

The simplest example of command-line argument processing is the following program that just echoes back all the arguments. The program was created with `cargo new args`, and the full source code is here:

Example 33.1. Printing out the command-line arguments

```
use std::env;

fn main() {
    let args: Vec<String> = env::args().collect();
    for (i, arg) in args.iter().enumerate() {
        println!("{}: {}", i + 1, arg);
    }
}
```

When this program is run, it will list all the command-line arguments as numbered strings:

```
% cargo run -q -- one two three
1: target/debug/args
2: one
3: two
4: three
```

Here we can see that the first command-line argument is actually the name of the executable program. In this case it is the debug version built and run by Cargo. This means that usually we will want to skip the first argument in the vector to get at the real arguments. The arguments are numbered from one onwards by adding one to the index value returned by the `enumerate`, which we first saw in Chapter 8, *Iteration and looping*.

Note also that the way to pass command-line arguments to programs we run with Cargo requires separating them from the arguments that are intended for Cargo, using the double dash. All arguments after the double dash go to the program being run, instead of Cargo itself. If we run the program directly from the command line, without using Cargo, the double dash does not apply, but the end result is the same:

```
% target/debug/args one two three
1: target/debug/args
2: one
3: two
4: three
```

For many simple programs, just having access to the command-line arguments is all we need. We may be able to use the arguments as is, as strings based on their positions on the command line. However, in command environments there are certain long-standing conventions regarding the use of options and flags on the command line. There are multiple sets of conventions, like the style of the GNU project, the POSIX standard, and the Microsoft Windows conventions. More information about these differences can be found at the Command Line Interface Guidelines website[1].

[1] https://clig.dev

If we want your command-line program to handle options and flags, and also Git-style subcommands, it will be a lot of work to implement the handling by ourselves. Luckily, Rust has several good options (pun intended) that we can delegate to, such as the `clap` crate.

Parsing command-line arguments with `clap`

The `clap` crate is one of the most popular crates for handling command-line arguments in Rust. We can describe our arguments either by using `derive` attributes or with the builder pattern that we looked at in Chapter 32, *Filtering events at the source*.

For a first taste of command-line argument handling, let's use the `clap` crate to implement an option to specify the month-day of the events we are interested in. Since we have already developed event filtering, we can use this argument as an option when we build a filter.

To begin using the `clap` crate we need to add it to our project and activate its `derive` feature. That is easy to do with the `cargo add` subcommand:

```
% cargo add clap -F derive
```

This will result in your `Cargo.toml` file having an entry like this in the `[dependencies]` section:

```
clap = { version = "4.6.1", features = ["derive"] }
```

(The version of `clap` may already be newer than this, of course.) This allows us to use the derive style for defining our command-line arguments.

The argument we are defining is called `--date`, or `-d` for short. We will allow both the long and the short form of the argument. The argument also needs a value, so that we can invoke the program in any of these ways:

```
% cargo run -q -- --date 0206
% cargo run -q -- -d 0206
% target/debug/today --date 0206
% target/debug/today -d 0206
```

To achieve that, we'll first define a struct called `Args` in our main program and use the facilities from the `clap` crate using the `derive` attribute and the `command` attributes (the latter is defined by `clap`):

Example 33.2. Using `clap` to process command-line arguments

```
use clap::Parser;

#[derive(Parser)]
#[command(name = "today")]
struct Args {
    #[arg(short, long, help = "Event date in MMDD format")]
    date: String,
}

fn main() {
    let args = Args::parse();

    // ... rest of the main function
}
```

If we now compile and run this program without any command-line arguments, we will see the following output (in color, if the terminal supports it):

```
% cargo run
error: the following required arguments were not provided:
  --date <DATE>

Usage: today --date <DATE>

For more information, try '--help'.
```

If we try the `--help` argument as suggested, this is the result:

```
% cargo run -- --help
Usage: today --date <DATE>

Options:
  -d, --date <DATE>  Event date in MMDD format
  -h, --help         Print help
```

With just a couple of lines we can get all of this for free from the clap crate's argument parser.

However, we don't want to force the user to always submit the date argument. If it is missing, we should default to the current date. This is easy to do with clap: just make the argument optional using the Option<String> type instead:

Example 33.3. Making the date argument optional

```
use clap::Parser;

#[derive(Parser)]
#[command(name = "today")]
struct Args {
    #[arg(short, long, help = "Event date in MMDD format")]
    date: Option<String>,  // optional, defaults to current date
}

fn main() {
    let args = Args::parse();

    // ... rest of the main function
}
```

Since we are going to use command-line arguments to control event filtering, we need to construct the event filter in the main function. This way we can collect all the relevant command-line arguments, construct a filter, and then pass it on to the run function in src/lib.rs. This allows us to add just one parameter to the run function, instead of several different criteria, like date, category or text content.

To do this, we'll bring the relevant items into scope and construct the filter in the main function with the information we have received from the command line so far:

Example 33.4. Constructing an event filter from the command-line arguments

```
use clap::Parser;
use chrono::{NaiveDate, Local, Datelike};

use today::events::MonthDay;
use today::filters::{EventFilter, FilterBuilder};

fn main() {
    let args = Args::parse();

    let month_day = if let Some(md) = args.date {
        MonthDay::from_str(&md).unwrap()
    } else {
        let today: NaiveDate = Local::now().date_naive();
        MonthDay::new(today.month(), today.day())
    };

    let filter: EventFilter = FilterBuilder::new()
        .month_day(month_day)
        .build();

    // ... to be continued
}
```

If the date command-line argument is present (is not None) we use it to construct a MonthDay; otherwise we make it from the current date. This makes the program work with or without the date argument.

This requires a small change to the signature of the run function in src/lib.rs. We add the filter parameter, so the signature becomes:

```
pub fn run(config: &Config, config_path: &Path, filter: &EventFilter)
        -> Result<(), Box<dyn Error>>
```

Any leftover code in the run function that constructs an event filter should also now be removed. (We need to be careful not to shadow the filter passed as argument with a local variable of the same name.) Finally, when we call the run function in the main program, we need to supply the filter parameter:

```
            if let Err(e) = run(&config, &path, &filter) {
```

```
            eprintln!("Error running program");
            return;
        }
```

We're sure to mention the `filters` and `events` modules in `src/lib.rs`:

```
// In src/lib.rs:
pub mod events;
pub mod filters;
```

Defining subcommands

The `clap` crate can also handle subcommands, as found in Git and many other tools. Let's implement a subcommand called `providers` to list all the event providers that are configured in the configuration file `today.toml` file, added in Chapter 29, *Configuration file*.

To define a subcommand with `clap` we need to refine the definition of the arguments a little bit. We'll add an enum called `Command` for the commands, and add a field to the `Args` struct with the `command` attribute:

Example 33.5. Defining subcommands with the `clap` crate

```
use clap::{Parser, Subcommand};

#[derive(Subcommand, Debug, Clone)]
enum Command {
    /// List all event providers
    Providers,
}

#[derive(Parser)]
#[command(name = "today")]
struct Args {
    #[command(subcommand)]
    cmd: Option<Command>,

    #[arg(short, long, help = "Event date in MMDD format")]
    date: Option<String>,
}
```

Note that we have made the subcommand optional, so that we can still run the program without any subcommand and get the normal behavior.

Note also that subcommands don't have a `help` text in the `arg` attribute like options do. Instead, the help text for the subcommand is expressed as a documentation comment, beginning with `///`.

Since the subcommand is optional, it will need to be handled accordingly. Where we would normally just call the `run` function we instead use a match expression on `args.cmd`:

Example 33.6. Using `match` to handle subcommands

```
match config_path {
    Some(path) => {
        let toml_path = path.join(format!("{}.toml", APP_NAME));
        println!("Looking for configuration file '{}'", &toml_path.display());
        let config_str = fs::read_to_string(&toml_path)
            .expect("configuration file should exist");
        let config: Config = toml::from_str(&config_str)
            .expect("configuration file should be valid");
        println!("config: {:#?}", config);

        match args.cmd {
            Some(Command::Providers) => {
                for provider in config.providers {
                    println!("{}", provider.name);
                }
            },

            _ => {
                if let Err(e) = run(&config, &path, &filter) {
                    eprintln!("Error running program: {}", e);
                    return;
                }
            }
        }
    },
    None => {
        eprintln!("Unable to configure the application");
        return;
```

```
    }
}
```

The trouble is, the `providers` field of `Config` is private, and so is the `name` field of `ProviderConfig`. We'll have to make a judgement call: should we make these fields public, or should we make accessor functions? In this case, since these are both kind of throwaway types, used only as helpers when parsing the configuration, we can just make them public by adding the `pub` keyword to the fields:

Example 33.7. Helper types for provider configuration

```
#[derive(Deserialize, Debug)]
pub struct ProviderConfig {
    pub name: String,
    pub kind: String,
    pub resource: String,
}

#[derive(Deserialize, Debug)]
pub struct Config {
    pub providers: Vec::<ProviderConfig>,
}
```

Now `cargo run` will give us the normal event listing, but `cargo run -- providers` will list all the event providers instead:

```
% cargo run -- providers
annual-events-csv
history
programming
computing
programming-csv
todayserver
rule-based
```

The contents of the listing will vary depending on the contents of the configuration file. Later we will augment this listing with information about which providers support adding events.

Chapter 34. Adding new event kinds

In this chapter we'll add new event kinds to augment the singular historical events we've used earlier. This will involve some refactoring of the Today program, but it can be done within the existing framework. By the end of the chapter we'll have three different kinds of events.

More than just singular events

So far, the only kind of event we have seen is the "singular" event, something that happened once in history. However, there are also other kinds of events that we might want to track with the Today program.

Annual events occur on the same day every year. Some examples of these include national holidays and various appreciation days. *Rule-based events* are events whose date is relative to months and weekdays, and so moves around in the year. They can be defined by a rule that involves ordinals, weekdays, and months. Examples of rules are "second Tuesday in May" and "last friday of November".

Annual events

We'll start with the annual events, and add a new variant to the `EventKind` enum:

Example 34.1. Adding a new event kind variant

```
use chrono::NaiveDate;

#[derive(Debug)]
pub enum EventKind {
    Singular(NaiveDate),
    Annual(MonthDay),
}
```

We'll also add a constructor function new_annual to create an annual event, and revise the year and month_day methods to handle the new variant:

Example 34.2. New constructor for creating annual events

```
impl Event {
    // ...

    pub fn new_annual(month_day: MonthDay, description: String, category: Category) -> Self {
        Self {
            kind: EventKind::Annual(month_day),
            description,
            category
        }
    }

    pub fn year(&self) -> i32 {
        match &self.kind {
            EventKind::Singular(date) => date.year(),
            EventKind::Annual(_month_day) => {
                let today: NaiveDate = Local::now().date_naive();
                today.year()
            },
        }
    }

    pub fn month_day(&self) -> MonthDay {
        match &self.kind {
            EventKind::Singular(date) => MonthDay::new(date.month(), date.day()),
            EventKind::Annual(month_day) => month_day.clone(),
        }
    }
}
```

The Display trait implementation for the Event struct needs to change a bit, because we can get the year for both enum variants using the year method:

Example 34.3. `Display` trait implementation for `Event`

```
impl fmt::Display for Event {
    fn fmt(&self, f: &mut fmt::Formatter) -> fmt::Result {
        write!(f, "{}: {} ({})",
            self.year(),
            self.description,
            self.category)
    }
}
```

Now we can create annual events if we get them from some outside source through an event provider. However, since an annual event has a month-day without a year, we also need to update our event providers to take that possibility into account.

A yearless date is expressed as `--MM-DD`, which is almost like a standard ISO 8601 date, but with the year replaced by a dash. An example would be `--05-01`, representing the first of May. This is how we can separate full dates from yearless dates when they occur in a text file.

Updating event providers to support annual events

Let's now update the text file and CSV file event providers to support annual events. First we'll add a new data file called `annuals.txt` in our operating system specific configuration directory, with the following sample content:

Example 34.4. Event text file with yearless dates

```
--04-25 ❶
World Penguin Day ❷
nature ❸
❹
--01-20
Penguin Awareness Day
```

```
nature

--06-05
World Environment Day
nature
❺
```

❶ The yearless date of the event.
❷ The event description.
❸ The category of the event, in technical format.
❹ Empty line separating the events.
❺ Empty line after the last event category makes the event record complete.

We'll make sure that we separate the event records with a blank line.

Now that we have a mechanism to configure the event providers, let's also add a new provider entry to our configuration file `today.toml`:

Example 34.5. Configuration entry for yearless event provider in `today.toml`

```
[[providers]]
name = "annuals-textfile"
kind = "text"
resource = "annuals.txt"
```

If we were to run the program now, the yearless dates would simply be ignored because the text file event provider was initially programmed to skip a record with a date that is not strictly in full ISO 8601 format. However, when all the changes above and those to follow are made, the program should pick up the new data file and parse also the yearless dates correctly.

In the `get_events` method, we are going to replace the `match` arm that handles `ReadingState::Separator` with the following:

Example 34.6. Creating a singular or annual event in `get_events`

```
ReadingState::Separator => {
    let is_yearless = date_string.starts_with("--");
    if is_yearless {
        let today: NaiveDate = Local::now().date_naive();
        let year_string = format!("{:04}-", today.year());
        date_string = date_string.replace("--", &year_string);
    }
    let event: Event;
    match NaiveDate::parse_from_str(&date_string, "%F") {
        Ok(date) => {
            let category = Category::from_str(&category_string).unwrap();
            if is_yearless {
                event = Event::new_annual(
                    MonthDay::new(date.month(), date.day()),
                    description.clone(),
                    category);
            } else {
                event = Event::new_singular(
                    date,
                    description.clone(),
                    category);
            }

            if filter.accepts(&event) {
                events.push(event);
            }
        },
        Err(_) => {
            eprintln!("Invalid date '{}'", date_string);
        }
    }
    state = ReadingState::Date;
},
```

If the date string starts with two dashes, we set a flag in the `is_yearless` variable, and replace those dashes with the year from the current date followed by a dash, to get a valid date for the ongoing year. This makes the date a complete ISO 8601 date string in the `YYYY-MM-DD` format. For example, if the original date string was `--01-20` and it is the year 2026, then the date string will end up as `2026-01-20`.

We then declare a variable of the `Event` type, called `event`, but we don't initialize it yet. Rust does require that all variables are eventually initialized, but that will eventually be the case here too, because the `match` arm that handles the `Ok` case will assign either a singular or annual event variant to this variable, based on the value of `is_yearless`.

The changes to the CSV event provider are almost identical, so they are not shown here. See the book's example repository on GitHub for the full code from this chapter.

Unfortunately the SQLite event provider can't be updated to support yearless dates, since SQLite does not support them. Also, the REST API of the web provider only handles only singular events.

Rule-based events

We've saved the trickiest case last. As mentioned at the start of this chapter, rule-based events are events that can occur on a slightly different date each year, determined by a rule like "last Thursday of April" or "second Sunday in November". To get from a textual rule like this to an actual calendar date turns out to be non-trivial, so let's walk through the code.

To be able to express rule-based events, we need to add one more variant to the `Event` struct:

Example 34.7. Adding a new event kind for rule-based events

```
use chrono::{
    NaiveDate,
    Datelike,
    Local,
    Month  // needed for the Rule in the RuleBased enum variant
};

#[derive(Debug)]
```

```
pub enum EventKind {
    Singular(NaiveDate),
    Annual(MonthDay),
    RuleBased(Rule),
}
```

To make a new rule-based event we need a new constructor function for the Event struct:

Example 34.8. Constructing a rule-based event

```
impl Event {
    pub fn new_rule_based(rule: Rule, description: String, category: Category) -> Self {
        Event {
            kind: EventKind::RuleBased(rule),
            description,
            category
        }
    }
}
```

The new RuleBased enum variant has an associated value of type Rule. We'll model the rule as a struct, with fields for the different components:

Example 34.9. Defining a struct for the event rule

```
#[derive(Debug, Clone, PartialEq, Eq, PartialOrd, Ord)]
pub struct Rule {
    ordinal: Ordinal,
    weekday: Weekday,  // not chrono::Weekday; see below
    month: Month,
}
```

The Ordinal type is intended to provide a type-safe variant for the specification of the ordinal in the rule:

Example 34.10. Enumerated type for the ordinals

```
#[derive(Debug, Clone, PartialEq, Eq, PartialOrd, Ord)]
enum Ordinal {
    First = 1,
    Second = 2,
    Third = 3,
    Fourth = 4,
    Fifth = 5,
    Last = 6,
}
```

We define a `Weekday` enumerated type for the `weekday` field since `chrono::Weekday` does not implement the `PartialOrd` or `Ord` traits; the `chrono` crate documentation states that this is because "the order of the days of week depends on the context".

Example 34.11. Enumerated type for the weekdays

```
#[derive(Debug, Clone, Copy, Eq, Ord, PartialEq, PartialOrd)]
pub enum Weekday {
    Monday = 0,
    Tuesday = 1,
    Wednesday = 2,
    Thursday = 3,
    Friday = 4,
    Saturday = 5,
    Sunday = 6,
}
```

Finally, the `month` field of the `Rule` struct is simply `chrono::Month`.

Note

After adding yet another enum variant the program will be in a non-compilable state. The Rust compiler will give various error messages about match expressions that do not cover all the enum variants. It will take some time to make all the changes required by the refactoring, but if we proceed methodically and keep a clear idea of what goes where, we will be able to restore error-free compilation soon.

The Rule struct will have an associated function called parse, which attempts to parse a string that contains a description of the rule, such as "last Thursday in April". Here is the code for the function, followed by a part-by-part walk-through:

Example 34.12. The parse function in the Rule struct

```
impl Rule {
    // Parse a rule of the following format:
    // first|second|third|fourth|fifth|last <weekday> in <month>
    //   weekday: Monday|Tuesday|Wednesday|Thursday|Friday|Saturday|Sunday
    //   month: January|February|March| ... |November|December
    pub fn parse(rule_string: &str) -> Option<Self> {
        let parts: Vec<String> = rule_string.to_lowercase().split_whitespace()
            .map(str::to_string).collect();

        // After splitting on whitespace, there must be exactly four parts.
        if parts.len() != 4 {
            eprintln!("invalid rule: {}", rule_string);
            return None;
        }

        let ordinal = match Ordinal::from_str(&parts[0]) {
            Ok(ord) => ord,
            Err(e) => {
                eprintln!("{}", e);
                return None;
            }
        };

        let weekday = match Weekday::from_str(&parts[1]) {
            Ok(wd) => wd,
            Err(e) => {
                eprintln!("{}", e);
                return None;
```

```
            }
        };

        if parts[2] != "in" && parts[2] != "of" {
            eprintln!("rule should specify `in` or `of`");
            return None;
        }

        let month = match parts[3].parse::<Month>() {
            Ok(m) => m,
            Err(e) => {
                eprintln!("{}", e);
                return None;
            }
        };

        Some(Self { ordinal, weekday, month })
    }
}
```

We first fold the string into lowercase so that we don't need to account for differences in character case (for example, "april" vs. "April"). Then we split the string by whitespace, and try to make sense of the individual pieces.

The first part must be one of the strings that correspond to a literal representation of one of the `Ordinal` values, while the second part must correspond to a literal representation of one of the `Weekday` values. The third part is expected to be the literal string `"in"` or `"of"` always. By allowing both literals we can cater for the Robustness Principle[1]. The fourth part is the name of the month.

To find out if the first part is valid we could implement a `from_str` method to convert a string into one of the `Ordinal` variants. However, the `strum` crate and its associated macros in the related `strum_macros` crate make this less of a chore, so we'll take advantage of those services.

We add both crates to the project's `Cargo.toml` file as usual, so that its `[dependencies]` section will contain these lines:

[1] Also known as Postel's Law, named after Jon Postel (1943-1988), American computer scientist. Formulated as: "Be conservative in what you do, be liberal in what you accept from others."

```
strum = "0.27"
strum_macros = "0.27"
```

Then we'll bring the necessary types into scope and add the `EnumString` type to the `derive` annotation of our `Ordinal` type. We also annotate the `enum` with the `#[strum(ascii_case_insensitive)]` attribute so that the conversions between literal strings and enum values are not affected by differences in character case. Then we do the same for the `Weekday`.

Example 34.13. Enriching the `Ordinal` and `Weekday` enums with the `strum` crate

```
use std::str::FromStr;
use strum_macros::EnumString;

#[derive(Debug, Copy, Clone, PartialEq, Eq, PartialOrd, Ord, EnumString)]
#[strum(ascii_case_insensitive)]
pub enum Ordinal {
    // ...
}

#[derive(Debug, Copy, Clone, PartialEq, Eq, PartialOrd, Ord, EnumString)]
#[strum(ascii_case_insensitive)]
pub enum Weekday {
    // ...
}
```

When we derive `EnumString` for the `Ordinal` and `Weekday` types, it automatically derives the `std::str::FromStr` trait for them as a convenience, so that we don't need to manually implement it. You still need to bring the trait into scope, as in the previous example.

The associated function `parse` is found in the `impl` block of the `Rule` struct. Using the `strum` crate to define the `Ordinal` and `Weekday` types as described earlier makes it easy to parse the ordinal and weekday parts and bail out in case of an error:

Example 34.14. Parsing the event rule

```
impl Rule {
    pub fn parse(rule_string: &str) -> Option<Self> {
        let parts: Vec<String> = rule_string.to_lowercase().split_whitespace()
            .map(str::to_string).collect();

        // After splitting on whitespace, there must be exactly four parts.
        if parts.len() != 4 {
            eprintln!("invalid rule: {}", rule_string);
            return None;
        }

        let ordinal = match Ordinal::from_str(&parts[0]) {
            Ok(ord) => ord,
            Err(e) => {
                eprintln!("{}", e);
                return None;
            }
        };

        let weekday = match Weekday::from_str(&parts[1]) {
            Ok(wd) => wd,
            Err(e) => {
                eprintln!("{}", e);
                return None;
            }
        };

        // ...
```

The third part is the "in" or "of" part, so we accept either one, but return `None` if neither is found. Finally, we parse the month, delegating to the `chrono` crate. As the final parsing step we collect the pieces into a value of type `Rule` that we return from the method:

Example 34.15. Parsing the rest of the rule

```
    if parts[2] != "in" && parts[2] != "of" {
        eprintln!("rule should specify `in` or `of`");
        return None;
    }

    let month = match parts[3].parse::<Month>() {
        Ok(m) => m,
        Err(e) => {
            eprintln!("{}", e);
            return None;
        }
    };

    Some(Self { ordinal, weekday, month })
}
```

Resolving the rule

Once the rule has been successfully parsed, it needs to be resolved into an actual calendar date. This date is most likely different from year to year, and some rules may not resolve to any date at all. That is why the method to resolve the rule can only practically return an optional value. We can use the `NaiveDate` type from the `chrono` crate, so the returned type will be `Option<NaiveDate>`.

We will naïvely assume that the resolved date will always land in the ongoing year, if it can be resolved at all. Still, to facilite testing, we will pass the year of the target event to the resolver. Any tests that we write to determine if the rule resolution works correctly will need to hard-code the year in them, but that also ensures that they keep working even after the new year.

All events have a year, at least conceptually, but it will be shown only for singular events. The `year` method of `Event` will need to handle all the enum varianta, and so does the `month_day` method. We implement the `EventKind::RuleBased` arm for both:

Example 34.16. Handling all the EventKind enum variants

```
impl Event {
    pub fn year(&self) -> i32 {
        match &self.kind {
            EventKind::Singular(date) => date.year(),
            EventKind::Annual(_month_day) => {
                let today: NaiveDate = Local::now().date_naive();
                today.year()
            },
            EventKind::RuleBased(rule) => rule.year(),
        }
    }

    pub fn month_day(&self) -> MonthDay {
        match &self.kind {
            EventKind::Singular(date) => MonthDay::new(date.month(), date.day()),
            EventKind::Annual(month_day) => month_day.clone(),
            EventKind::RuleBased(rule) => {
                match rule.month_day() {
                    Some(month_day) => month_day,
                    None => panic!("invalid month day resolved from rule"),
                }
            }
        }
    }
}
```

This means that Rule needs to have year and month_day methods too:

Example 34.17. The year and month_day methods of Rule

```
impl Rule {
    pub fn year(&self) -> i32 {
        Local::now().year()  // always use the year from the current local date
    }

    pub fn month_day(&self) -> Option<MonthDay> {
        if let Some(date) = self.resolve_date(self.year()) {
```

```
            Some(MonthDay { month: date.month(), day: date.day() })
        } else {
            None
        }
    }
}
```

Now we can finally implement tests for the rule resolution. We'll add a `tests` module in `src/events.rs` with some elementary tests:

Example 34.18. Tests for the event rule

```
#[cfg(test)]
mod tests {
    use super::*;
    use chrono::NaiveDate;

    #[test]
    fn rejects_invalid_ordinal() {
        assert_eq!(Rule::parse("sixth sunday in may"), None);
    }

    #[test]
    fn rejects_invalid_weekday() {
        assert_eq!(Rule::parse("first bloomsday in june"), None);
    }

    #[test]
    fn rejects_invalid_month() {
        assert_eq!(Rule::parse("first tuesday in remember"), None);
    }

    #[test]
    fn valid_date_from_rule() {
        let rule = Rule::parse("second tuesday of may").unwrap();
        assert_eq!(
            Some(rule.resolve_date(2026)),
            Some(NaiveDate::from_ymd_opt(2026, 5, 12)));
    }
}
```

Right now some of these tests will not compile, since we haven't even implemented the `resolve_date` method for `Rule` yet, so let's make a minimal placeholder implementation just so that we can run the tests. The rule resolution test will fail, but the rule parsing should already work. The following should be enough to run the tests:

Example 34.19. Stub method for resolving the rule

```
pub fn resolve_date(&self, year: i32) -> Option<NaiveDate> {
    None
}
```

Now running the tests should produce the following result:

```
running 4 tests
test events::tests::rejects_invalid_ordinal ... ok
test events::tests::rejects_invalid_month ... ok
test events::tests::rejects_invalid_weekday ... ok
test events::tests::valid_date_from_rule ... FAILED

failures:

---- events::tests::valid_date_from_rule stdout ----

thread 'events::tests::valid_date_from_rule' (617845) panicked at src/events.rs:391:9:
assertion `left == right` failed
  left: Some(None)
 right: Some(Some(2026-05-12))
note: run with `RUST_BACKTRACE=1` environment variable to display a backtrace


failures:
    events::tests::valid_date_from_rule

test result: FAILED. 3 passed; 1 failed; 0 ignored; 0 measured; 0 filtered out;
 finished in 0.00s
```

The `valid_date_from_rule` test failed because the `resolve_date` method simply returned `None`. We'll fix that next.

One possible implementation of `resolve_date` uses two helper functions, one to compute the each *nth* occurrence of a given weekday in some month, apart from the last, and another to compute the last occurrence:

Example 34.20. Resolving the rule to a date

```
pub fn resolve_date(&self, year: i32) -> Option<NaiveDate> {
    if self.ordinal == Ordinal::Last {
        last_weekday_in_month(year, self.month, self.weekday)
    } else {
        nth_weekday_in_month(year, self.month, self.weekday, self.ordinal)
    }
}
```

Computing the *n*th occurrence is done by counting the occurrences of the given weekday until we reach the desired count:

Example 34.21. Computing the *n* th weekday of the month

```
fn nth_weekday_in_month(year: i32,
                        month: Month,
                        weekday: Weekday,
                        ordinal: Ordinal) -> Option<NaiveDate> {
    let mut count = 0;

    for day in 1..=31 {
        if let Some(date) = NaiveDate::from_ymd_opt(year, month.number_from_month(), day) {
            if date.weekday() == weekday.as_chrono_weekday() {
                count += 1;
                if count == ordinal as i32 {
                    return Some(date);
                }
            }
        }
    }

    None
}
```

Computing the last occurrence is similar, but counting backwards from the end of the month, with a range reversed by its `rev` method:

Example 34.22. Computing the last weekday of the month

```
fn last_weekday_in_month(year: i32,
                         month: Month,
                         weekday: Weekday) -> Option<NaiveDate> {
    for day in (1..=31).rev() {   // note that the range is reversed!
        if let Some(date) = NaiveDate::from_ymd_opt(year, month.number_from_month(), day) {
            if date.weekday() == weekday.as_chrono_weekday() {
                return Some(date);
            }
        }
    }

    None
}
```

These two functions need a conversion from `Weekday` to `chrono::Weekday`, because we can only get the latter out of a `chrono::NaiveDate`. Since our own type is also called `Weekday`, we can avoid any confusion by bringing `chrono::Weekday` into scope with another name, as `ChronoWeekday`.

Example 34.23. Converting `Weekday` to `chrono::Weekday`

```
use chrono::Weekday as ChronoWeekday;

impl Weekday {
    pub fn as_chrono_weekday(&self) -> ChronoWeekday {
        match *self {
            Weekday::Monday => ChronoWeekday::Mon,
            Weekday::Tuesday => ChronoWeekday::Tue,
            Weekday::Wednesday => ChronoWeekday::Wed,
            Weekday::Thursday => ChronoWeekday::Thu,
            Weekday::Friday => ChronoWeekday::Fri,
            Weekday::Saturday => ChronoWeekday::Sat,
            Weekday::Sunday => ChronoWeekday::Sun,
        }
```

```
    }
}
```

The as_chrono_weekday method allows us to compare the two kinds of weekdays.

To build some confidence in these helper methods it is a good idea to add some more tests to the tests module to catch any corner cases:

Example 34.24. More unit tests for rule resolution

```
    #[test]
    fn last_weekday() {
        // last Monday in January 2026 should be 2026-01-26
        let target = NaiveDate::from_ymd_opt(2026, 1, 26);
        assert_eq!(
            Some(last_weekday_in_month(2026, Month::January, Weekday::Monday)),
            Some(target));
    }

    #[test]
    fn first_weekday() {
        // first Friday in May 2026 should be 2026-05-01
        let target = NaiveDate::from_ymd_opt(2026, 5, 1);
        assert_eq!(
            Some(nth_weekday_in_month(2026, Month::May, Weekday::Friday, Ordinal::First)),
            Some(target));
    }
```

These values were verified using the Unix cal command. Running the tests now should produce the following result (condensed):

```
running 6 tests
test events::tests::first_weekday ... ok
test events::tests::last_weekday ... ok
test events::tests::rejects_invalid_month ... ok
test events::tests::rejects_invalid_ordinal ... ok
test events::tests::rejects_invalid_weekday ... ok
test events::tests::valid_date_from_rule ... ok
```

This rounds up the rule implementation, but it is not used by anyone yet. In the next section we'll update the CSV file event provider to support rule-based events.

Updating the CSV file event provider to support rule-based events

We'll now proceed to update the CSV file event provider to support rule-based events. We can use the date column of the CSV row to determine if the event should be rule-based or date-based. Full dates always start with a digit, whereas yearless dates always start with a dash. However, a rule-based value always starts with a letter. We can use this information to decide whether to parse the date column as a full date, a yearless date, or a verbal rule. (Note that this would not work if you wanted to allow the ordinal to be expressed as 1st, 2nd, and so on.)

In the `get_events` method, right before checking for a yearless date, we check for letters:

Example 34.25. Checking for a rule-based event

```
for result in reader.records() {
    // ... collect the column values as before

    // Check if the date string starts with a letter:
    let is_rule_based = date_string.chars().next().unwrap().is_alphabetic();
    if is_rule_based {
        let rule = Rule::parse(&date_string).unwrap();
        let category = Category::from_str(&category_string).unwrap();
        let event = Event::new_rule_based(rule, description, category);
        if filter.accepts(&event) {
            events.push(event);
        }
        continue;
    }

    // ... handle the other event kinds as before
}
```

If we find a rule, we make a new rule-based event. If the current filter accepts it, we save it, and continue to the next record. The other event kinds are handled as before.

Chapter 35. Logging

Logging is an important part of program development and operation. Printing on the console here and there is not a substitute for proper logging, but fortunately Rust ecosystem has this part covered too. In this chapter we'll introduce logging in the Today program.

Leaving a log of the execution

During the development of the Today program we have quite casually printed out information about some of the internal variables of the program. While this is all right during development, the debugging output will interfere with the normal output of the program. Also, if we wanted to save the logging output somewhere to examine later we would need to direct it to a disk file.

The Rust ecosystem has good facilities for logging, with the `log` crate being some sort of standard. Together with the `env_logger` it gives a good way to log information about the operation of the Today program without messing up the normal output.

Adding the logging crates

The `log` and `env_logger` crates are added to the program in the usual way; either by manually editing the `Cargo.toml` file, or by using Cargo with

```
cargo add log env_logger
```

We bring the `log` crate into scope with the `use` statement. The environment logger is initialized by adding a call to `env_logger::init` as the first thing in your `main` function:

Example 35.1. Preparing for logging in the `main` function

```
use log;

fn main() {
    env_logger::init();

    log::info("today program execution starting");

    // ...
}
```

Above we have also issued our first logging statement, using the `log::info!` macro. Next we'll have a look at the various logging levels.

Logging levels and macros

Traditionally logging statements are classified according to their severity and function. The `log` crate uses the following logging levels, from lowest to highest priority:

- trace: for detailed tracing of program execution
- debug: for troubleshooting
- info: for non-critical information that does not need to appear in the program output
- warn: for warnings about potential problems during execution
- error: for errors that have occurred, possibly leading to the execution of the program halting prematurely

Conveniently the names of the levels are also the names of various macros in the `log` crate. These macros work very similarly to the `println!` macro.

The default log level is `info`, and we don't need to do anything special to have the informational log messages to appear. That is why, if we were to invoke the `log::info` macro as shown above, the program output would include a line similar to the following:

```
[2026-05-13T10:08:01Z INFO  today] today program execution starting
```

However, any `debug` or `trace` level logs would not appear.

We can control the log level with the `RUST_LOG` environment variable. Like any such variable, it can be set permanently in the shell configuration file, for the duration of the terminal session, or just for one run of the program. For example, if we invoke the `debug` macro like this:

Example 35.2. Adding some debug output to the program

```
use log;

fn main() {
    env_logger::init();

    let args = Args::parse();

    let month_day = if let Some(md) = args.date {
        MonthDay::from_str(&md).unwrap()
    } else {
        let today: NaiveDate = Local::now().date_naive();
        MonthDay::new(today.month(), today.day())
    };
    log::debug!("month_day = {:#?}", month_day);

    // ...
}
```

we would normally not see the debug output. However, if we invoke the program with a command prepended with the `RUST_LOG` environment variable, like this:

```
% RUST_LOG=debug cargo run
```

then we would see the value of the `month_day` variable printed out like this:

```
[2026-05-13T10:19:16Z DEBUG today] month_day = MonthDay {
        month: 5,
        day: 13,
    }
```

We would also see any debug output, since the `info` level would imply `debug`. The valid values of the `RUST_LOG` environment variable are the same as the log level names.

Converting `println!` output to logging macros

We'd like to clean up the output of the Today program so that we turn some of the helpful `println!` output into logging macros at a suitable level. This involves taking a look at the various places where we use the `println!` macro and determining whether it is intended to be shown during the normal operation of the program, or whether it is the result of some actual or potential problem.

For example, we are looking for the configuration directory and a TOML configuration file in the `main` function:

Example 35.3. Finding out and printing the configuration directory

```
const APP_NAME: &str = "today";
let config_path = get_config_path(APP_NAME);
match config_path {
    Some(path) => {
        let toml_path = path.join(format!("{}.toml", APP_NAME));
        println!("Looking for configuration file '{}'", &toml_path.display());
        let config_str = fs::read_to_string(&toml_path)
            .expect("configuration file should exist");
        let config: Config = toml::from_str(&config_str)
            .expect("configuration file should be valid");
        println!("config: {:#?}", config);
        match args.cmd {
            Some(Command::Providers) => {
                for provider in config.providers {
                    println!("{}", provider.name);
                }
            },
```

```
            _ => {
                if let Err(e) = run(&config, &path, &filter) {
                    eprintln!("Error running program: {}", e);
                    return;
                }
            }
        }
    },
    None => {
        eprintln!("Unable to configure the application");
        return;
    }
}
```

Some, but not all, of the println! macro invocations are clearly informational or debugging messages, while the eprintln! macro invocations are error messages. We can turn these into proper logging messages like this:

Example 35.4. Properly logging the configuration file search

```
const APP_NAME: &str = "today";
let config_path = get_config_path(APP_NAME);
match config_path {
    Some(path) => {
        let toml_path = path.join(format!("{}.toml", APP_NAME));
        log::info!("Looking for configuration file '{}'", &toml_path.display());
        let config_str = fs::read_to_string(&toml_path)
            .expect("configuration file should exist");
        let config: Config = toml::from_str(&config_str)
            .expect("configuration file should be valid");
        log::debug!("config: {:#?}", config);
        match args.cmd {
            Some(Command::Providers) => {
                for provider in config.providers {
                    println!("{}", provider.name);
                }
            },

            _ => {
                if let Err(e) = run(&config, &path, &filter) {
                    log::error!("Error running program: {}", e);
```

```
                        return;
                    }
                }
            }
        },
        None => {
            log::error!("Unable to configure the application");
            return;
        }
    }
```

For a comprehensive treatise on logging in Rust, see the excellent blog post series by Caroline Morton, starting with *Logs and tracing in Rust: Fundamentals*[1].

[1]https://www.carolinemorton.co.uk/blog/rust-tracing-logging-fundamentals/

Chapter 36. Adding new events

To get new events we have relied on someone editing the data files for the Today program, adding rows to the SQLite database, or updating the REST API. However, for local data in can be handy to be able to add events through some event provider. In this chapter we'll implement a subcommand to add an event to any event provider that supports adding. This will require some refactoring, of course.

New events from the command line

The Today program gets its events from various sources using event providers specialized for certain file formats, databases, and web services. The program operates mostly in "read-only" mode, and the responsibility of supplying events for the providers can be thought of being outside the scope of the program. However, since editing the various files can be cumbersome, we could add a feature that allows the user to add events to some event provider's repository if possible.

Adding an event can be implemented using an `add` subcommand with the same command-line argument handling mechanism that we saw earlier. The user of this subcommand needs to supply some information that also comes from the command line: the event provider where the new event is supposed to go, the textual description of the event, the date of the event (either absolute, month-day or text rule), and the category of the event in the agreed format.

In addition to command-line argument handling, supporting event adding also needs changes to other parts of the program. Here is a breakdown of the tasks and considerations:

- Revising the `EventProvider` trait to have a method for determining if an event provider supports adding events (say, `is_add_supported`, returning `bool`), and a method for adding an event (`add_event(event: &Event)`).
- Deciding which event providers actually support adding events, and revise their implementations to conform to the updated `EventProvider` trait.
- Revising the `providers` subcommand to show the information about the event provider supporting or not supporting event addition.

- Collecting the command-line arguments related to adding an event: event provider name, event description, event date, and event category.

Revising the `EventProvider` trait

The `EventProvider` trait needs some revision. We'll add a new method called `is_add_supported`. It has a default implementation which just returns `false`. Any event provider that supports adding events should override this to return `true`. Another new method, `add_event`, returns a `Result` with a custom error, so we'll also add an error type, which is just an enum.

Example 36.1. The revised `EventProvider` trait

```
pub trait EventProvider {
    fn name(&self) -> String;
    fn get_events(&self, filter: &EventFilter, events: &mut Vec<Event>);
    fn is_add_supported(&self) -> bool { false }
    fn add_event(&self, event: &Event) -> Result<(), EventProviderError>;
}

pub enum EventProviderError {
    OperationNotSupported,
    OperationFailed,
}
```

If someone attempts to add an event even though the event provider does not support it, `EventProviderError::OperationNotSupported` will be returned.

Implementing event addition for `TextFileProvider`

To implement event addition for the text file event provider, defined in `src/providers/textfile.rs`, we need to return `true` for the `is_add_supported` query, and then implement the `add_event` method so that the event is added at the end of the text file used by the provider:

Example 36.2. Adding an event to a text file

```
use std::fs::{File, OpenOptions};
use std::io::{BufReader, BufRead, BufWriter, Write};

impl EventProvider for TextFileProvider {
    // ... other trait method implementations done earlier

    fn is_add_supported(&self) -> bool { true }

    fn add_event(&self, event: &Event) -> Result<(), EventProviderError> {
        if !self.is_add_supported() {
            return Err(EventProviderError::OperationNotSupported);
        }

        let file = OpenOptions::new()
            .append(true)
            .open(self.path.clone())
            .expect("path to text file for writing");

        let mut writer = BufWriter::new(file);

        return match event.kind() {
            EventKind::Singular(date) => {
                writeln!(writer, "{}", date.to_string());
                writeln!(writer, "{}", event.description());
                writeln!(writer, "{}", event.category());
                writeln!(writer, "");
                Ok(())
            },
            _ => Err(EventProviderError::OperationNotSupported)
        };
    }
}
```

The method appends all the fields of the event to the end of the text file, and adds one blank line to separate the events. (Note that this blank line is only necessary for human inspection; without this line it would be difficult to see where one event starts and another begins.)

The `std::fs::OpenOptions` type is used to specify how the file should be opened. Here the most important option is `append`, which causes any writes to be added to the end of the file. Without this option, the existing file will be overwritten, which is definitely not what we want.

The `std::fs::BufWriter` type is used to buffer the writing. This is usually done for efficiency, even though in this case it hardly matters, since we are writing at most four lines to the end of the file. However, it is good practice to learn how to use buffered writing from the outset, for later more extensive output needs.

We have introduced a limitation here: we can only add singular events. With a little more work we could also support adding annual or rule-based events, but for now the method returns `EventProviderError::OperationNotSupported` if the event is not a singular event. Of course, this depends on what is passed in to this method by its caller.

Implementing event addition for `CSVFileProvider`

Adding events to a CSV file is even easier than to the multi-line format text file. First we need to override the `is_add_supported` method to return `true`. Then we add the implementation for the `add_event`:

Example 36.3. Adding an event to a CSV file

```
impl EventProvider for CSVFileProvider {
    // ... other trait method implementations done earlier

    fn is_add_supported(&self) -> bool { true }  // override the default implementation

    fn add_event(&self, event: &Event) -> Result<(), EventProviderError> {
        if !self.is_add_supported() {
            return Err(EventProviderError::OperationNotSupported);
        }

        let file = OpenOptions::new()
            .append(true)
            .open(self.path.clone())
            .expect("path to text file for writing");
```

```
        let writer = BufWriter::new(file);
        let mut csv_writer = csv::Writer::from_writer(writer);

        let date_string = match event.kind() {
            EventKind::Singular(date) =>
                date.format("%Y-%m-%d").to_string(),
            _ => {
                return Err(EventProviderError::OperationNotSupported);
            }
        };

        csv_writer.write_record([
            date_string,
            event.description(),
            format!("{}", event.category())
        ]).unwrap();

        csv_writer.flush().unwrap();

        Ok(())
    }
}
```

Just like the CSV file was read in using `csv::CSVReader`, writing is done using `csv::CSVWriter`. This ensures that the CSV columns are properly quoted and delimited, even if some event descriptions contain a comma. The `write_record` method takes an array of strings, which we construct from the fields of the event. Since we are using `std::io::BufWriter` to wrap the CSV writer, we are sure to flush when we are done.

Note

> It is never a good idea to read or write CSV records manually, if you have an existing library where all the hard work has already been done. All the problems that stem from the special cases regarding delimiters and quotes have been solved more than once.

With these changes, also the CSV file provider supports adding events, once we have a way to supply them from the command line.

Command-line arguments for adding events

In this section we will add the necessary command-line arguments to the `Args` struct in `src/main.rs`. We define the `add` subcommand with related arguments:

Example 36.4. Command-line arguments for adding an event

```
#[derive(Subcommand, Debug, Clone)]
enum Command {
    /// Lists all event providers
    Providers,

    /// Adds an event to an event provider
    Add {
        #[arg(short, long, help = "Name of event provider")]
        provider_name: String,

        #[arg(short, long, help = "Date of event. Format: YYYY-MM-DD")]
        date: String,

        #[arg(short = 'e', long, help = "Description of event")]
        description: String,

        #[arg(short, long, help = "Category of event. Format: primary[/secondary]")]
        category: String,
    },
}
```

The `add` subcommand has its own options, which are initially handled as strings.

Note that the `description` option has different short and long forms. The short option is `-e` because the `date` option already used up the short `-d`.

Next we'll add the match arm that handles the `add` subcommand:

Example 36.5. Handling the add subcommand

```
match args.cmd {
    Some(Command::Providers) => {
        for provider in config.providers {
            println!("{}", provider.name);
        }
    },

    // 0.36.0: add event
    Some(Command::Add { provider_name, date, description, category }) => {
        let category = Category::from_str(&category);
        let date = chrono::NaiveDate::parse_from_str(&date, "%Y-%m-%d").unwrap();
        let event = Event::new_singular(date, description, category);
        add_event(&config, &path, &provider_name, &event);
    },
    _ => {
        if let Err(e) = run(&config, &path, &filter) {
            log::error!("Error running program: {}", e);
            return;
        }
    }
}
```

The event is constructed from the command-line arguments, and added using the new add_event function in `src/lib.rs`. This function takes the same configuration parameters as the run function, because it needs to construct the event providers. (Technically it would only need to construct the one event provider that is going to be the target of the addition, but this will not be a performance bottleneck.)

Example 36.6. The add_event function in `lib.rs`

```
pub fn add_event(config: &Config, config_path: &Path, provider_name: &str, event: &Event) {
    let providers = create_providers(config, config_path);  // see below

    // Find provider by name
    let mut provider: Option<&dyn EventProvider> = None;
    for p in &providers {
```

```
        if p.name() == provider_name {
            provider = Some(p.as_ref());
            break;
        }
    }

    match provider {
        Some(p) => {
            if p.is_add_supported() {
                let _ = p.add_event(event);
            } else {
                println!("Adding events is not supported for provider '{}'", p.name());
            }
        },
        None => {
            eprintln!("Unknown event provider '{}'", provider_name);
        }
    }
}
```

In `src/lib.rs` we will also refactor the creation of the event providers into a dedicated function, so that both the `run` and `add_event` functions can use it:

Example 36.7. Function to create the event providers

```
fn create_providers(config: &Config, config_path: &Path)
        -> Vec::<Box<dyn EventProvider>> {
    // Try to create all the event providers specified in `config`.
    // Put them in a vector of trait objects.
    let mut providers: Vec::<Box<dyn EventProvider>> = Vec::new();
    for cfg in config.providers.iter() {
        let path = config_path.join(&cfg.resource);
        match cfg.kind.as_str() {
            "text" => {
                let provider = TextFileProvider::new(&cfg.name, &path);
                providers.push(Box::new(provider));
            },
            "csv" => {
                let provider = CSVFileProvider::new(&cfg.name, &path);
                providers.push(Box::new(provider));
            },
```

```
            "sqlite" => {
                let provider = SQLiteProvider::new(&cfg.name, &path);
                providers.push(Box::new(provider));
            },
            "web" => {
                let provider = WebProvider::new(&cfg.name, &cfg.resource);
                providers.push(Box::new(provider));
            },
            _ => {
                eprintln!("Unable to make provider: {:?}", cfg);
            }
        }
    }

    providers
}
```

Now both the run and add_event functions will create the providers using the following line of code:

```
let providers = create_providers(config, config_path);
```

With this refactoring done, we can present the entire add_event function:

Example 36.8. The add_event function

```
pub fn add_event(config: &Config, config_path: &Path, provider_name: &str, event: &Event) {
    let providers = create_providers(config, config_path);

    // Find provider by name
    let mut provider: Option<&dyn EventProvider> = None;
    for p in &providers {
        if p.name() == provider_name {
            provider = Some(p.as_ref());
            break;
        }
    }

    match provider {
        Some(p) => {
            if p.is_add_supported() {
```

```
                let _ = p.add_event(event);
            } else {
                eprintln!("Adding events is not supported for provider '{}'", p.name());
            }
        },
        None => {
            eprintln!("Unknown event provider '{}'", provider_name);
        }
    }
}
```

The function first creates all the event providers, and then finds the target of the addition by its name. An optional type is used for the provider, initialized as None, so if the provider is not found, it will remain None.

If a provider is found and it supports adding events, the event is added using the provider's add_event method.

Adding events to the SQLite database

Updating the SQLite event provider to support adding events is also easy with the help of the rusqlite crate. After making the is_add_supported method return true we can concentrate on the add_event method implementation.

The biggest task here is to check if the category of the event already exists in the database, and if not, add it there. For that we develop a helper function called find_category_id, which uses the database connection supplied to it to find the desired category, returning its category identifier, or None if not found:

Example 36.9. The find_category_id function

```
fn find_category_id(category: &Category, connection: &Connection) -> Option<CategoryId> {
    // Get the categories currently in the database.
    let category_map = get_categories(connection);

    // Use a brute force method where you iterate the hash map keys,
    // and stop if one of the values matches the category.
    for (id, cat) in &category_map {
        if *cat == *category { // found it!
```

```
            return Some(*id);
        }
    }

    None
}
```

This function does not need to be a method in the event provider, because it is not using the data members of the provider for anything. Free functions are often just as useful, and since Rust is not an object-oriented language as such, there is no need even to put everything inside a struct.

Example 36.10. The `EventProvider` implementation for `SQLiteProvider`

```
impl EventProvider for SQLiteProvider {
    // Override the default implementation from the trait:
    fn is_add_supported(&self) -> bool { true }

    fn add_event(&self, event: &Event) -> Result<(), EventProviderError> {
        let connection = Connection::open(self.path.clone()).unwrap();

        // Find out if the category of the event is already there.
        match find_category_id(&event.category(), &connection) {
            Some(category_id) => {
                // Found it, now insert the event to the database with this category ID:
                insert_event(&connection, event, category_id);
            },
            None => {
                // Add a new category first, then add the event
                let category = event.category();
                let primary_str = category.primary();
                match category.secondary() {
                    Some(secondary) => connection.execute(
                        "INSERT INTO category (primary_name, secondary_name) VALUES (?1, ?2)",
                        params![primary_str, secondary]).unwrap(),
                    None => connection.execute(
                        "INSERT INTO category (primary_name) VALUES (?1)",
                        [primary_str]).unwrap()
                };
```

```
                let category_id = connection.last_insert_rowid();
                insert_event(&connection, event, category_id);

                return Ok(());
            }
        }

        Err(EventProviderError::OperationNotSupported)
    }
}
```

This example shows how to use the facilities of the `rusqlite` crate to construct SQL queries, such as the `params!` macro (more information about it is available in the crate documentation).

The `add_event` method uses another free function, `insert_event`, to actually run the SQL INSERT query that adds the event. If the category exists, the event will be inserted right away. Otherwise a new category is added first, followed by the insertion of the event.

Example 36.11. The `insert_event` function

```
fn insert_event(connection: &Connection, event: &Event, category_id: CategoryId) {
    let event_date_str = format!("{:04}-{}", event.year(), event.month_day());
    connection.execute(
        "INSERT INTO event (event_date, event_description, category_id) VALUES (?1, ?2, ?3)",
        params![event_date_str, event.description(), category_id]).unwrap();
}
```

This function also uses an existing database connection. The category ID is also passed in as a parameter. It is either the ID of an existing category, or of a category that was just added (obtained from with the `last_insert_rowid` method of the database connection).

Trying to add an event from the command line

Now that we have implemented the `add` subcommand we can try adding an event from the command line.

If we ask for help about the add subcommand, we get this kind of output (courtesy of the clap crate):

```
% cargo run -- help add
Adds an event to an event provider

Usage: today add --provider-name <PROVIDER_NAME> --date <DATE> --description
 <DESCRIPTION> --category <CATEGORY>

Options:
  -p, --provider-name <PROVIDER_NAME>  Name of event provider
  -d, --date <DATE>                    Date of event. Format: YYYY-MM-DD
  -e, --description <DESCRIPTION>      Description of event
  -c, --category <CATEGORY>            Category of event. Format: primary[/secondary]
  -h, --help                           Print help
```

This tells us what command-line arguments to use when adding an event.

If we try to add an event to a provider that does not support adding, we will get an error message:

```
% cargo run -- add --provider-name todayserver --date 2026-05-13 --description "Test"
 --category test
Adding events is not supported for provider 'todayserver'
```

We need to use the `providers` subcommand to find which providers support adding events. We'll take a quick detour to fix that and then get back to adding events.

Updating the `providers` subcommand

To make it easy for users to know which event providers actually support adding events, we'll update the `providers` subcommand to show the kind of the provider, together with an asterisk (*) next to the name of any event provider that supports that feature. Initially this seems like an easy change to make; we just use the newly added `is_add_supported` method of `EventProvider`. However, that method is not available until the provider is actually constructed.

We already have a function called `create_providers` in `src/lib.rs`. It is used to construct the providers when the program is run without any subcommands.

By bringing it into scope we can reuse it to construct the providers also when the `providers` subcommand is used:

Example 36.12. Showing the listing of event providers

```
// Top of src/main.rs:
use today::{run, add_event, Config, create_providers};

// In src/main.rs, `main` function, in the match arm for the `providers` subcommand:
            match args.cmd {
                Some(Command::Providers) => {
                    let providers = create_providers(&config, &path);
                    for provider in providers {
                        println!(
                            "{} {} {}",
                            provider.name(),
                            provider.kind(),
                            if provider.is_add_supported() { "*" } else { "" });
                    }
                },
```

Our event providers don't yet have the `kind` method to get the information about the provider kind (text, CSV, SQLite, or web), so we'll add that to the `EventProvider` trait, and also add the implementations to the providers:

Example 36.13. Adding the `kind` for event providers

```
// In src/providers/mod.rs:
pub trait EventProvider {
    // ...existing method definitions

    fn kind(&self) -> String;   // added new trait method
}

// In src/providers/textfile.rs:
impl EventProvider for TextFileProvider {
    // ...existing method implementations

    fn kind(&self) -> String {
```

```
        String::from("text")
    }
}

// Other `kind` method implementations are almost identical:
// For CSVFileProvider: String::from("CSV");
// For SQLiteProvider:  String::from("SQLite");
// For WebProvider:     String::from("web");
```

This results in a listing like this, with several event providers, all defined in the `today.toml` configuration file:

```
annuals CSV *
history text *
computing text *
programming CSV *
sqlite SQLite *
todayserver web
holidays-japan CSV *
rustopedia SQLite *
```

The providers marked with an asterisk (*) support adding events.

Adding an event (finally)

Now that we can ask the program which event providers support adding events, we can try to add one again, this time picking the right kind of provider. We'll use the event provider named `programming` as the target, using the short argument forms this time:

```
% cargo run -- add -p programming -d 2026-04-16 -e "Rust 1.95.0 released" -c
 programming/rust
```

This version of the Today program does not give us any feedback if an event was added successfully. However, if we now query the events for the specified date, we can see that it is retrieved successfully:

```
% cargo run -- -d 0416
2026: Rust 1.95.0 released (programming/rust)
```

Seems like it worked! We can also manually check the data file for the event provider, as mentioned in the `today.toml` configuration file, to verify that the event data has indeed been appended to it.

Chapter 37. Grouping and sorting the events

In this penultimate chapter of Part III we will have a look at how to present the retrieved and filtered events to the user. This will also give us a glimpse of some of the functional programming features of Rust.

All the events, grouped and sorted

The Today program shows historical or observed events that occurred on today's date (or any date you specify on the command line). There are various kinds of events, and depending on the date there could be quite many of them. For a nicer output, the program should group and sort the events before displaying them to the user.

The following example show a revised `run` function in the `lib.rs`. It constructs the event providers based on the `today.toml` configuration file, and then sets up an event filter for either today's date or the one specified with the `--date` option.

The function then reads events from each provider, passing in the filter. Whatever is left in the `events` vector is the set of events that should be shown to the user. However, we wish to separate the singular events into their own group, and put the annual and rule-based events in a group of their own. This way we can show them better to the user. We set up two vectors, both of type `Vec<Event>`, and move the events into either one depending on its kind:

Example 37.1. The revised `run` function

```
pub fn run(config: &Config, config_path: &Path, filter: &EventFilter)
        -> Result<(), Box<dyn Error>> {
    let mut events: Vec<Event> = Vec::new();
    let providers = create_providers(&config, &config_path);
    for provider in &providers {
        provider.get_events(filter, &mut events);
    }

    let mut singular_events: Vec<&Event> = Vec::new();
    let mut annual_events: Vec<&Event> = Vec::new();
```

```
    for event in &events {
        match event.kind() {
            EventKind::Singular(_) => singular_events.push(event),
            _ => annual_events.push(event)
        }
    }

    // ... continued
```

Just to keep things interesting, we'll make a grammatically correct group heading with the help of the `pluralize` crate. We add the crate to the `Cargo.toml` file:

```
% cargo add pluralizer
```

and at the time of writing we get the following line in `Cargo.toml`:

```
pluralizer = "0.5.0"
```

We bring the `pluralizer` function from the crate into scope, and use it in the `run` function:

Example 37.2. Pluralizing the group headings

```
use pluralizer::pluralize;

    // ... run function continues

    let include_count = true;

    if !singular_events.is_empty() {
        singular_events.sort_by(|a, b| a.year().cmp(&b.year()));
        singular_events.reverse();
        println!("On this day in history ({}):",
            pluralize("event", singular_events.len() as isize, include_count));
        for event in singular_events {
            println!("{}", event);
        }
    }

    if !annual_events.is_empty() {
```

```
    println!("\nObserved today ({}):",
        pluralize("event", annual_events.len() as isize, include_count));
    for event in annual_events {
        println!("{} ({})", event.description(), event.category());
    }
}

Ok(())
```

We get the correct group heading based on the count of the elements in the vector using the `pluralize`, which takes the noun, the count, and a `bool` that indicates whether the count should be included in the result (we use a variable to make the intent clearer, since Rust does not have named function arguments). Note that the count is of type `isize`, so we need to explicitly convert the length of the vector, but the risk of there being more than `i32::MAX` events in either vector is rather small. The implementation of the `pluralize` crate is interesting and worth a look in the source code.

Running the program on May 13 with some test data defined earlier we get the following result:

```
On this day in history (1 event):
1991: Apple releases Macintosh operating System 7, codenamed 'Big Bang' (apple/macos)

Observed today (2 events):
IEEE Global Engineering Day (engineering)
International Hummus Day (food)
```

The events are split into two vectors by the kind of the event: one vector is for singular events (those that occurred once in history) and one is for annual events (both with an exact date or based on a verbal rule). Before showing their contents we check if there is anything worth showing, so that we don't show just a group title with no events following it.

If there are singular events, we then proceed to sort them in descending order by their year. This is achieved using a *closure*, a feature of Rust we saw earlier in the context of filters in Chapter 32, *Filtering events at the source*.

As a reminder, a closure is an anonymous function expression that can be specified on the spot when it is needed. The `Vec<T>` has a method called `sort_by` that takes a closure as a parameter, and applies the closure to each of the elements in the vector.

The `year` method of `Event` returns `i32`, and all the Rust machine types implement the `std::cmp::Eq` trait, so we can compare them using the `cmp` method. Note that we are not comparing the whole events, only what they report as their year.

The closure being passed to the `sort_by` method is defined as

```
|a, b| a.year().cmp(&b.year())
```

The parameters of the closure, if any, go between the pipe symbols, and the body of the function expression can refer to them. The Rust compiler is able to infer the types of the parameters, because the definition of the `sort_by` method in the `Vec<T>` type refers to the generic type `T`. So `a` and `b` are both known to be of type `&Event`.

The result of the `cmp` method is actually a value of the type `std::cmp::Ordering`. You can read more of how the comparison is done in the documentation of the `sort_by` method.

Partitioning the events

As a small taste of the functional programming features of Rust, let's group the events using an iterator's `partition` method instead of a `for` loop:

Example 37.3. Using the `partition` method of an iterator

```
let (mut singular_events, annual_events): (Vec<&Event>, Vec<&Event>)
    = events.iter().partition(|event| match event.kind() {
        EventKind::Singular(_) => true,
        _ => false
    });
```

Here we first get an iterator for the vector of all events. Then we call its `partition` method, passing a closure that determines one of two vectors the event should go to. If the closure returns `true`, the event goes to the first vector; if `false`, it goes to the second. The vectors are defined as a tuple with two components.

The `singular_events` vector needs to be mutable since we are going to sort its contents later on. However, the `annual_events` vector can remain immutable.

This code is very concise, maybe even slightly elegant, but it can also be hard to understand, since it combines many of the unusual features of Rust. There is nothing wrong with the earlier, more explicit version, but when we get more comfortable with Rust, we should certainly look deeper into iterators and their many uses.

Chapter 38. Today 1.0

First public version of Today

After over a dozen of chapters of incremental development, we have reached the end of this part, and also a point where we can declare Today 1.0 to be *feature complete.*

The program shows historical one-time events and recurring annual events from various local and online data sources, and can be directed with an outside configuration file. It also allows us to add new events to those sources that support it.

Today can also read the user's birthdate from the environment and compute their age in days, possibly with suitable commentary. Further command-line arguments allow the date of the events to be selected with a month-day combination. Adding an event is also possible to those event providers that support it.

Building a release version

By default, Cargo builds the debugging version of our program. As soon as we are confident that the program does what it is supposed to, we can prepare a release version for general use. This is done by adding a command-line argument to the `cargo` command:

```
% cargo build --release
```

This will build the program using the `release` profile. The release version will be significantly smaller in size because it does not contain debug information.

Installing the program

When we have successfully tested the Today program and built a release version, it can be taken into daily use. The way to do that depends on our chosen operating system.

In Microsoft Windows we copy the release version of the `today.exe` executable program (found under the project directory, in `target/release`) into some directory that is in the search path, as determined by the `PATH` environment variable. That allows us to easily invoke it from Command Prompt or PowerShell.

In Linux or macOS the same applies, except that the executable file is called simply `today`. It should already have execution rights for the current user, as prepared by the Rust compiler.

Cargo can also install Rust programs with applicable settings in the `Cargo.toml` so that they can be run with Cargo. Since we already have the Rust tools installed, the Cargo program is already in our search path. It is instructive to look into making the program installable with the command `cargo install`, using information found in *The Cargo Book*.

Configuring the program

If we run the program out of the box without any configuration, we will not see any events. In Chapter 28, *Configuration directories* we looked at operating-system specific locations for configuration files, and in Chapter 29, *Configuration file* we defined the contents of the program's configuration file, `today.toml`.

A minimal configuration has a `today.toml` file with at least one event provider configured. This could be any of the providers we have covered over various chapters, but a CSV file event provider is probably the easiest to arrange.

Here is an example of a configuration file that defines one CSV file provider called `rustopedia`. It contains events that mark the various releases of the Rust development tools. As we know by now, Rust is in constant development, and a new version the Rust tools are released roughly every six weeks.

Example 38.1. A minimal `today.toml` configuration file

```
[[providers]]
name = "rustopedia"
kind = "csv"
resource = "rustopedia.csv"
```

Here is the `rustopedia.csv` that was named as the resource of the CSV file provider:

Example 38.2. Rust tool releases in a CSV file called `rustopedia.csv`

```
2026-04-16,"Rust 1.95.0 released",programming/rust
2026-03-05,"Rust 1.94.0 released",programming/rust
2026-02-12,"Rust 1.93.1 released",programming/rust
2026-01-22,"Rust 1.93.0 released",programming/rust
2025-12-11,"Rust 1.92.0 released",programming/rust
```

If we prepare these two files and put them in the correct configuration directory, the next run of the program with a `--date` argument matching any of the dates above should show us the corresponding event:

```
% cargo run --quiet -- --date 0416
On this day in history (1 event):
2026: Rust 1.95.0 released (programming/rust)
```

Without the `--date` option the output of the program will of course depend on the event providers and the contents of their data files.

Part IV. Going Further than Today

This part is for additions that expand or improve the Today program.

Here are the topics that will be covered:

- Refactoring the `Event` struct based on the date
- Making an XML event provider
- Handling all the event providers with one event manager
- Refactoring the configuration file processing to specify active and passive (enabled and disabled) event providers

Table of Contents

Chapter 39. Refactoring the Event struct

A different kind of Event

In our first iteration, the `Event` struct had a field called `kind` of type `EventKind`, and that is a fairly traditional axis to be moving on. However, even though it uses the Rust enum type with associated values, it is maybe closer to traditional "object-oriented" than Rust typically embraces. In this chapter we will explore a different way of composing the events, and see how to refactor the Today program.

Focusing on the date

Every event has a date, but it is a different kind of date for each kind of event. Let's try refactoring the `Event` struct so that it has a `date` field of an enum type, `EventDate`:

Example 39.1. Refactoring `Event` by the date

```
#[derive(Debug, Clone, PartialEq, Eq)]
pub enum EventDate {
    Singular(NaiveDate),
    Annual(MonthDay),
    RuleBased(Rule),
}

/// Represents a historical or observed event.
#[derive(Debug, Clone, PartialEq, Eq)]
pub struct Event {
    date: EventDate,
    description: String,
    category: Category,
}
```

This naturally triggers a refactoring effort, but the Rust compiler and rust-analyzer can help to find the parts where changes are needed.

The first port of call is the construction of events. We currently have three different associated functions to construct events: `new_singular`, `new_annual`, and `new_rule_based`. With this refactoring we can get by with just one:

Example 39.2. Constructing an `Event` with an `EventDate`

```
impl Event {
    /// Makes a new event with date, description, and category.
    pub fn new(date: EventDate, description: String, category: Category) -> Self {
        Self {
            date,
            description,
            category
        }
    }
}
```

The next parts to fix are the `year` and `month_day` methods, which now need to match on the `date` field:

Example 39.3. Refactoring the `year` and `month_day` methods

```
impl Event {
    /// Gets the year of the event. For annual events, it is always
    /// the ongoing year.
    pub fn year(&self) -> i32 {
        match &self.date {
            EventDate::Singular(date) => date.year(),
            EventDate::Annual(_month_day) => {
                let today: NaiveDate = Local::now().date_naive();
                today.year()
            },
            EventDate::RuleBased(rule) => rule.year(),
        }
    }

    /// Gets the month-day of the event.
    pub fn month_day(&self) -> MonthDay {
```

```
        match &self.date {
            EventDate::Singular(date) => MonthDay::new(date.month(), date.day()),
            EventDate::Annual(month_day) => month_day.clone(),
            EventDate::RuleBased(rule) => {
                match rule.month_day() {
                    Some(month_day) => month_day,
                    None => panic!("invalid month day resolved from rule"),
                }
            }
        }
    }
}
```

The `kind` method can't be implemented because there is no `kind` field anymore. We'll replace it with a method called `is_singular`, which is enough to distinguish the events for grouping (see Chapter 37, *Grouping and sorting the events*):

Example 39.4. Adding the `is_singular` method

```
impl Event {
    /// Returns `true` if the event is singular, `false` otherwise.
    pub fn is_singular(&self) -> bool {
        match self.date {
            EventDate::Singular(_) => true,
            _ => false
        }
    }

}
```

If an event is not singular, it is either annual or rule-based. If the distinction between annual and rule-based matters, then there is a bit more work to do. However, for the same output as in Chapter 37, *Grouping and sorting the events* this is enough.

Next on the fix list are the places where the old constructor functions were used. These are in the event providers where new events are created. First up is the text file event provider.

The logic of the construction is now flipped; instead of using various constructors to create different kinds of events, we create different kinds of dates as enum variants and then construct the event with its `new` function. We'll also take the opportunity to make the code a little more idiomatic by using the `if` expression when initializing the event date:

Example 39.5. Creating a new-style event in the text file provider

```
ReadingState::Separator => {
    let is_yearless = date_string.starts_with("--");
    if is_yearless {
        let today: NaiveDate = Local::now().date_naive();
        let year_string = format!("{:04}-", today.year());
        date_string = date_string.replace("--", &year_string);
    }

    match NaiveDate::parse_from_str(&date_string, "%F") {
        Ok(date) => {
            let category = Category::from_str(&category_string).unwrap();
            let event_date = if is_yearless {
                let month_day = MonthDay::new(date.month(), date.day());
                EventDate::Annual(month_day)
            } else {
                EventDate::Singular(date)
            };
            let event = Event::new(event_date, description.clone(), category);
            if filter.accepts(&event) {
                events.push(event);
            }
        },
        Err(_) => {
            log::error!("Invalid date '{}'", date_string);
        }
    }
    state = ReadingState::Date;
},
```

Next we will fix the `add_event` method of `TextFileProvider`:

Example 39.6. Adding a new-style event to a text file

```
impl EventProvider for TextFileProvider {
    // ... other trait method implementations

    fn add_event(&self, event: &Event) -> Result<(), EventProviderError> {
        if !self.is_add_supported() {
            return Err(EventProviderError::OperationNotSupported);
        }

        let file = OpenOptions::new()
            .append(true)
            .open(self.path.clone())
            .expect("path to text file for writing");

        let mut writer = BufWriter::new(file);

        return if event.is_singular() {
            let _ = writeln!(writer, "{}", event.date());
            let _ = writeln!(writer, "{}", event.description());
            let _ = writeln!(writer, "{}", event.category());
            let _ = writeln!(writer, "");
            Ok(())
        } else {
            Err(EventProviderError::OperationNotSupported)
        };
    }
}
```

The CSV file provider changes are almost the same. These methods do not need many changes, but writing the date without unnecessary friction requires us to implement the `Display` trait for `EventDate`:

Example 39.7. Implementing the `Display` trait for `EventDate`

```
impl fmt::Display for EventDate {
    fn fmt(&self, f: &mut fmt::Formatter) -> fmt::Result {
        match self {
            EventDate::Singular(date) => write!(f, "{}", date),
            EventDate::Annual(month_day) => write!(f, "--{}", month_day),
            EventDate::RuleBased(rule) => write!(f, "{}", rule),
        }
    }
}
```

This causes something of a ripple effect. We have already implemented the `Display` trait for `MonthDay`, but not for `Rule`. That struct, in turn, has components of type `Ordinal` and `Weekday` that don't have the `Display` trait implementation either. We could use the debug placeholder, but there happens to be an easy way to convert enum variants to strings, using the `strum_macros` crate that we already know. Just add `strum_macros::Display` to the `#[derive]` attribute of `Ordinal` and `Weekday`. See the full source code in the GitHub repository for details.

Simplified

This refactoring has already simplified the code quite a lot. There is one more thing to do: fix the collecting of the events in the `run` function:

Example 39.8. Collecting events with `partition` and closure

```
    let (mut singular_events, annual_events): (Vec<&Event>, Vec<&Event>)
        = events.iter().partition(|event| event.is_singular());
```

That's it!

If we enjoyed a small challenge, why not make it possible to add also annual and rule-based events from the command line, and not just singular events? We might want to start with a function that parses a string and returns an `EventDate` variant or `None`. That function could then be reused in the event providers.

Chapter 40. Making an XML event provider

Making an XML event provider

The Today program can already get events from ordinary text files, CSV files, SQLite databases, and REST APIs as JSON. One important format is still missing, and depending on your domain it could be essential one: XML or Extensible Markup Language.

XML is a recommendation from the World Wide Web Consortium, and it is actually a misnomer to say we would like to support the XML format, because XML is a language for making markup languages. Whatever we would be supporting is an *application of XML*, meaning a document that conforms to structural rules laid down by XML, and sometimes also expressed in another application of XML (like XML Schema).

In this chapter we're going to define an XML-based format for our events, make some documents that adhere to that format, and then make an event provider that can read events from the document, working just like the other event providers on the surface, but handling XML markup beneath.

Defining an XML Schema

XML documents can be *well-formed*, or both well-formed and *valid*. Well-formed means that the document is correctly structured according to XML, but that does not necessarily mean it makes any sense. Valid means that the XML document has only certain elements and attributes, that they occur in a certain order, and have only certain values. The most common way to ensure this is to define a *schema* that lays down the rules about our application of XML, and then use that schema to validate the document.

We're going to define our document format using XML Schema, another W3C recommendation. It is itself defined in XML, and we'll use its elements and attributes to define our document. If you are familiar with XML and schemas, the following should be straightforward, but if you need more information, the W3C XML Schema Primer[1] is a good read.

[1]https://www.w3.org/TR/xmlschema-0/

Some tools can make XML schema from an instance document, but since our format will be quite simple, we can just start with the schema definition and create some instance documents later. The following example is the complete XML Schema for our event documents:

Example 40.1. The XML Schema for the event document

```
<?xml version="1.0"?>
<xs:schema xmlns:xs="http://www.w3.org/2001/XMLSchema">
    <xs:element name="events">
        <xs:complexType>
            <xs:sequence>
                <xs:element ref="event" minOccurs="0" maxOccurs="unbounded"/>
            </xs:sequence>
        </xs:complexType>
    </xs:element>

    <xs:simpleType name="fullDateType">
        <xs:restriction base="xs:date"/>
    </xs:simpleType>

    <xs:simpleType name="monthDayType">
        <xs:restriction base="xs:gMonthDay"/>
    </xs:simpleType>

    <xs:simpleType name="dateRuleType">
        <xs:restriction base="xs:string">
            <xs:pattern value="(first|second|third|fourth|fifth|last)\s+(Monday|Tuesday|Wednesday
Thursday|Friday|Saturday|Sunday)\s+(in|of)\s+(January|February|March|April|May|June|July|August|
September|October|November|December)"/>
        </xs:restriction>
    </xs:simpleType>

    <xs:simpleType name="eventDateType">
        <xs:union memberTypes="fullDateType monthDayType dateRuleType"/>
    </xs:simpleType>

    <xs:element name="event">
        <xs:complexType>
            <xs:sequence>
                <xs:element name="date" type="eventDateType"/>
```

```
                <xs:element name="description" type="xs:string"/>
                <xs:element ref="category"/>
            </xs:sequence>
        </xs:complexType>
    </xs:element>

    <xs:element name="category">
        <xs:complexType>
            <xs:sequence>
                <xs:element name="primary" type="xs:string"/>
                <xs:element name="secondary" type="xs:string" minOccurs="0"/>
            </xs:sequence>
        </xs:complexType>
    </xs:element>
</xs:schema>
```

We won't go deep into the schema here; for more information see the W3C material or Eric van der Vlist's book *XML Schema*. The most important thing about this schema is that it supports all the three different event date kinds that we defined in Chapter 39, *Refactoring the Event struct*: singular, annual, and rule-based.

If we were to define an instance document based on this schema, it would look something like this:

Example 40.2. An instance document with some XML-related events

```
<?xml version="1.0" encoding="UTF-8"?>
<events>
  <event>
    <date>1998-02-10</date>
    <description>XML 1.0 becomes a W3C Recommendation</description>
    <category>
      <primary>computing</primary>
      <secondary>xml</secondary>
    </category>
  </event>

  <event>
    <date>2026-05-05</date>
    <description>Testing the XML event provider</description>
```

```
    <category>
      <primary>test</primary>
    </category>
  </event>

  <event>
    <date>2008-11-26</date>
    <description>XML 1.0 Fifth Edition published</description>
    <category>
      <primary>computing</primary>
      <secondary>xml</secondary>
    </category>
  </event>

  <event>
    <date>2004-02-04</date>
    <description>XML 1.1 published</description>
    <category>
      <primary>computing</primary>
      <secondary>xml</secondary>
    </category>
  </event>

  <event>
    <date>2006-08-16</date>
    <description>XML 1.1 Second Edition published</description>
    <category>
      <primary>computing</primary>
      <secondary>xml</secondary>
    </category>
  </event>

</events>
```

As we can see from the example, XML is often much more verbose than, say, CSV, but it is much better specified. XML documents are often more suited to reading and writing completely, instead of inserting elements. For example, to add an event to the XML document would essentially require us to read the full document into memory, parse it into a Document Object Model (DOM) tree, insert the event in the three, and write the document back to disk. This is not excessive, but our XML file event provider will not support adding events.

Now that we have an XML instance document, we need to parse it.

Making the XML provider

The architecture of the Today program makes it easy to add new event providers. We only need to create a new struct and implement the `EventProvider` the way we want based on the data you are reading. To get the provider registered we'll need to add it to the configuration file. If we want to add a new provider kind, we need to handle it when the event providers are being created. In the case of the XML event provider we'll want to have a new kind, `xml`.

Here is a placeholder implementation of the XML event provider, called `XmlFileProvider`. We'll create a new file `src/providers/xmlfile.rs` to host its source code.

Example 40.3. Placeholder implementation of `XmlFileProvider`

```
use std::path::{Path, PathBuf};

use crate::events::{Event, Category};
use crate::providers::{EventProvider, EventProviderError};
use crate::filters::EventFilter;

pub struct XmlFileProvider {
    name: String,
    path: PathBuf,
}

impl XmlFileProvider {
    pub fn new(name: &str, path: &Path) -> Self {
        Self {
            name: name.to_string(),
            path: path.to_path_buf()
        }
    }
}

impl EventProvider for XmlFileProvider {
    fn name(&self) -> String {
```

```
        self.name.clone()
    }

    fn get_events(&self, filter: &EventFilter, events: &mut Vec<Event>) {
        todo!("Getting events from XML not implemented yet");
    }

    fn is_add_supported(&self) -> bool { false }

    fn add_event(&self, _event: &Event) -> Result<(), EventProviderError> {
        Err(EventProviderError::OperationNotSupported)
    }

    fn kind(&self) -> String { String::from("XML") }
}
```

Parsing XML

There are several established ways of parsing XML documents, many of which originate from the Java programming community. SAX (Simple API for XML) is one notable example, as is an implementation of the DOM (Document Object Model). The Java SDK was an early supporter of XML, and there are many essential high quality XML libraries in the Java Development Kit, and also created by third parties.

Rust does not have as much choice as Java when it comes to parsing XML, but there are several useful crates that implement similar XML parsing techniques as the Java packages for XML. One of these techniques is the *streaming API*, where the client repeatedly reads "events" from the stream maintained by the parser. Here is some potential for confusion, because we are dealing with historical events, but "event" in stream parsing terminology means the occurrence of some significant construct in the document. Examples of parse-time events are the start of an element, the end of an element, and character data in the document.

We'll use the `xml` crate for parsing XML with a stream. This crate was inspired by the StAX API in Java. We'll keep track of the various XML element contents using a selection of local variables which are reused as the parser events come in from the stream. The following example uses the `log::debug!` macro (see

Chapter 35, *Logging*) liberally to show the elements and their content as the parsing proceeds:

Example 40.4. Parsing XML events

```
use std::fs::File;
use std::io::BufReader;
use std::str::FromStr;

use chrono::{NaiveDate, Local};
use xml::reader::{EventReader, XmlEvent};  // 1.2.0
use log;

use crate::events::{Event, EventDate, Category};
use crate::providers::{EventProvider, EventProviderError};
use crate::filters::EventFilter;

impl EventProvider for XmlFileProvider {
    // ...other trait method implementations

    fn get_events(&self, filter: &EventFilter, events: &mut Vec<Event>) {
        let file = File::open(self.path.clone()).expect("path to XML file");
        let file = BufReader::new(file);
        let parser = EventReader::new(file);

        // Set up some reusable event parts with default values.
        // When we encounter XML elements, we set these values with their content.
        let today: NaiveDate = Local::now().date_naive();
        let mut event_date = EventDate::Singular(today);

        // Holds the description of the pending event
        let mut pending_description: String = String::new();

        let mut event_category: Category = Category::from_primary("test");
        let mut pending_category_string = String::new();

        let mut new_events: Vec<Event> = Vec::new();

        let mut content = String::new();  // also reused inside the loop
        for e in parser {
            match e {
                Ok(XmlEvent::StartElement { name, .. }) => {
```

```
            content.clear();
            match name.local_name.as_str() {
                "events" => new_events.clear(),
                "description" => pending_description.clear(),
                "category" => pending_category_string.clear(),
                _ => {}
            }
        },
        Ok(XmlEvent::EndElement { name }) => {
            log::debug!("end element {}", name);
            match name.local_name.as_str() {
                "events" => events.append(&mut new_events),
                "event" => {
                    let event = Event::new(
                        event_date,
                        pending_description.clone(),
                        event_category.clone());
                    log::debug!("New event: {}", &event);
                    if filter.accepts(&event) {
                        new_events.push(event);
                    } else {
                        log::debug!("Filter rejects event");
                    }
                },
                "date" => {
                    log::debug!("content = '{}'", &content);
                    event_date = EventDate::parse(&content)
                        .expect("invalid date");
                    content.clear();
                },
                "description" => {
                    pending_description = content.clone();
                    content.clear();
                },
                "category" => {
                    log::debug!("pending_category_string = '{}'",
                        &pending_category_string);
                    event_category = Category::from_str(&pending_category_string).unwrap
                },
                "primary" => {
                    log::debug!("content = '{}'", &content);
                    pending_category_string.push_str(&content);
```

```
                },
                "secondary" => {
                    log::debug!("content = '{}'", &content);
                    pending_category_string.push('/');
                    pending_category_string.push_str(&content);
                },
                _ => ()
            }
        },
        Ok(XmlEvent::Characters(text)) => {
            log::debug!("characters: '{}'", text);
            content.push_str(&text);
        },
        Err(e) => {
            eprintln!("Error: {e}");
            break;
        },
        _ => {},
    }
  }
 }
}
```

The match expression handles the various XML parser events. When an element starts, we reset the scratch variables. When we get character content, we save it for later. When an element ends, we either update the scratch variables with new values, or use them to create a new event.

Note that the debug messages are not seen unless we run the program with the RUST_LOG environment value set to debug. In that case the output from the program would look something like this:

```
[2026-05-15T07:37:58Z DEBUG today::providers::xmlfile] characters: '2023-09-19'
[2026-05-15T07:37:58Z DEBUG today::providers::xmlfile] end element date
[2026-05-15T07:37:58Z DEBUG today::providers::xmlfile] date content=2023-09-19
[2026-05-15T07:37:58Z DEBUG today::events] not rule-based
[2026-05-15T07:37:58Z DEBUG today::events] not yearless
[2026-05-15T07:37:58Z DEBUG today::providers::xmlfile] characters: 'Java SE 21
 released'
[2026-05-15T07:37:58Z DEBUG today::providers::xmlfile] end element description
[2026-05-15T07:37:58Z DEBUG today::providers::xmlfile] characters: 'programming'
```

```
[2026-05-15T07:37:58Z DEBUG today::providers::xmlfile] end element primary
[2026-05-15T07:37:58Z DEBUG today::providers::xmlfile] content = 'programming'
[2026-05-15T07:37:58Z DEBUG today::providers::xmlfile] characters: 'java'
[2026-05-15T07:37:58Z DEBUG today::providers::xmlfile] end element secondary
[2026-05-15T07:37:58Z DEBUG today::providers::xmlfile] content = 'java'
[2026-05-15T07:37:58Z DEBUG today::providers::xmlfile] end element category
[2026-05-15T07:37:58Z DEBUG today::providers::xmlfile] pending_category_string =
 'programming/java'
[2026-05-15T07:37:58Z DEBUG today::providers::xmlfile] end element event
[2026-05-15T07:37:58Z DEBUG today::providers::xmlfile] New event: 2023: Java SE 21
 released (programming/java)
[2026-05-15T07:37:58Z DEBUG today::providers::xmlfile] Filter rejects event
```

That is just for one historical event, so the debug information can quickly get excessive. However, during program development it can be very helpful.

During XML parsing we collect all the events we get into the local vector `new_events`. When we encounter the end of the `events` element, we append all the new events to the function argument `events`.

The `get_events` uses the helper function `EventDate::parse` to parse an event date. This method can deal with singular, annual, and rule-based dates. It was presented as a challenge at the end of Chapter 39, *Refactoring the Event struct*, and is shown here:

Example 40.5. Parsing the many forms of event dates in `EventDate::parse`

```
impl EventDate {
    pub fn parse(date_string: &str) -> Option<EventDate> {
        if date_string.is_empty() {
            log::warn!("empty date string");
            return None;
        }

        let is_rule_based = date_string.chars().next().unwrap().is_alphabetic();
        if is_rule_based {
            match Rule::parse(&date_string) {
                Some(rule) => return Some(EventDate::RuleBased(rule)),
                None => {
                    log::error!("error parsing rule");
                    return None;
                }
```

```
            }
        }
        log::debug!("not rule-based");

        let is_yearless = date_string.starts_with("--");
        if is_yearless {
            let md_string: String = date_string.chars()
                .filter(|c| *c != '-')
                .collect();
            log::debug!("md_string = '{}'", &md_string);
            match MonthDay::from_str(&md_string) {
                Ok(month_day) => return Some(EventDate::Annual(month_day)),
                Err(e) => {
                    log::error!("error parsing yearless date: {}", e);
                    return None;
                }
            }
        } else {
            log::debug!("not yearless");

            match NaiveDate::parse_from_str(&date_string, "%F") {
                Ok(date) => return Some(EventDate::Singular(date)),
                Err(_) => {
                    log::error!("Invalid date '{}'", date_string);
                    return None;
                }
            }
        }
    }
}
```

The function returns an optional value, which will be `None` if the parsing fails. The `get_events` method does not have a specific handling in this case, but going forward we may wish to think about how to deal with an invalid date so that the XML parsing continues from the next `event` element in the XML file. A simple `continue` statement would only take us the next XML parsing event. (As mentioned earlier, there is real potential for confusion between events as our domain objects and events that the XML parser produces.)

The handling of invalid dates will actually be a non-issue if we validate our XML instance document before parsing. We could use the XML Schema shown earlier to do that. The state of XML Schema validation libraries in Rust is currently not as good as in Java, for example, but there are crates like `fastxml` that we could try out. We could also just use an established non-Rust-related tool like `xmllint`[2] to do out-of-band validation, like so:

```
% xmllint --xinclude --noout --schema events.xsd xml-events.xml
xml-events.xml validates
```

[2]https://gnome.pages.gitlab.gnome.org/libxml2/xmllint.html

Chapter 41. One final refactoring

In this chapter we'll do one more refactoring to the Today program. We'll add a configuration item to turn event providers on or off. That triggers an update to the provider listing. Finally we'll collect all the event processing to one event manager, to make the program architecture even cleaner and easier to update.

Configuration of event provider activity

When we have many event providers, we may sometimes wish to turn some of them off, either for testing purposes, or just to control which events are shown, depending on how we have organized the content between the providers.

Since our configuration file is in TOML format, it is easy to add a new setting that is essentially a switch to turn an event provider on or off. This setting naturally has a Boolean value, and it will default to `true`, so that we will need to explicitly turn off an event provider.

This is how an entry for an event provider will look when it has been turned off:

Example 41.1. The `is_active` setting for an event provider

```
[[providers]]
name = "rustopedia"
kind = "csv"
resource = "rustopedia.csv"
is_active = false
```

Here the last row has the new setting `is_active`, and for this provider it has the value `false`.

We don't need to do anything special to have this setting parsed from the TOML file, but we do need some place to put it at runtime, so we'll make a small addition to the `ProviderConfig` struct in `src/lib.rs`:

Example 41.2. The new configuration setting

```
#[derive(Deserialize, Debug)]
pub struct ProviderConfig {
    pub name: String,
    kind: String,
    resource: String,
    is_active: Option<bool>,  // field for new setting added
}
```

The setting is optional. However, we won't use the setting yet, because we have one more refactoring to do.

Introducing the event manager

We have already refactored the events and related data types in Chapter 39, *Refactoring the Event struct*, but the program logic is still the same as it was when it was initially programmed in Chapter 24, *Modules*. It is time to consolidate all the event handling under a single entity, called `EventManager`.

`EventManager` is a struct that holds the configuration path and the event providers. When it is created using its associated `new` function, it will prepare the event providers based on the configuration. It will also have a method to get information about the providers in response to the `providers` subcommand entered at the command line. Most importantly, it will have a `get_events` method that gets events from any active event providers and filters them.

The following is a partial implementation of `EventManager`. The complete code is in the book's GitHub repository, where the necessary `use` statements are also shown. We'll put the code in a new source file, `src/manager.rs`.

Example 41.3. `EventManager` partial implementation

```
pub struct EventManager {
    config_path: PathBuf,
    providers: Vec::<Box<dyn EventProvider>>,
}

impl EventManager {
    pub fn new(config_path: &Path) -> Self {
```

```
    log::debug!("Making new EventManager, config_path = '{:?}'",
        config_path.to_str());
    Self {
        config_path: config_path.to_path_buf(),
        providers: Vec::new(),
    }
}

pub fn create_providers(&mut self, config: &Config) {
    for cfg in config.providers.iter() {
        let found = self.providers.iter().any(|p| p.name() == cfg.name);
        if found {
            eprintln!("Event provider {} already exists", &cfg.name);
            continue;
        }

        let path = self.config_path.join(&cfg.resource);
        match cfg.kind.as_str() {
            "text" => {
                let provider = TextFileProvider::new(
                    &cfg.name,
                    &path,
                    cfg.is_active.unwrap_or(true));
                self.providers.push(Box::new(provider));
            },
            "csv" => {
                let provider = CSVFileProvider::new(
                    &cfg.name,
                    &path,
                    cfg.is_active.unwrap_or(true));
                self.providers.push(Box::new(provider));
            },
            "sqlite" => {
                let provider = SQLiteProvider::new(
                    &cfg.name,
                    &path,
                    cfg.is_active.unwrap_or(true));
                self.providers.push(Box::new(provider));
            },
            "web" => {
                match Url::parse(&cfg.resource) {
                    Ok(url) => {
```

```
                        let provider = WebProvider::new(
                            &cfg.name,
                            &url,
                            cfg.is_active.unwrap_or(true));
                        self.providers.push(Box::new(provider));
                    },
                    Err(e) => {
                        eprintln!("Error in URL for provider {}: {}",
                            &cfg.name, e);
                    }
                }
            },
            "xml" => {
                let provider = XmlFileProvider::new(
                    &cfg.name,
                    &path,
                    cfg.is_active.unwrap_or(true));
                self.providers.push(Box::new(provider));
            },
            _ => {
                eprintln!("Unable to make provider: {:?}", cfg);
            }
        }
    }
}
```

The provider constructors now have an additional parameter that has the `is_active` setting from the configuration file.

Checking for active providers

The constructors of the providers now need an additional field to hold the activity information. We will soon be adding those.

Since the `is_active` setting is optional, it could be missing from the TOML file. If we try to use it but it's not there, it will be a problem. That is why we use the `unwrap_or` method of `Optional` to get it, and specify `true` as the value to use if the optional doesn't have a value. If the setting is missing, its value in the provider will default to `true`.

Often refactoring triggers a ripple effect across the codebase. We may well notice that some additional functionality is needed. For example, since we now have a setting that tells us if the event provider is active or not, we should also be able to ask about it. The `EventProvider` trait needs a new method `is_active`:

Example 41.4. New `is_active` method for the `EventProvider` trait

```
pub trait EventProvider {
    fn name(&self) -> String;
    fn get_events(&self, filter: &EventFilter, events: &mut Vec<Event>);
    fn is_add_supported(&self) -> bool { false }
    fn add_event(&self, event: &Event) -> Result<(), EventProviderError>;
    fn kind(&self) -> String;
    fn is_active(&self) -> bool;  // new trait method
}
```

Every event provider struct will also need a field to hold this information, initialized when the provider is created with settings from the configuration file. Here is an example from `CSVFileProvider`:

Example 41.5. New struct field to hold provider active status

```
pub struct CSVFileProvider {
    name: String,
    path: PathBuf,
    is_active: bool,  // new field
}

impl CSVFileProvider {
    pub fn new(name: &str, path: &Path, is_active: bool) -> Self {
        Self {
            name: name.to_string(),
            path: path.to_path_buf(),
            is_active
        }
    }
}
```

```
impl EventProvider for CSVFileProvider {
    // ...other trait method implementations

    fn is_active(&self) -> bool {   // new method
        self.is_active
    }
}
```

Now when we loop through the event providers we check if a provider is active, and will move immediately to the next one if it isn't:

Example 41.6. Checking if the event provider is active

```
impl EventManager {
    pub fn get_events(&self, filter: &EventFilter) -> Vec<Event> {
        let mut result: Vec<Event> = Vec::new();

        let mut count = 0;

        for provider in &self.providers {
            if !provider.is_active() {     // OK, don't bother with this provider
                log::info!("Provider '{}' is not active, skipping",
                    provider.name());
                continue;
            }
            provider.get_events(&filter, &mut result);
            let new_count = result.len();
            log::info!(
                "Got {} events from provider '{}'",
                new_count - count,
                provider.name());
            count = new_count;
        }

        result
    }
}
```

Note

> The is_active field of an event provider is not public, so we need to get its value using the is_active method. It may seem like it would be easier to just mark the field as pub and use it directly. However, that would make it possible to set the field of some provider to true accidentally, even if that provider is marked as inactive in the configuration file (or the other way around). Also, in some cases a method like this could actually use several fields of the struct, maybe with some other information, to compute the return value. Therefore direct access to struct fields may not be a good idea, even though in some cases it is justified.

We should also check if the provider is active or not when adding an event. Of course, this only applies to event providers that support adding. Clearly both conditions need to hold, but it is a matter of taste whether to check for active first, and then check for addition support, or the other way around. We'll go for the following implementation of the add_event method, which now lives in EventManager:

Example 41.7. Checking for active and add support in a provider

```
impl EventManager {
    pub fn add_event(&self, provider_name: &str, event: &Event) -> bool {
        // Find provider by name
        let mut provider: Option<&dyn EventProvider> = None;
        for p in &self.providers {
            if p.name() == provider_name {
                provider = Some(p.as_ref());
                break;
            }
        }

        match provider {
            Some(p) => {
                if p.is_active() {
                    if p.is_add_supported() {
                        let _ = p.add_event(event);
                        return true;
                    } else {
```

```
                    eprintln!("Adding events is not supported for provider '{}'", p.name());
                    return false;
                }
            } else {
                eprintln!("Provider '{}' is not active", p.name());
                return false;
            }
        },
        None => {
            eprintln!("Unknown event provider '{}'", provider_name);
            return false;
        }
    }
  }
}
```

If we start to think that the add_event should return a Result<T, E> value instead of bool, then that is a sign that our thinking is beginning to align with Rust. That is yet another refactoring to try out, but we'll leave that for some future session.

Updating the provider information

Since event providers have gained new and interesting information, we should update the implementation of the providers subcommand. For that we'll add a new struct and a method that fills it in:

Example 41.8. Support for getting provider information

```
pub struct ProviderInfo {
    pub name: String,
    pub kind: String,
    pub is_add_supported: bool,
    pub is_active: bool,
}

impl EventManager {
    pub fn get_provider_info(&self) -> Vec<ProviderInfo> {
```

```
        let mut result = Vec::new();

        for provider in &self.providers {
            result.push(ProviderInfo {
                name: provider.name(),
                kind: provider.kind(),
                is_add_supported: provider.is_add_supported(),
                is_active: provider.is_active() });
        }

        result
    }
}
```

The `main` function uses this method in the implementation of the `providers` subcommand. While we are refactoring, let's actually make a function that runs the subcommand in the `src/lib.rs` file:

Example 41.9. Implementing the `providers` subcommand

```
pub fn run_providers(manager: &EventManager) {
    log::debug!("run_providers: for the `providers` subcommand");

    println!("! = active   + = supports add");
    let provider_info = manager.get_provider_info();
    for info in provider_info {
        println!(
            "{:20} {}{} {}",
            info.name,
            if info.is_active { "!" } else { " "},
            if info.is_add_supported { "+" } else { " " },
            info.kind);
    }
}
```

This is a free function that takes an `EventManager` as its parameter, so that it can be used to retrieve the provider information. One example of the output of this function could be:

```
! = active    + = supports add
xml-events            !  XML
java-xml              !  XML
annuals               !+ CSV
history               !+ text
computing             !+ CSV
programming           !+ CSV
todayserver           !  web
holidays-japan         + CSV
rustopedia            !+ SQLite
```

We'll also make a similar function in `src/lib.rs` for running the `add` subcommand:

Example 41.10. Implementing the `add` subcommand

```
pub fn run_add(manager: &EventManager, provider_name: &str, event: &Event) {
    log::debug!("run_add");

    if !manager.add_event(provider_name, event) {
        eprintln!("Unable to add event to provider '{}'", provider_name);
    }
}
```

Finally, the `run` function, used to run a session without a subcommand, can be refactored like this:

Example 41.11. The revised `run` function

```
use pluralizer::pluralize;

pub fn run(manager: &EventManager, filter: &EventFilter)
        -> Result<(), Box<dyn Error>> {
    log::debug!("run");

    let events = manager.get_events(&filter);

    let (mut singular_events, annual_events): (Vec<&Event>, Vec<&Event>)
```

```
        = events.iter().partition(|event| event.is_singular());

    let include_count = true;
    let mut print_separator = true;

    if !singular_events.is_empty() {
        singular_events.sort_by(|a, b| a.year().cmp(&b.year()));
        singular_events.reverse();
        println!("On this day in history ({}):",
            pluralize("event", singular_events.len() as isize, include_count));
        for event in singular_events {
            println!("{}", event);
        }
    } else {
        print_separator = false;
    }

    if !annual_events.is_empty() {
        if print_separator {
            println!();
        }
        println!("Observed today ({}):",
            pluralize("event", annual_events.len() as isize, include_count));
        for event in annual_events {
            println!("{} ({})", event.description(), event.category());
        }
    }

    Ok(())
}
```

Most of this code is already familiar, but the headings for singular and annual events are now grammatically correct, also in cases where there is just one event, thanks to the `pluralize`, which we of course include in the `Cargo.toml` and bring into scope. The `pluralize` function does the legwork.

Final `main` function

With the introduction of `EventManager` and the resulting refactoring, the latter part of the `main` function ends up looking like this:

Example 41.12. The revised `main` function

```
use today::{run, run_providers, run_add, Config};
use today::events::{Event, EventDate, Category, MonthDay};
use today::filters::FilterBuilder;
use today::manager::EventManager;

fn main() {
    env_logger::init();

    let args = Args::parse();

    let month_day = if let Some(md) = args.date {
        MonthDay::from_str(&md).unwrap()
    } else {
        let today: NaiveDate = Local::now().date_naive();
        MonthDay::new(today.month(), today.day())
    };
    log::debug!("month_day = {}", month_day);

    let filter = FilterBuilder::new()
        .month_day(month_day)
        .build();

    const APP_NAME: &str = "today";
    let config_path = get_config_path(APP_NAME);
    match config_path {
        Some(path) => {
            let toml_path = path.join(format!("{}.toml", APP_NAME));
            log::debug!("Looking for configuration file '{}'", &toml_path.display());
            let config_str = fs::read_to_string(toml_path).expect("existing configuration file")
            let config: Config = toml::from_str(&config_str).expect("valid configuration file");
            log::debug!("config: {:#?}", config);

            let mut manager = EventManager::new(&path);
            manager.create_providers(&config);

            match args.cmd {
                Some(Command::Providers) => run_providers(&manager),

                Some(Command::Add { provider, date, description, category }) => {
                    let category = Category::from_str(&category).unwrap();
```

```
                let date = chrono::NaiveDate::parse_from_str(&date, "%Y-%m-%d").unwrap();
                let event = Event::new(EventDate::Singular(date), description, category);
                run_add(&manager, &provider, &event);
            },

            _ => {  // no subcommand given, normal run
                if !args.no_birthday {
                    today::birthday::handle_birthday();
                }

                if let Err(e) = run(&manager, &filter) {
                    eprintln!("Error running program: {}", e);
                    return;
                }
            }
        }
    }
    None => {
        eprintln!("Unable to configure the application");
        return;
    }
  }
}
```

There is one new thing: the `--no-birthday` or `-n` option suppresses the age calculation and commentary when specified. The option is added to the `Args` struct at the top of `src/main.rs`, along with the `--date` / `-d` option. See the GitHub repository for the full source code.

Chapter 42. Future development ideas

The Today program is already fairly complete for its purpose, but that doesn't mean it can't be improved. Here are some future development ideas to try out.

Localized category names

Currently the event categories are shown in their technical format, like `programming/rust`. It is perhaps worth it to devise a mechanism where the program could show the category names translated to the user's local language. This could be determined from the environment settings.

The localization mechanism could be realised using an implementation of a system like Fluent[1]. Missing translations could fall back on the technical category names.

Category exclusions

The event filter mechanism could be extended to support categories to be excluded. For example, you could give a list of categories to exclude on the command line, like `"test,test/fake"`, or possibly even wildcards like `"test/*"`.

Year count for events

The event output could be enhanced by showing how many years ago the historical event occurred (only for singular events, of course). The year display could be suppressed for events that happened in the ongoing year.

Showing upcoming events

A feature that could possibly trigger a large refactoring involves showing upcoming events. For this the program would essentially need to read all events and then retain those that are in the past, and those that are into the future by some specified cutoff date (a week, two weeks, a month).

[1]https://projectfluent.org

Color terminal display

The output of the Today program is decidedly monochrome. The Rust ecosystem has numerous crates that are able to colorize terminal output, like `termcolor`[2] or `colored`[3]. By using colored output tastefully the Today program could be made more vibrant.

Yes.

Many other enhancements could be devised, but now it is time to wrap up this book. The Today program will be developed further in its own public GitHub repository, separately from the book examples.

```
% today --no-birthday
On this day in history (1 event):
2026: The Learn Rust Programming Today book is completed (programming/rust)

Observed today (1 event):
Bloomsday
```

[2]https://crates.io/crates/termcolor
[3]https://crates.io/crates/colored

Appendix A. About this book

This book was written in DocBook XML 5.0 markup using Microsoft Visual Studio Code on an Apple MacBook Air (13-inch, M4, 2025). The markup was converted to XSL-FO using the DocBook XSL Stylesheets, and further converted to print-ready PDF using Apache FOP. Fun fact: it takes about six seconds to render the whole book from DocBook XML to PDF.

The programming examples were developed on the same machine with Visual Studio Code and rust-analyzer, compiled with the latest Rust compiler (version 1.94.1 at the time of the book's completion), and tested in macOS 26.5.1 Tahoe and also in Linux Mint 22.3 Cinnamon on a Lenovo Ideapad Slim 3.

The first part of the book mostly addresses you directly. In the second and third parts it shifts to an inclusive "we" form of addressing the reader. Each of the parts has its own table of contents for easy reference. All chapters start on the right hand page, sometimes leaving a good amount of space on the left for notes.

The headings use sentence case instead of title case for better readability. The body font is Source Serif 4, and the title font is Source Sans 3. The code font is Inconsolata.

The cover image was designed by the author. The colored backgrounds are combined so that the title can be read several ways, including "learn Rust", "learn programming", "Rust programming", and "programming Today" (or "today"). The note and tip icons are from Icons8.com[1], with the backlink requested appearing in the footnote.

Large language models (LLM) or other Artificial Intelligence (AI) assistants were not used in the production of this book's text or code examples. ChatGPT (GPT-5.5) was used to generate the fake event data for testing, and to troubleshoot some problems with the PDF production toolchain.

[1]https://icons8.com

Appendix B. About the author

Jere Käpyaho is a Finnish software developer and author who currently works as Lecturer in Computing at the Tampere University of Applied Sciences. He is also the founder of Conifer Productions Oy[1], a software and media company.

Jere started programming in 1984 on a Commodore VIC-20 home computer, and has since then worked in journalism, standardization, consulting, and education. He first heard about Rust in 2014 in the context of bioinformatics, and picked it up seriously in 2021. He is the author of a popular Finnish-language Python programming book called *Selkeästi Python,* but his favorite programming language is actually Ada.

He likes old and new digital music synthesizers and electronic music, spends a lot of time programming MIDI System Exclusive utilities, and publishes the DigitalSynth.net website[2]. He lives in Tampere, Finland with his wonderful wife, a big bookcase and a small, serene garden. He's all right.

[1]https://coniferproductions.com
[2]https://digitalsynth.net

Further reading

[Bla2021] Jim Blandy, Jason Orendorff, Leonora F. S. Tindall, *Programming Rust, 2nd Edition*. O'Reilly, 2021.

[Gje2022] Jon Gjengset, *Rust for Rustaceans*. No Starch Press, 2022.

[ISO2019] *ISO 8601-1:2019. Date and time — Representations for information interchange*. International Organisation for Standardisation, 2019.

[Ker2019] Brian Kernighan, *Unix: A History and a Memoir*. Kindle Direct Publishing, 2019.

[Kla2026] Steve Klabnik, Carol Nichols, Chris Krycho, *The Rust Programming Language, 3rd Edition*. No Starch Press, 2026.

[McN2021] Tim McNamara, *Rust in Action*. Manning, 2021.

Index

Symbols

A

B

C

D

E

F

N

O

P

R

S

T

U

V

W

X

Z